JAMES STOKES LECTURESHIP ON POLITICS

NEW YORK UNIVERSITY

STOKES FOUNDATION

American Diplomacy and Emergent Patterns

AMERICAN DIPLOMACY

AND

EMERGENT PATTERNS

Kenneth W. Thompson

NEW YORK UNIVERSITY PRESS   1962

TO

Kenny C. Thompson

AND HIS GENERATION

CONTENTS

PREFACE

A CRITICAL ESSAY that affirms a definite viewpoint concerning the theory and practice of American diplomacy can be misleading. It may convey a sense that the manifold problems and dilemmas of foreign policy are easily resolved if only the author's counsel is heeded. Yet bold is the writer who presumes to offer a complete blueprint for building the edifice of peace. This essay, alert to the close link between action and circumstance, leaves to others the perplexing task of proposing policy. Its aim is more modest, if equally elusive. It has proceeded on the assumption that the style, the management, and the techniques of diplomacy are amenable to inquiry and research. They can be sorted out, assessed, and applied. It asserts that those who formulate policy today labor within an established framework of institutions and practices drawing on a fixed body of ideas and doctrine. While such a framework sets limits, the diplomat more often than not is free to choose the stage on which the drama will be enacted, the *dramatis personae* who will play the parts, and the main themes of the drama. In any given historical era, the choice is influenced but not determined by facts in the minds and the real world of the actors.

Ideas, institutions, practice, and problems intermingle and provide the raw content of this essay. The most baffling relationship, of course, continues to be that between ideas and practice. In recent American history, men of ideas have played an awkward if essential role in shaping institutions and programs. It must be said that while seldom at the front of the stage, they have never been entirely crowded from it. Yet in candor you have only to ask yourself what recent administration has found a place for the brooding, searching, and inquiring mind of the philosopher. The nearest approximation may have been "the braintrust" of President Franklin D. Roosevelt, but it is not without significance that its members one by one fell by the wayside. More often, a President or Secretary from the outset turns to men who by instinct recognize the difference between a decision and a conclusion, are not immobilized by complexity, and can work in the uncertain realm where policy-makers must choose among lesser evils. They must carry the marks of the man of action; they must both be and appear decisive, matter-of-fact, and to the point. They should be confirmed in their original premises, use short sentences and an economy of words, and resist too much dispersion of thought and unbridled intellectual curiosity. And yet, as they measure up to these requirements, they run the risk of being clever rather than wise, proficient rather than profound, and active rather than articulate. Only a handful of American leaders are exceptions to the rule that philosophy and decision-making are incompatible, and fewer still can be counted successful. Yet somewhere at the heart of every regime there is need for a philosopher. Presidents Abraham Lincoln and Woodrow Wilson are, of course, the prime examples of leaders who in living political philosophy spoke not for the moment but for the ages. While both could act, they could also shine the spotlight of powerful minds into the murky corners of ignorance and illusion. By their exposition of the great issues of national life they were able to bring light out of darkness, hope out of despair, and courage out of fear.

Many confess to a growing uneasiness concerning the state of contemporary political leadership. They ask whether we can marshal the human and material resources essential to the present crisis if leadership is mute on the issues that most need changing. The words "technician of power" have crept into the vocabulary, and ordinary men and women not content with mere efficiency and dispatch call for guidance, particularly in areas of greatest controversy. The Achilles heel of an approach that dampens out debate, that smooths over conflicts, and that hesitates to take the public into its confidence on the dilemmas with which it daily contends is its failure in preparing the people for the struggles ahead. President Lincoln never flinched when the moment came to speak of the pathos and tragedy of the struggle to preserve the Union. As he approached the noble goal of emancipating the slaves, he outlined the scale of values with which he as President had to work. If he could save the Union by freeing all the slaves, he said, he would do so. If he could preserve it by freeing some and leaving others enslaved, he was obliged to do that. If to save it he could not free any of the slaves, he would do that. As guardian of the republic, his first allegiance was to the Union. These harsh truths, which opened windows into the President's official mind, enabled the people to share some of the burdens that weighed too heavily for any one man to bear alone. To shield the people from the realities of the great choices that leaders make and the reasons for their choices may offer short-run political advantages in blunting the edges of partisan criticism. In the long run, this posture is unlikely to serve the public interest. The disease that gnaws at the vitals of a free society stems from the widening gap between public understanding and responsible leadership. Two languages evolve: one for statesmen and another for the people. While it is true that a major burden of public office is to spare the people answering "yes" or "no" on successive issues on which facts are obscured or restricted, a twentieth-century public is bound to grow restless and confused if its image of the world is based on fiction and shrouded in mystery and illusion. If its diet lacks the staple of reality, the prospects are scant of its developing moral fiber for the long voyage ahead. While leaders may think of slow and steady progress and the skillful avoidance of catastrophe, false prophets may beguile the people through talk of total victory.

A discourse on American diplomacy that left an impression

that practitioners were free to choose as wisely and well as circumstances permitted without more than a glance at the public would be wide of the mark. Within a democracy the people choose and in choosing must know. I find no evidence that the need for public understanding stops at the water's edge. If the problems are baffling, the stakes are even greater than within a single national arena. Surely complexity and uncertainty are no excuse for ignorance.

Somehow in the American system ways must be found to make partners of our diplomats and the people they serve. Both must seek this partnership, recognizing from the start that they are not equals. Their inequality extends to both sources of information and professional competence, but in this diplomacy is not unique. The people repose their trust in city managers, public-service commissions, and administrative and quasi-judicial bodies. The public stakes its hopes on the responsibility of a network of executive and administrative officials. The parallel with the men who administer foreign policy is imperfect at various points, but broadly speaking we leave to a corps of responsible officials the business of implementing policies and programs grounded in widely accepted national goals and purposes. Their task gains acceptance and approval as the framework within which they labor is more widely understood.

It remains for the President to give content to national aims and policies, to educate the people both in ends and means, to interpret the route his administration is following, and to account for inevitable detours and bypasses along the way. Periodically, he must sketch in for the people the landscape and the terrain that comprise the world scene. He must review the state of the Union and the world. He must close the gap as much as he can between his own grasp of affairs and that of the people as a whole. At times, he may survey the future from the mountaintop of great national and international purposes, renewing thereby the common faith. But on other occasions he will have no choice but to descend into the valley of painful choices, unpleasant sacrifices, and insoluble problems that at best can be ameliorated through wit and good fortune. It is at times like these that technical skill is not enough, that mere finesse and facility will not suffice, and that only the statesman who draws on the deepest human and spiritual resources will come out all right. In Western civilization we remember Washington and Lincoln, Marshall and Bevin, and Roosevelt and Churchill because they were leaders in good times and bad, and because they seldom faltered in formulating either towering principles or practical guidelines as necessity required.

The present decade will see in countries around the globe a new generation of political leaders. They will be forming governments of their own choosing, drawing on experience and talent dedicated to programs to which they are pledged. Some of these leaders may be tempted to shortcut the lessons of the past. They may look for others to share the burdens of national leadership. They may assume that someone else—a popular Secretary or a famous personality in Congress—can speak for the administration. Or they may imagine that political leadership need involve no more than the recitation of the great truths on which the republic is founded. They will find that, if they leave to others the expression of all the hard facts and stubborn problems that face them along a crowded avenue of national self-fulfillment, they will lose control. A driverless vehicle will careen recklessly along, driven now here and now there by forces of circumstance. If the head of state is not in control, accountable to the people for the nation's course, no one else can be his surrogate. He must know his objectives and the route by which he can reach them, and be able to chart the course for those who accompany him along a difficult and often confusing highway. Similarly, the President must, with his trusted lieutenants, grasp the functions and limits of institutional patterns in contemporary diplomacy. He may be tempted to erect a single institution into an end in itself. Under pressure of political debate, he may accord to one pattern or another a measure of final validity. Yet he must know that diplomacy is an empirical art and that he who sacrifices flexibility and freedom of maneuver is likely to come a cropper in the end.

The channels of parliamentary and personal diplomacy lie open to him and so do the time-tested channels of traditional diplomacy. He can ill afford to plead ignorance to their several uses by affirming uncritical loyalty to one or the other in advance. The novelty and the promise of present-day patterns of diplomacy are no excuse for viewing them any differently than the instruments and agencies with which the successful political leader must work. Each calls for the same mastery of rules and procedures required by the politician who seeks his ends in the Congress or in appeals at the hustings. Too much sentimentalism or an excess of cynicism are equally destined to be self-defeating. Since the latest forms of diplomacy, including the United Nations, are not as solidly established as the more durable national institutions, those who strive to gain for them a legitimate place in the sun may understandably cross the line separating reason from emotion. Experience in the end may prove the best antidote to extravagant praise or blind criticism of patterns of diplomacy, whether novel or traditional.

If the President, in the face of the great burdens he carries and the harsh storms of conflict and conscience that envelop him, is able to pursue a wise and steady course, diplomats will more likely be freed to carry on the daily business of foreign affairs. They must never assume that they and not the President are the principal spokesmen for the nation's policy. Neither must they be misled by the opposite illusion to suppose they are not through him publicly accountable. Much of the diplomat's work need not be a subject for continuous debate and review. His day-by-day decisions are seldom appropriate subjects for a plebiscite. But if he would conduct his affairs with the wisdom and skill that the circumstances require, he cannot for a moment ignore the constitutional framework within which he operates. And the President in turn must remain vigilant to the needs of public education and leadership.

Thus the broad lines of democracy and the requirements of diplomacy converge and become compatible. In the mid-twentieth century, free institutions and successful diplomacy are on trial together. If one is to survive, the other must grow ever more viable. A study of the patterns of American diplomacy is thus a study of democratic diplomacy. A proper review of the techniques and management of American diplomacy cannot end without a reminder of this truth. At this point, the concerns of the political philosopher are identical with those of the diplomatic analyst. Democratic diplomacy is for better or worse a central theme of contemporary political theory.

Since this is true, the diplomacy of each successive national administration will be judged both in terms of its management of international relationships and the depth of its grasp of the root principles of democratic diplomacy. It must call therefore no less on skilled practitioners than on trenchant philosophers. It must find a place for both the man of action and the man of ideas. Neither the pragmatist reacting instinctively with an unerring sense of the possible nor the thinker who would recast the problem or the setting within which choices are made dare be excluded. An administration must find a place within the inner workings of government, if you will, no less for a George F. Kennan or a C. B. Marshall than for a "Chip" Bohlen or a Robert Murphy.

It would be premature to judge the administration of President John F. Kennedy by these standards. The straws in the wind leave a picture that is neither all black nor all white. By comparison with some of the preceding regimes, this administration's pragmatic approach and grasp of essentials cannot but be impressive. But there remain gaps and deficiencies of which other observers have spoken. Will the government in power provide leadership both in word and deed? Can it close the gap between the public and its leaders? Is there a sure sense and enough freedom of action to assure the wise choice of the most appropriate and effective institutions of diplomacy? Will diplomats and the President himself take seriously the injunction contained in his greatest foreign policy address—at the University of Washington in November of 1961? Is there the moral stamina to persist over decades in the face of adversity? Can President Kennedy rally the people for the sacrifices that a protracted struggle entails, while simultaneously preparing them for compromises and adjustments when they are necessary and possible? Beyond this, can any government whose differences are open for public notice and which periodically engages in vigorous debate with itself persuade the rest of the world that its cause is just and its forms and values are the wave of the future? Can we affirm our goals without disparaging the aims of others, particularly our friends in the uncommitted world? Are we able to point with pride to genuine accomplishments without lapsing into self-righteousness?

These problems are not the business of President Kennedy's administration alone. They are broader national opportunities open to all. As such, they will prove in the end the measure by which we shall all be judged. We are all of us implicated in the challenge of American diplomacy. Our response must therefore be thoughtful, decisive, and constructive. Civilization will not forgive, nor for that matter survive, anything less than a full response to this challenge.

INTRODUCTION

THE UNDERLYING PURPOSE of these lectures, which I was privileged to give at New York University in the important James Stokes series, is suggested by two cogent sentences in a recent commentary by Don K. Price, Dean of Harvard's Littauer School. He observes: "In our general approach to international affairs, we have changed from utopians to realists. . . . But we have not yet taken the same step with respect to the ways by which our policies are to be made and the means by which they are to be carried out." [1] Diplomacy, like politics, is preeminently a realm of ways and means. It is the avenue along which ideals and objectives are realized. At some point the philosopher, however amateur in matters affecting the organization of the state, must venture across the line that separates thought and action. As he does, he is likely to stumble, if he fancies himself able in one brief foray to discover the truth about diplomacy. Yet if he would command a hearing, must he not do more than speculate and idealize, or criticize and condemn? Is there a point at which he must grapple, vicariously at least, with the stubborn issues of statecraft? Is the sole task of the philosopher to stand in judgment, or must he take in his hands the raw matter that resists ideal solutions for the diplomat? Is there common ground on which the philosopher and the practitioner can join, or is their relationship one in which the twain shall never meet? What can we say of the enduring and the changing character of diplomacy?

[1] The American Assembly, Columbia University, *The Secretary of State*, ed. Don K. Price (Englewood Cliffs, N. J.: Prentice-Hall, Inc., 1960), p. 170.

The notion is frequently advanced that the intellectual stops being an intellectual by being practical. In becoming a practitioner, he ceases to be the conscience of society, becoming instead its ideologue. Yet a conscience that has never known the deep pathos of social action and the tragic choices of statesmen inevitably views the political scene from the false security of moral and intellectual superiority. Much of present-day social and political criticism rings with a note of "holier than thou." When the organic connection is destroyed between the philosopher's world and the world of shadows and imperfections, he loses a zest for discrimination in practical affairs and declares a plague on every man's house. Intellectuals speak to intellectuals not of truth but of the dire shortcomings of men of affairs; they ask not what were the alternatives, but was an action, as measured by absolute standards, simultaneously successful, wise, and good. Critical analysis becomes a beginning and an end; constructive proposals are left to the "social engineer." The scholar becomes a specialist in postmortems condemning, denouncing, and viewing with alarm. Thus the true wellspring of social and political innovation dries up; the deepest resources of human wisdom lie impotent and unused. Practitioners, in turn, speak in derision of intellectuals who offer little help with problems that crowd their agendas. If there is a germ of truth in this diagnosis of the unhealthy state of American intellectual life, then we are justified in approaching rather in the spirit of a dialogue the continuing interplay between philosophy, diplomacy, and politics. No subject lends itself to this viewpoint more completely than the unfinished story of the emerging patterns of American diplomacy.

I propose to approach my topic of "American Diplomacy and Emergent Patterns" by discussing, first, the Ideas and Institutions (Part One), and second, the Practice and Procedures in Diplomacy (Part Two). In Chapters I and IV, I shall introduce the two general concepts with a broadly philosophical and historical analysis. Thereafter, my aim is to explicate as best I can the ways and means of American diplomacy, where its origins lie, and how it appears to be evolving. If such a survey should bring the reader to a clearer, more realistic grasp of the forms of American diplomacy, the influence of ideas, morality, and politics, and the specific problems that face the government in determining the functions of the secretary of state, ambassadors, special envoys, and representatives to international bodies, then Dean Price's injunction will have been heeded.

The objective of the Stokes Lectures, in the words of their founder, is "the inculcation of the obligation and necessity of maintaining a high moral standard in politics and legislation and administration of political affairs" in the United States. In reviewing my predecessors' lectures, I am impressed that they all have sought to fulfill this mandate by approaching the subject obliquely. They have treated morality and politics not abstractly but in the context of certain fundamental problems pressing in on the nation and its leaders. In recent American history, the problems of paramount importance have been organizing our government for domestic affairs, rallying the American people to meet their international responsibilities, and defining the relationship between government and important sectors of national life such as science or social change. The themes of successive lectures reflect these broad concerns and the willingness of a group of American leaders to grapple with moral questions embedded in the great issues that face the republic.

The problems of American diplomacy take on an importance in the mid-twentieth century surpassing those of earlier decades. Foreign policy truly has become a matter of life and death. The nation's leaders are obliged to formulate wise policies and execute them through a myriad of evolving diplomatic institutions. The patterns of American diplomacy are evolving, not fixed. One problem with which we must cope is determining how much of the past may be relevant to the present. What precepts and rules are meaningful today that have applied in the past? When and how do novel institutions call for a changing style of international diplomacy, and when and how do they require the faithful pursuit of traditional methods? Where in the developing patterns of our relations with the rest of the world can we put our finger on standards that differentiate right from wrong, wisdom from folly, and success from failure? If we look to the future, what can we say of the prospects for tomorrow's diplomatic patterns? What are the chances for health and survival of democratic diplomacy in a world of crisis and conflict, armaments and force, tyranny and deception, and revolutionary change?

I am persuaded that a study of ideas, institutions, and policies provides a broad avenue along which to trace the relationship between morality and politics. The connection between what men do and say is one important yardstick of the relevance and substance of moral principles. So are a succession of problems that arise in shaping institutions to serve the requirements of efficiency while meeting the needs of public responsibility. Even a cursory survey of the patterns of American diplomacy gives us a text and workbook for the examination of theory and practice relating moral principles and the imperatives of successful foreign policy.

I am grateful to New York University for affording me the incentive to comment on these great problems. I am particularly indebted to Professors Thomas M. Hovet and Marshall E. Dimock of the Department of Government at New York University. Their colleagues who have given warm encouragement and friendly criticism include President James M. Hester, Chancellor George D. Stoddard, Dean Russell D. Niles, Dean Ray F. Harvey, and Professor Bayrd Still. Needless to say, they share no responsibility for my conclusions. I should also thank those who have made possible the completion of the manuscript, including Miss Catherine L. Tolles, Mrs. Ethel Wellman, Mrs. Ethel Williams, and Miss Betty Heitman. The main burden of assistance fell to Miss Janet Weaver, who brought to her task high intelligence, extraordinary professional competence, and great devotion. Above all, I appreciate the patience and forbearance of my family through months of preparation and grave inroads on our life together.

I

IDEAS AND INSTITUTIONS

1

Philosophy, Diplomacy, and Politics

PERENNIAL TRUTHS *VS.*
CHANGING PATTERNS

*Lord Salisbury's realism was "to face the facts, keeping
hypotheses in the background; to eschew chimeras, to
abominate cant and sentimentality, while conforming to
moral law and the trend of events. . . ."*
A. L. KENNEDY

A NYONE WITH THE TEMERITY to analyze patterns of American diplomacy must inevitably ask where he should com-
mence. Ought he direct attention to the most recent diplomatic
crisis on grounds that in a revolutionary age the current alone
is relevant? Or should he, by treating its historical antecedents,
cut through to the root forces which shape the present? Are
the patterns of diplomacy embedded in the practice, as contrasted with the theory, of statecraft? Are the prime lessons of
international affairs to be gleaned from philosophers, diplomatists, or statesmen? If the world view of the diplomatist is
incomplete, are scientists and humanists a better source for
illuminating the underlying principles of our policies? Could
it be that when Sir John Maynard Keynes wrote of the role of
academic scribblers as the fountainhead of all the great movements in history, he faithfully described the circumstances of

world politics as well? What should we say of the statesman-philosophers who help fashion the course of foreign relations in each succeeding period? Is philosophy, diplomacy, or politics the best focus for understanding American diplomacy, and how are we to proceed in giving each aspect its due? Any observer is obliged at the very least to write a note to himself setting forth the main elements of his credo on these basic issues. If I were to comply with this, my *aide-mémoire* on how I meant to proceed would read somewhat as follows:

I would suggest that the point that needs stressing at the beginning and end of a study like this is the fact of the shortcomings and limits inherent in any of these approaches alone. No one approach will suffice. If the observer focuses too narrowly on ideas and philosophies, he may lose sight of the dominant and sometimes determining influence of events. If the stress is placed exclusively upon the contemporary, to the exclusion of relevant historical background, he runs the risk of imagining that problems are wholly novel, that statesmen stand alone in confronting issues which have no parallels in past experience, and that those who guide the ship of state move over uncharted water which no one before them has traveled. Whether we approach our problem then through philosophy, statecraft, or politics, insights are shaped by prevailing viewpoints and by underlying assumptions and experiences. If American diplomacy is seen through the eyes of the philosopher who has never known the harsh choices with which the statesman must learn to live, or by the man of ideas as distinct from the man of action, an important dimension for the understanding of diplomacy will be missing. But difficulties and problems reappear in other ways of viewing international events. If the solitary statesman is left with the task of describing American diplomacy, he may well omit crucial and important judgments that a scholar once removed from the clash of events will more likely take into account. Thus for the discussion of American diplomacy no single viewpoint seems sufficient. The ideas of peoples and statesmen, the forces of international politics, and the procedures and pressures of diplomatic practice all come into play, all interact with one another.

Moreover, the uncertainties of chance and fate hang like a dark and forbidding cloud over those who seek by logic or understanding to pierce the future or explain the past. We are reminded that in foreign relations, "the statesman must cross the Rubicon not knowing how deep and turbulent the river is, nor what he will find on the other side. . . . He must face the impenetrable darkness of the future and still not flinch from walking into it, drawing the nation behind him." [1] More often than not, he must stake his country's future on a hunch. Neither more advice nor additional information can close the gap between what he knows and what he might wish he knew. The diplomatist, like the soldier, moves across *terra incognita*— a vast realm of uncertainty and chance—never able to chart the landscape with the knowledge and confidence of the national political leader. In his vivid account of the struggle for Anzio in World War II, Mr. Wynford Vaughan-Thomas writes: "Battles are not won entirely by logistics, vitally important though they are. There are always other imponderables—surprise, daring, bluff, imaginative leadership." [2] After any great event in the annals of war or statecraft, the nagging doubt persists that some influence or force no one had foreseen may have been decisive. Each new "science" of human behavior partakes at some point of the hope that social phenomena can be isolated and studied through observations so numerous that all exceptions and "disturbances" will be eliminated. Periodically, we are told that statistics, decision-making, or some other promising theoretical advance throws more light on the study of man or social relations than all past or present approaches, bringing prediction and prophesy within man's reach.

Philosophers or statesmen who are persuaded that their perspective constitutes a kind of master discipline for the

---

[1] Hans J. Morgenthau, "The Trouble with Kennedy," *Commentary*, XXXIII, No. 1 (January 1962), 52.

[2] Vaughan-Thomas, *Anzio* (London: Longmans, 1961), Epilogue.

analysis of all diplomacy may profit from Arnold J. Toynbee's discerning remark: "In the world of scholarship, to give and take criticism is all in the day's work and, each in our day, we may criticize our predecessors without becoming guilty of presumption so long as we are able to look forward without rancour to being criticized in our turn by our successors when our day is past." [3] We need to recall that history in general, and diplomatic history in particular, is essentially unpredictable. The soundest predictions and estimates will be disturbed and confounded by elements of chance and contingency. No one can say in advance what the conduct of this president or that secretary of state will be, however deeply he may perceive their philosophy or the circumstances within which they live and work. You have only to ask yourself what kind of president you expected Harry S. Truman or Dwight D. Eisenhower to be and compare it with the way things turned out. The extravagant and cheerful expectations that surround the formulation of a challenging new approach are inevitably cut down to size by the grim reaper of unfolding events.

Therefore, an interpretation of American diplomacy in terms of ideas, procedures, or political forces may serve as a broad outline for discussion and thought. It can never provide a Euclidean demonstration. This is so because such a large part of diplomacy takes place in the interstices of interstate relations, on the hidden side of the curtain of human relations, that any hoped-for comprehensive analysis of the whole is virtually doomed to failure. The best writers and historians give us firefly flashes of insight. They cite and evaluate the dispatches. They project what leaders have said or done and relate this to a concrete event. But even the participants in moments of great decision are unlikely to know or remember all the steps leading up to an action. Who can tell us precisely what factors prompted the United States to intervene in Korea, or who can say what forced our leaders to choose not to intervene in Cuba?

[3] Royal Institute of International Affairs, *Survey of International Affairs, 1931* (Oxford: Oxford University Press, 1933), pp. 13–14.

I do not consider these cautionary words a counsel of despair. The sensitive and intelligent philosopher or the spokesman of any other viewpoint can tell us much. But he and all the rest of us who seek to explain and interpret should be conscious of the nature, scope, and restrictions of the framework within which we think and write. One example may help to dramatize the point. The goal of philosophy is truth; the goal of statesmanship is a decision. Justice Louis Brandeis, who to an exceptional degree had attributes both of the philosopher and man of action, felt called upon to observe: "Some questions can be decided even if not answered." General George C. Marshall spoke in much the same vein when he advised: "Don't fight the problem, decide it." The classic case of the anguish and mental torture to which the philosopher who must act is subjected is, of course, the figure of Hamlet. To decide is to cut off at some point, sooner rather than later, the dialogue in which the searcher-after-truth engages himself and reality. Dean Acheson, whose intellectual capacities surpassed those of most secretaries of state, confessed that "decision and self-analysis are incompatible." Decisions in diplomacy or politics —or for that matter in administration—involve action on fragmentary knowledge before all the evidence is in. To transpose Sören Kierkegaard's graphic phrase from the religious to the political sphere, a decision is a "leap," or an act of faith that what we can know and see, insufficient as it may be, foreshadows a wider sector of reality and justifies action "as if" all were true. Writing in 1890, Woodrow Wilson observed: "Principles, as statesmen conceive them, are threads to the labyrinth of circumstances. . . . Throw the conceiving mind, habituated to contemplating wholes, into the arena of politics, and it seems to itself to be standing upon shifting sands, where no sure foothold and no upright posture are possible." [4]

The radical difference between philosophy and action is a continuing theme in the literature on American diplomacy or

[4] Quoted in Arthur Walworth, *Woodrow Wilson, American Prophet* (New York: Longmans, Green & Co., 1958), I, 287.

government and politics throughout the world. Intellectuals in particular should be aware that the broad sweep of modern thinking on foreign policy, in which they participate and of which they are a part, views diplomacy as a problematical endeavor. For some, it may seem slightly less odious than politics, but for the most part modern culture has been consistently sanguine that superior forms of state relations were soon to be discovered. Indeed, from the popular standpoint, diplomacy, like politics, is basically a highly questionable activity. It is what is left over when more responsible functions of government like law and administration are extracted. It is the unsavory aspect of man's collective life tarnished by ambition, rivalry, and open strife.

The examples of this attitude are numerous. During and following World War I, a handful of diplomats plying their trade in secrecy beyond the reach of public opinion were identified as a principal cause of war. The Nye Committee, in conducting an investigation into the role of munition makers in leading the United States to the brink of war, inferred that this group was allied with a handful of "secret diplomatists." Following World War II, well-informed journalists and popular writers applauded the fact that new and more broadly based forms of United States representation abroad were being established. Specialists in economics, cultural affairs, agriculture, and the information services had taken the place of, or been added to, the working of United States diplomacy. For many, the new programs had the effect of substituting economics, reason, law, or science for the ambiguous art of politics and diplomacy.

This trend of thought had expressed itself in liberal or Marxist forms at the turn of the century. According to Marxism, more peaceful times would follow once the bourgeois exploiters were overthrown and the domination of men by men was replaced by the administration of things. Liberal economists such as Cobden and Bright held one view in common with Marx. They too looked forward to the day when old forms of international diplomacy were supplanted, in this case by new patterns of international trade. In our own day, some proponents of economic development and technical assistance advance a similar view. Thus an architect of the Marshall Plan recently observed that the success of the program was due to the fact that "considerations of the cold war never entered into its planning."

Not surprisingly, the defenders of reason or law or science have been equally outspoken in claims that something better could take the place of diplomatic procedures. Science, which daily is propelling men and nations into the twenty-first century at a dismayingly rapid pace, has its own outspoken critics. The scientist, appalled by the tortuous pace of negotiations and conciliation, and sensitive to the awesome nature of discoveries in which he has personally had a hand, is tempted to urge that science replace diplomacy. C. P. Snow's *Two Cultures,* the scientific and the humanistic, presents a fairly explicit choice for those confronted with the issues of foreign policy. The scientist can point to a superior method illustrated by recent Soviet and American successes in outer space. The one thing common to these projects has been the tendency to think through the problem as a whole, from beginning to end, or from countdown to pickup. With astronauts or cosmonauts, scientists measure the forces available against those that have to be overcome. They determine not only how to shoot an object or man through space but also how to bring him back to earth. In the language of foreign policy, the scientist balances objectives against capacity and proceeds when he is clear that the needed resources are at hand.

Sensing the superiority of this method, scientists, like Isador Rabi of Columbia University, have called for an educational program under which diplomatists and statesmen were exposed to the truths of science at an early stage. They maintain that wise policy in the mid-twentieth century is no longer possible in the absence of full knowledge of scientific realities. To have the scientific expert on tap is no longer enough; the policy-maker must himself be a scientist. Against this viewpoint, Professor Rabi's Columbia University colleague, Professor Richard Neustedt, asserts that in fact there is a third culture mediating between science and the humanities, which is politics or statesmanship itself.

The evidence multiplies that diplomatists or foreign policy-makers in moments of candor express grave doubts as to the contributions of scientists and philosophers. Willingness to use "academically or analytically trained men" seems stronger in theory than practice. Thus the late John Foster Dulles once announced that he would "welcome assistance" from scholars with experience and knowledge of world problems comparable to his own. But he went on to ask, with greater candor than tact, "Where are there such people?" [5] Even philosophers or theorists of diplomacy have not always proven their worth. Two recent secretaries of state, Dean Acheson and John Foster Dulles, commented on the importance of deeper understanding of the philosophy of foreign policy. Mr. Dulles stated that: "No nation's foreign policy can be ascertained merely from what its officials say. More important are the philosophy of its leaders and the actual manifestation of that philosophy in what is done." Yet the philosophies in action of individual leaders are seldom systematized and often not articulated, though no less powerful for that. Former President Harry S. Truman, according to his closest associates, had one underlying conviction. Briefly, it was that expansionism and aggression must be resisted at its source before reaching the proportions of the massive agglomeration of power that was Nazi Germany. President Truman's simple and clear-cut philosophy was an outgrowth of one man's experience between World Wars I and II, but as such it reflects the lesson that embedded itself in the consciousness of a whole nation.

Beyond this, some leaders and diplomatists maintain that intellectuals and philosophers exaggerate the influence of di-

[5] John Foster Dulles, "Thoughts on Soviet Foreign Policy and What to Do about It," *Life*, XX (June 3, 1946), 113.

vergent philosophies as they affect decisions in specific cases. In a crisis like the one leading up to the Korean War, the nature of the problem that faced the men who had to make the far-reaching choice to intervene or stand aside had a great unifying effect. Men of quite different persuasions united on a single line of action. The weight of this criticism suggests that outsiders, whether scientists or philosophers, unfairly ignore the context and setting in which foreign policy decisions must be made. Doctrines shape policies less than facts. A leading American columnist observed a common human coloration in the top executive officials of the Kennedy administration who "are not doctrinaire. They accept no limitations, except the limitations that the hard facts impose. Their simple, highly pragmatic aim is to deal with the hard facts in whatever way will be most likely to safeguard and promote the great interests of the United States." [6]

Intellectuals, including philosophers and scientists, are prompt to respond. They assert that professional diplomatists are too often wedded to the status quo. Diplomats instinctively react by rolling with the punch or allowing themselves to be carried along by events. Within a given country, they operate from too narrow a base, and their contacts are limited to select groups in the diplomatic community and in the government in power to which they are assigned. Professionals underestimate the power of tides of change. For example, how many ambassadors have predicted the overthrow of a particular regime? In the years following World War II, what diplomat foresaw the impending changes in Korea, Iran, Iraq, Cuba, or Lebanon?

Humanists and scientists also maintain that diplomatists all too often disparage the role of human relationships in dissolving tensions and conflicts. They say that the professionals are the group most likely to question the value, for example, of Soviet-American scientific exchange. The importance of

° Joseph Alsop, "Matter of Fact: The Level of Competence," *New York Herald Tribune,* December 28, 1960, p. 20.

human relationships in removing mutual fears and misunderstandings is frequently given short shrift by full-time representatives abroad. They lose touch with the day-by-day developments that shape the country in which they live. Philosophers remind us that the professionals opposed India's independence, attacked the support of principles of international law in the Suez crisis, and criticized self-determination as the foundation of policy for Africa and Asia.

Finally, philosophers and scientists ridicule those aspects of diplomacy associated with stilted language and outmoded procedures. There is something grotesque about the degree to which diplomacy is restricted and shackled by its formality. Some of the empty procedures that celebrate the practices of an earlier day divert responsible officials from their most important constitutional task. Intellectuals call attention to the endless round of diplomatic receptions, particularly in great centers like New York, Washington, and London—all at the expense of the diplomatists' most precious resource, time. Incidentally, philosophers who reason this way must remind themselves that the added burdens of contemporary diplomats are partly a result of the widening scope of foreign policy, which now emphasizes culture, economics, and agriculture, along with negotiation and conciliation.

Sir Harold Nicolson, the British historian, who can hardly be dismissed as an unfriendly critic of professional diplomacy, speaks of the functional defects the diplomatist may develop. He is aware of the risk that the diplomat

has seen human folly or egoism operating in so many different circumstances that he may identify serious passions with transitory feelings and thus underestimate the profound emotion by which whole nations can be swayed. He is so inured to the contrast between those who know the facts and those who do not know the facts, that he forgets that the latter constitute the vast majority and that it is with them that the last decision rests. He may have deduced from experience that time alone is the conciliator, that unimportant things do not matter and that important things settle themselves, that mistakes are the only things that are really effective, and he may thus incline to the fallacy that on the whole it is wiser, in all circumstances, to do nothing at all.[7]

In eras of profound change, these functional defects may restrict the professional diplomat to a restraining rather than an innovating role. They may hamper him in responding to great forces of history that must be appraised before they reach full tide. His predispositions and much of his professional apprenticeship may endanger the diplomat's capacity for decisive action and creative leadership in a day and age when such qualities are essential.

It seems obvious then that a wide gulf separates philosophers and diplomatists. A former colleague took occasion more than once to caution a younger, overzealous associate: "Some issues and differences won't settle themselves in your time or mine." The divergence between approaches to the problems of American diplomacy may be a case in point. How does one measure the validity of the contending viewpoints, and how call on one or the other school of thought to help us understand our problems and meet the challenges of the days ahead? How strike a balance between the claims of philosophers and diplomatists?

The philosophers and scientists and men of thought are undoubtedly right on at least three counts. Diplomatists and statesmen are subject to winds of change far more than they know. History, which has never stood still, is now in almost continuous flux. Today's allies are yesterday's foes; sturdy political institutions are transformed within a decade. For example, the United Nations, formed to institutionalize the ability of the great powers to police the world, has now come under the sway of the Afro-Asian world. The timetable of independence for countries around the globe has been advanced to a degree no one expected. The order of magnitude of foreign policy problems has multiplied by many factors with the

[7] Harold Nicolson, *The Evolution of Diplomatic Method* (New York: The Macmillan Co., 1954), p. 78.

threat of nuclear war. And with the nuclear stalemate the problem of poor and rich states has come to preoccupy if not obsess hard-bitten realists on both sides of the Iron Curtain. So far-reaching has been the transformation of contemporary world politics, so profound and sweeping the changes in situations with which statesmen and diplomats must cope, that ancient wisdom and time-tested procedures are called into question. Are there ways in which diplomats can approach the implications of today's events that may be manifest five, ten, or more years in the future?

Secondly, pure or narrow professionalism, if it ever existed, is undoubtedly a thing of the past. Decisions have gravitated to top political leaders who must rally public support for what they do. Participation in policy formulation requires talent mobilized across a wide front—armaments specialists, economists, legislators, and seasoned negotiators. A purely political or diplomatic question is a thing of the past, and the structure and content of today's diplomacy may bear little relationship to present forms.

Finally, a more orderly and systematic approach to diplomatic problems is needed, and in this the scientists' warning may be worthy of note. Foreign policy should never result from mere "bull sessions." The elements that make up a decision in diplomacy no less than science should be weighed, and policy and power brought into line. The commitment of resources must be commensurate with objectives pursued. Our record is not beyond constructive criticism in this regard. The task of foreign assistance, for example, in one writer's terse description, has to the present involved an effort to help two-thirds of the world's population in a program requiring a twenty-year design with a five-year plan executed by two-year personnel operating on the basis of one-year appropriations. Perhaps the new foreign aid legislation will ease this difficulty, but the problem in varying guises will undoubtedly haunt our leaders into the foreseeable future.

At the same time, diplomatists and statesmen are right in

saying that foreign policy is an inexact science. It requires compromises, judgments, and the willingness to live with all the uncertain consequences of a decision. The intellectual processes are by no means the same. In the words of the famous Arabic classic, the *Muqaddima* of Ibn Khaldun:

Scholars are of all men those least fitted for politics and its ways. The reason for this is that they are accustomed to intellectual speculation, the search for concepts, and their abstraction from sense data and clarification in the mind. All these operations aim at attaining the universal aspect of things, not those particular to their material content, or to a person, generation, nation, or particular class of men. . . . Politics are tortuous and may contain elements which prevent the subsumption of a given event under a universal concept or maxim or its comparison with another similar event. In fact, no social phenomenon should be judged by analogy with other phenomena, for if it is similar to them in certain respects it may yet differ from them in many others. . . . The same is true of the sharper and more brilliant men of the world, who because of their quick wits tend to behave like men of learning in their search for concepts and in their use of analogy. The ordinary sound man of average intelligence, however, whose mind is unaccustomed to such speculation and incapable of practising it, judges each case on its own merits. . . .[8]

The problem of the decision-maker, paradoxically enough, is to master "the last detail" while accepting the fact that his knowledge remains incomplete. He must recognize always that the most remote of any set of possibilities may occur. Intellectuals share a certain contempt for administrative detail—or else would they speak in such mournful tones of university administration, which sets the framework within which they live and work? Need I remind you of prevailing attitudes in many universities toward the labors of administrative leaders, deans, and departmental chairmen? When the intellectual comes on the firing line, this viewpoint may reflect itself in an impatience with the homework needed to "get on top of any prob-

[8] *An Arab Philosophy of History*, rendered in Issawi (New York: Charles P. Taplinger, 1950), p. 64.

lem." Mere brilliance in spinning off novel ideas is not sufficient for diplomacy. At some point a conclusion must become
a decision with which an executive must be prepared to live.

Moreover, intellectuals all too often are passionately devoted to "manageable research." Unfortunately, most policy
questions are anything but manageable. An American secretary
of state was asked what form of training was best suited to a
young man aspiring to foreign service. He pointed to the wide
expanse of his office and said, "Turn loose one hundred white
mice and ask the candidate to deal with them." However useful
useless science may prove in the long run, it is often a luxury
in the short run in which the policy-maker cannot indulge
himself.

Finally, the skills and qualities appropriate to foreign
policy and other policy fields may be those which tend to be
undervalued by pure scholars. The patronizing phrase "merely
technical" is frequently on the lips of intellectuals, but the
technical man more often than not is indispensable. Modern
government requires technicians who bring skills to an endless
range of public duties. Thus the diplomatist today must be a
parliamentarian to carry out his functions within multilateral
agencies. He must be an international lawyer, or at least have
knowledge of the principles of law. He must know the country
in which he works and the limits of working there. And all
these resources and many more must be summoned up on
very short notice. Someone has said that the expert or intellectual advising the diplomat is much like a friend calling direc-
tions to the man on a crowded subway platform. The friend
has no dearth of good intentions; yet for the man on the platform the facts of the situation are controlling. The friend may
urge that the victim of a subway rush move this way or that,
but the crush of the crowd is more compelling than the well-
meant advice of the friend. Intellectuals, if they are to contribute, must cleanse themselves of the thought that by "listening to reason" the problems of diplomacy will be eased. They
must recognize that men act in diplomacy because they must,

their alernatives are restricted, their choices hedged about, and the ground on which they stand seldom is wholly of their own choosing. Decisions are made oftentimes not for want of other more desirable intentions but because the range of practical choice excludes them.

I believe if philosophers and diplomatists in turn were able to place themselves in one another's position, their debate might be less rancorous, their understanding of divergent viewpoints more compassionate. As we unfold the scroll of American diplomatic history and consider its central problems, the evidence for this assertion may become clearer. But even if this were not the case, we can ill afford in the nuclear age too deep and profound a schism between men of thought and men of action. Our problems are too great, our numbers too few. However we mobilize resources, our problems make pygmies of us all.

1. Philosophy, Purpose, and Diplomacy

THE importance of philosophy to American diplomacy has been more or less obvious from the beginnings of our history. The Founding Fathers were practical political philosophers whose views on federalism, representative government, taxation, and public authority grew out of their political philosophies. The Federalist Papers are among the most enduring documents in political philosophy in Western civilization. Our early leaders were clear that a system of government and foreign policy had to be based on a clear-cut conception of the nature of man, the state, and of the world. They were the inheritors of two thousand years of discussion on the political consequences of the nature of man. Their own principles and beliefs in government and foreign policy were derived from the principles and beliefs preserved in the thought and experience of the West. The institutions of free government had been tested on other soil; the problems that arose, either when individual rights were abridged or when too little power was available to govern, were understood vicariously from the beginning.

The goals of early leaders insofar as they affected foreign relations were simple and limited. They stemmed from the primary objective of establishing a society in which freedom and equality could be pursued. The uniqueness and importance of this objective and past memories of being deprived of its fruits led Americans to see themselves as a chosen people. Moreover, the quest for freedom and self-determination seems to require that states claiming freedom for themselves proclaim their purposes in universal terms. In the words of Washington's Farewell Address, the goal of America was to "give to mankind the magnanimous and too novel example of a

people always guided by an exalted justice and benevolence."
America from its birth was to be an example and model. Even
while claiming a universal purpose, this nation had to recognize that the form and content of its benevolence would be
colored by its particular conception of national destiny. Time
and circumstance shape virtue itself. The exalted justice of
Washington's "no entangling alliances" became neither just
nor exalted in Wilson's or Roosevelt's administration.

In the first years of our history, the national purpose beyond national boundaries was chiefly to protect American lives
and interests abroad and to safeguard the Western Hemisphere
from outside interference and control. The Monroe Doctrine
became the classic statement of this latter goal and purpose.
With the growth of interests abroad, these comparatively
simple purposes were expanded and multiplied.

A philosophy which can be helpful in shaping American
programs at home and abroad must not only state political purposes and goals; it must also provide some idea about the
nature of man, his aims, and his limitations. The most significant attribute of our earlier writers may have been the
stress placed on the nature of man. Democracy was linked
both to the frailties and the possibilities of man. Thus, it was
argued that if men were wholly evil, government would be
impossible; if men were wholly good, government would be
unnecessary. Since man is both good and evil, the best system
of government is one which harnesses his virtues to serve good
purposes and limits his vices through legal and institutional
restraints. Those who argued against a government of unlimited powers did so on grounds that no one was virtuous enough
to hold such power. Those who argued for stronger national
government maintained that only the state representing the
nation as a whole would act to advance the common good while
safeguarding the interests of weak and strong alike.

The early debate about the form and institutions of American government was in essence a debate over the qualities and
attributes of man. If man was to realize himself and the capac-

ities he enjoys, free institutions of government were needed. If he was to achieve the best of which man is capable, provisions respecting the dignity of man, the rights of the individual, and the consent of the governed had to be institutionalized. It would be a mistake to imagine that views on the nature of man and government put forward by early leaders were uniquely or even primarily American. John Marshall, the first Chief Justice, could write: "There are principles of abstract justice which the Creator of all things has impressed on the minds of His creature, man, and which are admitted to regulate in great degree the right of civilized nations." These general principles were not ones that had an exclusive American parentage. A stream of thought going back to Graeco-Roman and Christian philosophy marked out the principles on which the Union was based.

From the Declaration of Independence to the present, philosophers have, of course, contributed to the vision and definition of America's objectives and goals. Yet it is only in the seventh decade of the twentieth century that an explicit and deliberate attempt has been made to summon philosophers, statesmen, and scientists as a group to state more clearly where we are and where we must go. At no time has so direct and organized an attack been made on defining the State of the Union. A President's Commission on National Goals and a *Life-New York Times* series on the national purpose were organized in part to rally American intelligence to the task of stating what we are and what we strive to become. Walter Lippmann has written: "The critical weakness of our society is that for the time being our people do not have great purposes which they are united in wanting to achieve." [9] The quest for these purposes, whether lost or forgotten goals of the past or novel objectives for the future, has recently become a dominant preoccupation of individuals and groups. It may be that in

[9] *The National Purpose*, ed. *Life* magazine (New York: Holt, Rinehart and Winston, 1960), p. 1.

the process contemporaries run the risk of forgetting that the
national heritage is as often the slow deposit of experience
as the outcome of broad decrees. Some may misconceive the
birth and growth of national goals. They may wait in vain for
resounding and ennobling affirmations that provide something
of the framework of documents like the Declaration of Independence. Yet it is significant that outstandingly able Americans are engaged in this task.

However, there are also dangers inherent in the mobiliza-
tion of America's intellectuals to search for a doctrine. For
some, the one lesson of the Soviet challenge to the West is the
need for a comprehensive doctrine that can match that of the
Soviet Union. We run a dual risk in the present-day struggle
with a powerful and unscrupulous adversary. There is danger,
on one side, of assuming that the rival is politically backward,
handcuffed by tyrannical forces, incapable through indigenous
resources of enterprise and initiative, and beyond the pale of
responsibility and trust in every form of international relationship. We tended to view the Soviet Union in this light at the
end of the McCarthy period. Today nearly all of us find it
more fashionable to examine objectively the principal sources
of Soviet strength—its leadership in science, educational progress, respect for intellectuals, and political and ideological
skills. Most of us do not credit the average Russian with being
nine feet tall, but we are nonetheless disposed to measure our
national assets as reflected in the Soviet mirror. For example,
how many worthy men have not rallied around programs designed to match or master the Soviet Union in some field or
other of human endeavor?

Not surprisingly, we sense the superior Soviet ideological
position in many parts of the world playing its fateful role in
the struggle for men's minds. The democratic world can boast
no equivalent of the Communist Manifesto; the democratic
dogma is forever unfolding and the great epochs in American
history are the years in which new ground was broken. Presi-

dents like Washington, Jefferson, and Lincoln, in response to the needs of their age and in partnership with the people, raised up from the warp and woof of national experience the purposes that carried us through a stormy past. Their purposes were living goals, not abstract ends or fixed doctrines. Indeed, the great expressions of national purpose were the products of the gravest moments of crisis, whether in 1776, 1861, or 1939. Paradoxically, the conflict, doubt, and tragedy that preceded the great statements are inseparable from their abiding value. Our history suggests it must always be thus in a vast pluralistic society where ends as well as means compete, and the government and the people give them substance, proportion, and meaning along the way.

For the United States as world leader, this truth obtains today as it has throughout our history. The goals of a "troubled past" cannot be the aims of an uncertain present. But neither are modern goals sufficient as commonly formulated. For example, freedom may be too individualistic, sophisticated in its requirements, and restrictive to have much meaning for nearly two-thirds of the world's people. For the vast agrarian societies of Asia and Africa, predominantly illiterate, only partially escaped from feudalism, and pressing in on limited resources for survival, the doctrine of majority rule seems often a distant goal. Even the leaders of those societies that are relatively mature politically and can point to the beginnings of democratic institutions are compelled periodically to remind us that "order" must precede "liberty."

This is true of countries like Egypt and Tunisia, to say nothing of countries with less political modernization. If the treasure we have to offer the rest of the world is conceived too narrowly as freedom or equality or individual rights, our words and deeds may fall on barren ground. But the soil may prove more fertile if, from our political storehouse, we rediscover the broader tradition we share with Western civilization of "order and liberty." These are the working principles with which Western man has sought political justice and which he has weighed and balanced in an endless variety of political contexts.

The Soviet scheme by contrast has no place for the balancing of political or ideological claims. All goals and interests within the Communist state are subordinated to one transcendent purpose; all means are appropriate to a single all-consuming end. For the sake of a solution to the economic problem, millions of Kulaks were sacrificed. No democratic society would pay the price of lifting a single national purpose to these heights; the fury and ruthlessness of political action within Russia are a product of its very clarity and single-mindedness of national purpose. Therefore, the Soviet example, far from demonstrating the importance of consensus on one overarching goal for society, sends up ominous warning signs for all those who would slavishly follow its lead.

The Soviet lesson is at best problematical for any free people. It is true in broader terms that political philosophies have faced their severest test in attempting to relate the specific or unique to the general and universal. The problem persists not only in totalitarian systems, but also with more modest and limited historical propositions. The charge is frequently made that recent American foreign policy has been exclusively preoccupied with discussion of means as against the ends of national life. But surely the broad national tendency has been precisely the opposite. The grand purposes of international action have been articulated far more often than the limited goals of world affairs.

Consider the basic policies recent presidents have espoused: peace and justice, collective security, the outlawing of war, national self-determination, a war to make the world safe for democracy, support for the United Nations as the cornerstone of American policy, the world rule of law, the Fourteen Points, and the Atlantic Charter. The leaders who expressed these purposes were hardly involved in nitpicking over means and techniques. Were they not rather putting forward a grand design with which they intended to resolve all the troublesome problems that baffle and confound the people and their policy-makers?

From Woodrow Wilson to John F. Kennedy, historians note a succession of doctrines, proclamations, and overall plans that tend to comprise the overwhelming majority of the dialogues between the leaders and the people. Some may say that the grand purposes chosen were misguided or ill-designed, short-sighted or utopian, but no one can or should confuse them with technical military or diplomatic contrivances. If anything, these approaches suffered from the contempt and disdain idealists frequently display as they confront the problems of painful details.

President Wilson, for example, had no comprehensive plan for the realization of the objectives of the Fourteen Points nor of his world organization. He was largely indifferent to the territorial and political factors that were a precondition to his "grand and noble illusion." Yet who would question that Wilson succeeded in formulating a grand design and noble purpose that captured the imagination of millions of ordinary people. If there was lack of clarity, it was hardly in the realm of ends. Those who base their appeal on broad and simple principles, avoiding commitments on specific measures, often fall prey to cynics like Clemenceau who, far more than Wilson, was the architect of the ill-fated peace.

Another difficulty that plagues understanding and confounds the dialogue between leaders and followers in any free society is the gap that periodically develops between them. Leaders oftentimes speak in two languages. To the people, they express foreign policy in terms of moral purpose, of ultimate goals, and towering intentions. To one another, they speak in the practical language of alliances, deterrents, and the balance of power—the selfsame purposes repudiated in public discussions. The public philosophy, far from thriving on such discrepancies, is weakened and enfeebled, much as children come to doubt loving parents who have prepared them only for a world of social relations free of conflicts, frustrations, and despair—a preparation that bears scant resemblance to the real world.

Hence, if danger and political failure await those who see the nation's course too narrowly in terms of means and techniques, the opposite danger persists for those who speak only of noble purposes. I suspect this is the reason why some of our wisest observers writing in the American context agree with Walter Lippmann that if the moral philosopher or the architect of national purpose "is to deserve a hearing among his fellows, he must set himself this task which is so much humbler than to command and so much more difficult than to exhort: he must seek to anticipate and to supplement the insight of his fellow men into the problems of their adjustment to reality."

Many who engage in the current debate run the risk of confounding means and ends. The risk is considerably aggravated by the nature of the present crisis. The West in its struggle with world communism is called upon to be specific if its counsels are to carry weight, for the Communists have ready-made solutions alluring in the simplicity of their appeal to the peoples of Asia and Africa. All goals are subordinated to a single purpose; every policy is rationalized by its link with the end of economic development and social justice. The temptation is nearly overpowering to put forward an equally simple and specific design for the world. Since we have lost a good measure of the subtlety and depth of our earlier philosopher-statesmen, we fall prey to the perennial disease of giving grand and utopian answers to complex, practical issues and offering this as our national purpose.

The conflicts and contradictions that result come quickly to the surface. Thus one interpreter of national purpose would rally Americans to a massive counterpolitical strategy making use of trained cold war specialists. He sees a political West Point or a Liberation Force "drawn largely from among refugees from captive nations" as instruments in "a strategy for victory." At the same time he rather piously declares:

"Whenever the United States tried to act without moral conviction or contrary to our basic beliefs, it found itself inhibited and ultimately had to rechart its course."

The mediating role of prudence, that ancient political virtue known to the classical philosophers and to many of the Founding Fathers, finds no place in a strategy which supplants ends with autonomous moral means. The function of those who plot concrete political strategies is more modest but no less essential than that of the moral philosopher. They must search for ways of balancing competing moral and political claims, never losing sight of ultimate purposes. Yet at the point they assert too sharply the prerogatives of the moralist they debase both the virtue of their humble task and the credit of the ultimate ends of society.

In practical politics, a realm of intermediate moral and political purposes exists, each serving a valued moral function. In this realm, we discover the sensitive conscience of the responsible leader grappling with himself and the harsh realities to chart a course that is morally responsible within a set of existing circumstances. In the book *The National Purpose*, the first clear statement of this problem appears on page 96. At this point, Mr. Albert Wohlstetter writes that:

the limitation of the questions raised so far is that they ask for very general answers, for a statement of ends without any explicit weighing of means or costs. They sometimes seem to imply . . . that our difficulties are not really complex, deep or particular, and that they can be solved by a simple reaffirmation—and of some one thing at that.[10]

Mr. Wohlstetter, after arguing that what is needed at the working level is hard analysis of what we want and what we can do and the efforts needed, then concludes: "While we may talk about national purpose in the singular, the first thing to observe about our aims is that we have many of them. They are connected; some depend on others; many conflict." [11]

At the level at which he writes, his conclusion seems un-

---

[10] *The National Purpose, op. cit.*, pp. 95–96.
[11] *Ibid.*, p. 96.

exceptional. The proximate aims and purposes of the American Republic are manifold and interrelated. Some oppose others; thus while we seek the "common defense," we likewise search for present satisfaction. Efforts to safeguard ourselves and our allies from self-destruction may be at odds with getting the utmost in production of civilian goods and services. We strive to increase democracy everywhere, but this conflicts with our resolution to avoid interference in the internal affairs of other nations. It will not do to insist that no conflicts exist, that policy-makers are free to choose peace over justice, or national self-determination over noninterference. Common sense should tell us that "to make fundamental choices, we must understand specific means as well as general ends." [12] We should expect to be faced with unpleasant and even tragic judgments. Failure to admit this accounts for the rather pious and irrelevant nature of so much of both private and public discussion of national purpose.

I sense at the heart of the debate a vast and perhaps unbridgeable gap between those who would affirm the final ends of society and let it go at that and those who strive to relate means and ends. It is no distortion of truth to point to sacred texts like the Declaration of Independence as the American dream. Yet men like Walter Lippmann and Reinhold Niebuhr are also right in saying that professing devotion to historic goals does not exhaust our responsibility in a changing world. Somehow, doctrines of a radical individualism or American messianism are not sufficient to the hazards and opportunities of the cold war. New formulae, policies, and programs are called for, and innovation is as vital now as in the days of Lincoln, Wilson, or the two Roosevelts. In Walter Lippmann's words:

> The innovator for whom the country is waiting will not come with a new revelation of the ultimate ends and commitments of our society. The ultimate ends are fixed. They are lasting and they are not disputed. The nation is dedicated to freedom. It is dedicated to the

[12] *Ibid.*, p. 97.

rights of men and to government with the consent of the governed. The innovation . . . will be in the means, in the policies and programs and measures, by which the ultimate ends of our free society can be realized in the world today.[13]

Affirming our ultimate ends, like standing erect at the playing of the national anthem, may bring a flush of moral self-satisfaction but it is hardly a substitute for giving content to purposes in a changing historical context.

Furthermore, greater attention to means alongside devotion to ends might safeguard us against self-righteousness in lecturing other peoples and especially newly independent states on the goals they should follow. The great strength of a society that is rigorous and flexible in the way it pursues its goals stems from the breadth of its vision of the manifold institutions and measures through which states seek their goals. It is the beginning of wisdom for Americans to know that the problem of individual rights, which in the eighteenth and nineteenth centuries involved protecting the individual from the state, today has become the issue of making individual freedom compatible with national stability and justice for the collective interest of classes and races. Knowing this, the light of our national experience illuminates far more the problems of new nations than would the mere recitation of national texts. The great virtue of discussing the means and policies by which national ends are pursued lies in their tentative, pragmatic, and evolving character. All nations suffer periods which Professor Walt W. Rostow has called "neurotic fixations of history" when, confronted by radically new situations, they cling to timeworn policies increasingly divorced from reality. The realm of means enjoys benefits that the more sanctified domain of ultimate ends cannot boast.

For the most part, the national purpose finds expression in the words and deeds of its historic leaders. The goals of American life have not been given us on tablets of stone. They

---

[13] *Ibid.*, p. 127.

have rather been plucked out of the ebb and flow of national existence by leaders who gave them form and content. James Reston wryly observes: "If George Washington had waited for the doubters to develop a sense of purpose in the 18th century, he'd still be crossing the Delaware." [14] The Declaration of Independence, the Emancipation Proclamation, and the Four Freedoms were existential, not philosophical, statements. The large ideas that comprise national purpose were extracted from the national experience by leaders who could command the full attention of the American people. They dipped down, as it were, into the stream of experience and brought forth classic statements of lasting truth about immediately relevant problems of our collective life. If we say that the people become bored with the glittering generalities that infect much of the discussion of national purpose, we should remind ourselves of two features of the great historic statements. First, they were propositions linked closely to urgent needs and problems. There was an organic relationship between means and ends. Second, they resulted from attempts by responsible leaders to help men frame the issues to better understand the choices that lay before them. The powers of the presidency in fixing national attention should never be underestimated. In Woodrow Wilson's words: "His is the only national voice in affairs. Let him once win the admiration and confidence of the country and no other single force can withstand him. . . . His is the vital place of action in the system." [15] The evidence is impressive that once the President expresses the national need, his propositions and his acts vitally affect the spirit and direction of the nation. When the sense of purpose lags, the likelihood is greater that the President has failed to call on the people than that they have refused to do what they have been asked to do.

This feature of our constitutional system is often perplex-

---

[14] *Ibid.*, p. 109.
[15] Woodrow Wilson, *Constitutional Government in the United States* (New York: Columbia University Press, 1908), pp. 67 ff.

ing both to ourselves and to friends abroad. We tend to forget that "most of the great crises of the American past have been resolved, not by the zeal and purpose of the people, but usually by the will power or obstinacy of their leaders." James Reston reminds us that "John Adams estimated that one-third of the population was against the American Revolution, one-third for it, and one-third indifferent." [16] Democracy is not only compatible with strong leadership, it is dependent upon it. If this is true in a nation richly endowed with a cultured and self-conscious people, it should be yet more obvious in nations struggling to reach some degree of minimum literacy. A remnant of leaders who loved wisdom and could bring together ideas and politics has been the fountainhead of national progress. They have stood above the "prosperities, idolatries, oppression, luxury [and] pleasures" of the majority and in so doing shaped lasting national purposes. They have not flinched at the responsibility of defining our tasks. In a world of two billion hungry people seized with the passion of rising expectations, statements of national purpose must be as real and meaningful for their problems as was the Emancipation Proclamation to the long-term needs of 31,000,000 Americans at the outbreak of the Civil War.

The opportunity that beckons is one of stating a national purpose that will be relevant here and abroad. As a great hegemonial power, we speak not alone for ourselves but for others: for De Gaulle, who stakes his political life on the hazardous movement toward Algerian self-determination; for Britain, which grapples with the baffling problems of the Central African Federation; and for the new states, which yearn for the beginnings of individual rights while they compress into years and months achievements that required nearly two centuries within our borders. Is it any wonder that our leaders speak of new opportunities and purposes or assert that our national ends must become international in scope?

In this setting, the broader moral and philosophical prin-

---

[16] *The National Purpose, op. cit.,* pp. 109–10.

ciples have meaning. Natural law at its best has much to contribute to the debate over changing national purpose. At its worst, it can impair understanding and progress. The perennial temptation of moderns is to fix proximate moral goals into rigid natural law categories. The imperatives of practical politics are sanctified prematurely as final moral truth. For this reason, contemporary writers all too frequently assert that natural law is irrelevant to present-day problems, as when some of its champions call for a holy war to the death against the injustice of communism.

However, hidden away in at least some of the current debate are more legitimate references to natural law. Thus John K. Jessup maintains: "Democracy, though we have treasured it, is not the highest value known to man. Indeed, it is only because enough Americans have had still higher allegiances that we have made democracy work." [17] Because democracy is at some points at least in harmony with a higher order, it enjoys a special moral sanction. Archibald MacLeish pays homage to this truth when he argues:

> To be free is not, perhaps, a political program in the modern sense, but from the point of view of a new nation it may be something better. The weakness of political programs—Five Year Plans and the like—is that they can be achieved. But human freedom can never be achieved because human freedom is a continuously evolving condition. It is infinite in its possibilities—as infinite as the human soul which it enfranchises.[18]

When James Reston speaks of "the outer, quieter America, which has either kept its religious faith or at least held on to the morality derived from religious tradition," he points to a layer of ideals the Founding Fathers comprehended in the claim that the moral idea came before the political.

The higher law has englobed American political life, defining the framework within which political debate and

[17] *Ibid.*, p. 17.
[18] *Ibid.*, p. 27.

change were possible. Because there was broad agreement on ends, debate over means became possible. America could tolerate diversity because the bonds of unity had been forged— as, incidentally, they have not been forged in many parts of the world. The ends of American society are not difficult to discover. They touch the corporate ends of the nation and were first stated in our great fundamental documents like the Declaration of Independence. One of our ablest scholars, Professor Hans J. Morgenthau, has described them as freedom expressed in equality. The same goals are restated in the Preamble and Articles I and II of the United Nations Charter. These great ideas have been illumined by "flashes of documentary lightning," but their sources lie buried in more than two thousand years of Western experience, thought, and reflection. For the United States, they were the slow deposit of English and Colonial experience, drawing upon the maxims of the Greeks and Romans. An ancient dialogue lay behind them. In this historic sense, American purposes were grounded in natural law and allied with Judaeo-Christian moral principles. Their content remained to be hammered out on the anvil of successive decades of unfolding history.

2. Diplomacy and American Culture

ALEXIS de Tocqueville wrote of the United States: "I think that in no country in the civilized world is less attention paid to philosophy. . . ." [19] We ask ourselves whether or not we have turned a corner, whether the organized concern with national values would lead de Tocqueville to alter his claim, or whether we remain a society seldom, if ever, disposed to speculation and philosophy? If such a charge respecting philosophy could be made in the nineteenth century, a similar remark is possible in the twentieth century for diplomacy. Indeed, diplomacy until quite recently has been the orphan of organized international studies. It is not without symbolic significance that most young Americans who study international relations approach diplomacy with a backward look. They survey the topic through diplomatic history. By contrast, international law, international organization, and international economics are the wave of the future. Diplomacy by implication was a thing of the past. A few archaic customs might persist, but diplomacy as such, so heavily encrusted with the wars and conflicts of the past, was doomed to pass from the picture.

What accounts for the sharp rejection of diplomacy in American culture? Why have we gone so far in turning our backs on this ancient art? In part, the American viewpoint may stem from the continuous flux and movement that agitate a democratic society. Diplomacy embraces traditional procedures, and we are far from traditional in outlook. On the contrary, it has been said of Americans: "The tie that unites one generation to another is relaxed or broken; every man . . .

---

[19] Alexis de Tocqueville, *Democracy in America*, trans. Henry Reeve (New York: Alfred A. Knopf, Inc., 1954), II, 3.

readily loses all traces of the ideas of his forefathers or takes no care about them." [20] The burden of proof is heaviest in our culture on those who would show that the traditional is superior.

Nor have we perpetuated the notion of an aristocratic elite, even Jefferson's "aristocracy of talent." Diplomacy presupposes that the judgment of the few is best since they are continuously seized with the subtleties and complexities of the problem. Our version of democratic dogma with its social and intellectual equalitarianism forces us to be at odds with every expression of aristocracy. Writing of this, Tocqueville could say: "It is not only confidence in this or that man which is destroyed, but the disposition to trust the authority of any man whatsoever. Everyone shuts himself up tightly within himself and insists upon judging the world from there." [21]

Yet these clues to a prevailing American attitude are probably insufficient in themselves. The fundamental question that adds confusion is the apparent conflict between an essential pragmatic approach to politics in the United States and its denial in international affairs. In democratic countries, the busy citizen eagerly lays hold of broad general ideas that spare him the trouble of studying particulars. Significantly, this applies most to subjects that are not habitual objects of thought. Thus businessmen accept uncritically the broad and sweeping views that seem to explain in a phrase philosophy, politics, or the arts, while rejecting grand simplifications in commerce, industry, or trade. Within a federal system where political decisions are more often resolved locally than on a national level, politics for many remains sufficiently a daily concern to moderate excessive taste for grand theories. International politics is far more an alien undertaking, and the practical and discriminating views that businessmen and private citizens bring to issues of immediate concern are more difficult to sustain the more distant and remote the problem. Virtuous and dedicated men, who find their virtue is never

[20] *Ibid.*, p. 4.
[21] *Ibid.*

complete in problems of daily concern, project their full sense of virtue to the international sphere.

At the heart of this problem is a moral dilemma. We are never as moral as we claim to be. This is true of the parent who disciplines the child "for its own good" no less than of the powerful nation that works its will on less powerful, but no less virtuous, states. Even when justice is the goal of a loving father, it invariably becomes mixed with coercion, caprice, and injustice. Nations with few exceptions have seen their cause and supremacy as equivalent to universal justice. The Archbishop of Canterbury, at a time Britain hoped to rally resistance to Italian aggression in Ethiopia, admonished the French: "We are animated by moral and spiritual considerations. . . . It is . . . no egoist interest driving us forward, and no consideration of interest should keep you behind." Yet serious historians, looking today on the paralysis of French policy and its failure to act, point not to her moral depravity, but to a tragic and tangled procession of events that includes the American refusal to give guarantees, France's pathological fear of Germany, and her plausible but ill-fated attempt to gain security in the northeast through an entente with Italy in the south. Nevertheless, as partners in two world wars with the British, we find her claims more plausible than those of a prominent National Socialist in 1935: "Anything that benefits the German people is right, anything that harms the German people is wrong."

Nor is American history lacking in comparable examples. It provides the story of President McKinley, who spent the night in prayer for divine guidance before deciding, as one might have expected, to annex the Philippines. Or President Wilson, who, following the bombardment of Vera Cruz in 1914, assured the world that "the United States had gone to Mexico to serve mankind," [22] and who shortly before our entry

[22] Woodrow Wilson, *The New Democracy:* Presidential Messages, Addresses and Other Papers (1913-17), eds. Ray Stannard Baker and William E. Dodd (New York, 1926), I, 104.

into World War I identified American principles and American policies as "the principles of mankind . . . [which] must prevail." [23] We are reminded of Tocqueville's words:

> If I say to an American that the country he lives in is a fine one, aye, he replies and there is not its equal in the world. If I applaud the freedom its inhabitants enjoy, he answers "freedom is a fine thing but few nations are worthy of it." If I remark on the purity of morals that distinguishes the United States he declares "I can imagine that a stranger who has witnessed the corruption which prevails in other nations would be astonished at the difference." At length I leave him to a contemplation of himself but he returns to the charge and does not desist until he has got me to repeat all I have been saying. It is impossible to conceive a more troublesome and garrulous patriotism.[24]

It must, of course, be obvious that every nation has its own form of spiritual pride. Our version is compounded, I would suppose, of at least three factors.

The first derives from the role of the immigrant who had turned his back on the vices of Europe and was making a new beginning. Having shaken the dust of the Old World from his feet, he was anxious to prove that none of its ancient failings were his failings. Their purposes, often sullied by the ambiguities and compromises bound up with national existence in the cockpit of Europe, were not his purposes. And strikingly enough, his affirmations of moral purity—or more specifically, those by which national leaders appealed to his virtue—seemed to be confirmed by early American social history. In the first phases of this history, the frontier saved us from the acrimony of class struggle and, later, our superior technology gave new outlets to the ambitious and adventurous. Beyond this we were freed from international responsibility by the fortuitous coincidence of our geographic isolation and a European equilibrium of power which British policy and naval power were dedicated to preserve. In such a world, it was natural to as-

---

[23] *Ibid.*, II, 414.
[24] Tocqueville, *op. cit.*, p. 236.

sume that domestic policies were more important than foreign policy and that the alliances so prevalent on the European scene were an expensive and pernicious nuisance. These objective conditions have passed, but the psychology they inspired lingers on, as in the recent sweeping and indignant denunciations of the exercise of power by European or Asian states, followed abruptly by our own decision to use force unilaterally if necessary in the Middle East and in Cuba.

A second factor shaping the American outlook results from the fact that our prevailing philosophy of international relations has been a curious blending of legalism and rationalism. Law and reason are, of course, indispensable ingredients of an orderly life. They are precious fruits of the flowering of a free community and the good life. And ultimately peace becomes possible in any permanent sense only when law and order prevail. However, the tragedy of much of our thinking has been to assume that this ultimate end was either realized or shortly realizable and to tailor our words and sometimes our deeds to fit this mistaken assumption.

American lawyers whose influence on our foreign relations has been immense have confused the realities of municipal law with the hopes of international law. They have imposed on the international system burdens it could not bear. If the problem was war, it must be outlawed (the Kellogg-Briand Pact). If the peril was aggression, a legal formula proscribing it and defining it was the goal—even though a United Nations Commission recently gave up this task in despair. If states trembled in a state of insecurity, reassure them with security pacts heaped one upon the other! If a state threatened the peace, pass a resolution! Some observers believe that if the United Nations should fall into decline, a major cause will have been this obsession with broad, sweeping resolutions carrying little prospect of observance. All these acts, so frequently a positive force in organized and integrated communities, have on balance weakened the feeble system of international order, for pacts, declarations, and formulas at odds with the realities of international life tempt the lawless to reckless adventures and the law-abiding to a whole chain of emotional responses beginning with self-righteousness and indignation, shading off into disillusionment and finally into despair.

Legalists brush aside the limits of international law and the fact that it is still in a laissez-faire stage of development. J. L. Brierly, one of a handful of international lawyers in the twentieth century whose writings give signs of enduring, begins his little classic, *The Outlook for International Law*, with the following quotation from John Morley:

> Success in politics, as in every other art, obviously before all else implies both knowledge of the material with which we have to deal, and also such concession as is necessary to the qualities of the materials. Above all, in politics we have an art in which development depends upon small modification. . . . To hurry on after logical perfection is to show oneself ignorant of the material. . . . To disdain anything short of an organic change in thought or institution is infatuation.[25]

Then Brierly concludes:

> . . . The part that international law can play, or the conditions on which we can hope to make it one of the pillars of a more stable world, cannot be determined by reasoning in the void or by wishful thinking. Too many people assume, generally without having given any serious thought to its character or history, that international law is and always has been a sham. Others seem to think that it is a force with inherent strength of its own, and that if we only had the sense to set the lawyers to work to draft a comprehensive code for the nations, we might live together in peace and all would be well with the world. Whether the cynic or the sciolist is the less helpful is hard to say. . . .[26]

Unhappily for us, historians often search in vain for this modesty and maturity in the legalist approach to American foreign policy. At times the very virtues of the legal approach in a

[25] John Viscount Morley, *On Compromise* (London: Watts & Co., 1933), p. 112.

[26] J. L. Brierly, *The Outlook for International Law* (Oxford: Clarendon Press, 1944), p. 1.

society with effective legislatures and courts have become the vices of international life, e.g., case-by-case diplomacy.

If we have suffered from legalism, the price of liberal rationalism has been still greater. It has been said of the League and the United Nations that for some they represent an attempt to apply the principles of Lockean liberalism to the machinery of international order. They carry into world affairs the outlook of an ordered democratic society. One rather acute critic has noted in some rational spokesmen the tendency to believe that there can exist a card index of situations or events to be consulted for the appropriate and prescribed action whenever the event or situation turns up. Standardized procedures are valued more than prudence; the perfection of machinery more than political wisdom.

This is not the place to discuss these problems except to suggest that where prestige of states is involved, rational discussion is not necessarily served by open forums. Mr. Lester Pearson has written with great insight and judgment of the problems of diplomacy in a "goldfish bowl." Moreover, we know after four decades of experience that responsible international conduct is not the necessary result of gathering together representatives of some one hundred states differing widely in size, power, and political, economic, and cultural development. States not affected by events and not required to sacrifice vital interests can more easily strike poses than those whose security is in jeopardy. Nations with limited interests in a question may band together to outvote states whose survival may be at stake. For example, it would be helpful to know how often uninstructed United Nations delegates, on matters of no concern to their governments, capriciously throw their votes to the support of a resolution for which they would be unwilling to accept direct national responsibility. It would be useful to discover how often states turn to the United Nations when they are unwilling or unable to evolve a viable foreign policy of their own.

To ask such questions is not to detract from the vital, constructive, and continuing role of the United Nations. However, if this relatively new international institution is to contribute, survive, and grow, its members must face the hard problems. They must recognize that it provides a set of methods and procedures and embodies certain fundamental aims and goals. However, it can contribute only what its members bring to its affairs in the form of commitments, policies, resources, and loyalties. It will not, in the foreseeable future, be a substitute for foreign policy, and we should remind ourselves constantly of this when we are tempted to drop the hard issues and unsolved problems in its lap.

According to the liberal or rationalist world view, evil in history is largely ascribable to social institutions, or ignorance, or some other manageable defect in the human environment. It is *not* the product of human nature. Correct the institution and man's problems are solved. The United Nations was designed to rectify the evils of diplomacy and traditional world politics. Therefore, when we have redress to the methods and measures by which states continue to make their way, the rationalist is offended.

Indeed, nothing has been more disabling in America's adjustment to her new world responsibilities than the over-dependence on a too simple liberal rationalist point of view.

A third source of American pride is the regnant theme of our sectarian religious outlook. Whether for New England Calvinism and the deism of Jefferson in Virginia, or more recently for much of modernist Protestant and Catholic thought, this land has been identified as God's "American Israel." With all its pessimism about human nature, Calvinism, in the words of Edward Johnson in "Wonder Working Providence of Zion's Savior" (1650), found here "the place where the Lord would create a new heaven and a new earth, new churches and a new commonwealth." Here the Protestant Reformation had reached its culmination and here God had made a new beginning for mankind. The deist's God was nature's God, and Jefferson, whose thought was a blending of religious faith and

Enlightenment rationalism, could assert: "Before the establishment of the American States nothing was known to history but the man of the old world crowded within limits . . . and steeped in vices which the situation generates." Superior virtue was an outgrowth of favorable social circumstances and the distinction between Europe and America was an absolute one.

It is the religious dimension of America's pride that brings us to the crux of the problem. Historically, ethics and religion when they have not been used as an instrument of self-righteousness have provided a firm base from which to view man's moral dilemma. This is true because religion gives the resources for reconciling the majesty and misery of life. It accepts sin and salvation as a datum of life, and in its profoundest insights is not forever consumed in proving that through this artifact or that we can escape from the moral dilemma. Yet religion and life have not always manifested this relationship in American society.

This dilemma in foreign policy is but a special, though a particularly flagrant, example of the moral dilemma facing men on all levels of social action. Man cannot help sinning when he acts in relation to his fellow men; he may be able to minimize that sinfulness, but he cannot escape it. For no social action can be completely free of the taint of egotism which as selfishness, pride, or self-deception claims for the actor more than is his due. Man's aspiration for power over other men, which is of the essence of politics, tends toward the denial of the very core of Judaeo-Christian morality. At the heart of the West's ethical tradition is the historic precept of respect for man as an end in himself.

The power relation in any ultimate sense is a denial of this precept, for power at root involves the use of man as a means to the end of another man. The full pathos of this appears on the international scene where the civilizing influence of law, morality, and mores is less effective than on the domestic political scene. And paradoxically, while nations take this for granted and appraise the power drives of others for what they are, or worse, they blind themselves to their own aspirations, which appear as something different and nobler—justified by necessity and ethics. The Founding Fathers were more sensitive to this than some moderns, for it was John Adams who wrote:

> Power always thinks it has a great soul and vast views beyond the comprehension of the weak and that it is doing God's service when it is violating all His laws. Our passions, ambitions, avarice, love and resentment, etc., possess so much metaphysical subtlety and so much overpowering eloquence that they insinuate themselves into the understanding and the conscience and convert both to their party.

Religion and ethics have not only contributed the intellectual and spiritual resources for understanding the moral dilemma, they have also at times in Western history checkmated the extravagances of temporal authority. The struggles between emperors and popes are only the most dramatic expression of the use of countervailing moral and political power. Probably this resistance has been most successful when the claims of princes and rulers were made in the name of higher moral principles, which could be judged by certain accepted moral and legal standards based on an objective external authority. With the passing of the *corpus Christianum* this explicit authority, at least for parts of the world, seems to have disappeared. The substitutes thus far discovered are but pale reflections, for they no longer rest on a substantial moral consensus. It is symptomatic of the times that during the conflict over Suez between Egypt and Israel and its allies, Ambassador Douglas Dillon, then Ambassador to France, perhaps indiscreetly reported that the French withdrawal from Suez was due, not to the pressure of moral force, but to the Russian ultimatum. It may also have resulted from economic coercion and political pressure in the West.

If nations are obliged to consider their own interests, they also must attend to the interests of others. This note is struck in *The Federalist*, No. 63:

An attention to the judgment of other nations is important to every government for two reasons: the one is, that, independently of the merits of any particular plan or measure, it is desirable on various accounts, that it should appear to other nations as the offspring of a wise and honourable policy; the second is, that in doubtful cases, particularly where the national councils may be warped by some strong passion or momentary interest, the presumed or known opinion of the impartial world may be the best guide that can be followed. What has not America lost by her want of character with foreign nations; and how many errors and follies would she not have avoided if the justice and propriety of her measures had, in every instance, been previously tried by the light in which they would probably appear to the unbiased part of mankind? [27]

[27] Alexander Hamilton, John Jay, and James Madison, *The Federalist* (New York: E. P. Dutton & Co., 1911), p. 320.

3. The Political and Moral Setting
of American Diplomacy

THE setting for American diplomacy continues to be the realm of world politics. Thus diplomacy is subject to many of the constraints and considerations that mark national politics. Pure reason or ultimate ethical principles have their impact therefore in the long run rather than in each immediate circumstance. Diplomacy, like politics, is an area of give and take, of compromise with cherished principles, and of continued adjustment to practical possibilities. Both realms provoke the impatience of those who look for more clear-cut and less ambiguous choices. Principles in diplomacy and politics compete with one another, and the statesman more often than not must balance out the weight and force of contending objectives. Even in international institutions whose preamble and charter state clear and simple moral objectives, realization of such goals seldom moves along a straight line. In politics the conflict between legitimate goals is virtually endless. How is a president to weigh the success of his efforts to achieve support for tariff reduction or foreign aid legislation against success or defeat for programs of civil rights or federal aid to education? When should he sacrifice the support in one field of a political coalition in order to attain a particular goal to which part of the coalition may be opposed? What are the rules by which he can be guided in seeking support for a legislative program now extending from rivers and harbors through civil rights to widening the membership of the United Nations? How far can he go in publicly endorsing programs which are anathema to a decisively important sector of his own party? In the field of diplomacy, when does he act in representing the legislative voice of the voters on some delicate but sensitive issue, more complicated than the people know, and when must he

speak as the people might speak if they had all the evidence
to which he is privy? When does he represent the voters in
the narrow sense of the word, attending to their more immediate and petty interests, and when does he fail to represent
in the hope that by the next presidential election they may
recognize that he acted in the national interest?

These questions and many others pose fundamentally the
problem common to politics and diplomacy of principles in
relation to decisions. Partly because this sphere is one on which
political philosophers offer conflicting advice and partly because enunciation of principles raises more questions than
philosophers and moralists recognize, many observers have
grown increasingly cynical about the relation of ethics to politics and foreign policy. They ask whether ethics in the political
sphere is something like the weather, about which everyone
speaks, but without any practical or visible effect. Some say
that ethical principles in the ever more complex mid-twentieth
century are like a living organism which in a changing environment has lost its earlier function. Others maintain that
while the ethical sphere is more difficult to delineate, the role
of principle is nonetheless unmistakably clear.

I would align myself with the second group and point to
at least four domains where principles and ethics have a central role to play.

The first domain is often obscured by the complexities and
uncertainties of which I have spoken. In the same way that
personality is extinguished by the pressures bearing in on the
organization man, human qualities of honesty, judgment, and
responsibility fall victim to demands for national conformity.
"A diplomat is a man sent abroad to lie and deceive in the
interests of his country," wrote an early diplomatic observer.
Harold Nicolson has amended the statement by adding, "but
he must return to negotiate another day." Thus the qualities
by which men measure their friends are not wholly irrelevant
for diplomacy. A strong, trustworthy, and responsible diplomat is more likely than a palpably deceitful colleague to build

up that intangible nexus of solid human relations from which understanding can grow.

One can point to a complex of such personal qualities memorialized by writers in ancient maxims, virtues not exclusively in the realm of personal ethics but political qualities by which the extraordinary individual is measured. One such virtue is courage: "In politics courage is the master virtue and without it there can be no others." Another is the capacity for leadership: "There is this to be said for a strong and scrupulous man; when he gives his word he can keep it." Professionalism in the broadest sense is also a hallmark of responsible politics: "The worst blunders of practitioners are less dangerous than the sciolism of the amateur." Resourcefulness coupled with a sense of Providence transcending all fragmentary human virtues is a quality well exemplified by Lincoln and Washington: "Do as if everything depended on you while knowing that all depends on God." When joined and brought together, qualities like these make for firmness free of arrogance, idealism devoid of hypocrisy, and justice unsullied by claims of purity. In this way personal ethics, which so frequently seem alien in the clash of great collective groupings, are rediscovered and embodied in individual representatives and leaders.

The second domain includes the values men cherish most as they reflect on the social and political order within which they live and move. What is the good society? What is the current state of national life, and what ought it to be? Moralists need to remember that religious and ethical values are never the sole support for a more tolerable collective order. History offers too many examples of "rightest" monarchical states that have exploited and used religion for their own purposes in suppressing individual rights and making tyranny legitimate. American democracy, by contrast, is the product of a happy confluence of Judaeo-Christian precepts and liberal humanitarian values. Both have contributed to the needs of a free society; each furnishes a vital corrective for the other's excesses, with liberalism giving to the secular order a mood of tentativeness and civilized conduct that fosters political give and take.

If political issues were arbitrated solely in moral terms, political debate would soon deteriorate into internecine strife and open civil war. The classic instance of such a breakdown was the American "War between the States," when both sides framed their positions in the absolute righteousness of Biblical texts. On the other hand, secularists need to recall that compromise on means and politics is made possible because there has first been agreement on overarching moral and political ends. The higher law that englobes the United States Constitution provides the framework within which sharp but acceptable debates are pursued on the methods of achieving justice. In Paul H. Nitze's well-chosen words: "Over and above the values of any particular array . . . of human beings there exists an ethical framework which has objective validity, of which men can aspire to have some degree of understanding— not perfect, but approximate—and which can give a measure of insight and of guidance to those who seek it." [28]

A third domain concerns the ethical principles that carry meaning for the hard realities of international politics: power struggles, armaments races, self-interest in national security. Moralists and international lawyers, out of genuine concern for the predicaments that confound the participants in world politics, often contrive rules and standards meant to reduce international conflict—but when external standards run athwart the natural aims and drives of men and states, they find ways of abridging or destroying them. If standards and limitations can be made to serve the purposes of states, they will be honored and observed for long periods of time. One significant example stands out in the realm of treaties. Nations keep their inter-

[28] Paul H. Nitze, *The Recovery of Ethics* (New York: The Church Peace Union, 1960), p. 24.

national commitments when it is in their mutual self-interest to do so. The Rush-Bagot agreement settling the Canadian-American boundary dispute has been long-lived because the parties found it served their national interests. Other agreements, particularly in the armaments field, have been scrapped when their terms conflicted with national interests. Today our disarmament negotiators face above all the task of picking out standards that will be self-enforcing, because on balance they serve both East and West.

Beyond this, however, the observer can point to general moral concerns that have meaning in the interstate system. One is the concept of forgiveness and another the principle of charity. After every war the victors have essentially two alternatives as guides in the drafting of the peace. The one is to approach this task in a spirit of understandable *revanche* and vindictiveness, in an effort to wipe from the earth the evil force responsible for the conflict. Unlimited war aims and demands for unconditional surrender embody this approach. The trouble with such a conception is that almost inevitably it sows the seeds of the next conflict. The destruction of one great power creates a political vacuum into which another ambitious state extends influence and control. Not only does the laying waste of a nation assure that the reestablishment of internal order will be more difficult—a situation that extremist political groups will exploit—it also constitutes a standing invitation for outside power to flow into the vacuum, as exemplified by Soviet expansionism since World War II.

Forgiveness in world politics presumes that most international struggles take the form of a tragic predicament. However much one nation's cause may be more just than another's, neither side is wholly right and neither is totally at fault. They break off diplomatic relations and take up arms when neither can afford to yield on the points at issue; after long contention they have found themselves at a point of no return. Once at war, they abandon the tentativeness of the political process for full-scale moral and military crusades; and when they approach the peace table in the same spirit, the chances are very remote that they can establish conditions of lasting peace.

In certain historic peace settlements, forgiveness has been combined with political realism. At the Congress of Vienna, France almost immediately was reinstated to the councils of state, partly on moral grounds but primarily because the order of Europe required it. Realists such as Metternich, Castlereagh, and Talleyrand recognized the rising threat of czarist Russia and the states of Germany. To stem this threat, the peace was drawn with an eye to the new danger no less than to the ancient foe, now vanquished and powerless in defeat. With the possible exception of the Japanese Peace Treaty after World War II, Bismarck's settlement at the end of the Austro-Prussian conflict may have been the last genuinely conciliatory peace. The fruits of the new approach are apparent in a succession of devastating wars.

Charity is another moral purpose that on its face seems too gentle and civilized for the brutalities of international life. Yet the rise of new nations crying out for aid and respect may well be the dominant problem of the second half of our century. In sheer self-interest, but no less from moral impulse, the wealthy nations are assuming responsibility to aid impoverished states. Walter Lippmann may be stretching a point when he draws an analogy from American life where the rich, through taxes and gifts, now plainly bear responsibility for helping the poor; yet his comparison is sufficiently close to the mark to point up a lesson. The "have-not" states ask and receive technical assistance from the "haves" because in this era of rising expectations the powerful must aid the weak if they would maintain any form of international peace and order.

The fourth and last domain is the international community itself. This comprises subcommunities that hold values deserving of respect. Paul H. Nitze has observed of the secretary of state that he "has a primary obligation . . . to the interests of the United States as a nation state," but "in representing the coalition system and alliance systems of which the United

States is a leading member, [he] has obligations . . . to a much wider . . . group. . . . If the thesis is accepted that a principal task of United States foreign policy is today the construction and defense of a world system of order to replace that shattered in two world wars, then the values to be pursued by the Secretary of State include those associated with a . . . group virtually coterminous with mankind as a whole." [29]

Mr. Nitze points to layers of responsibility which, taken together, make for an international order. In part, the building of an international system is a public and governmental act. Underlying these measures, however, and often preceding them, private groups and individuals build up networks of common interests. Church groups, voluntary agencies, universities, and foundations may lay more solid groundwork, at deeper levels of reality. The growth of a regional system like the British Commonwealth resulted from an infinite number of individual acts. Some of these were sufficiently sound so that, on independence, states such as India and Nigeria continued to embrace many inherited values. The growth of an international order may equally depend on a succession of small actions taken by men who try to give humane values a fair chance of survival. The United States government in one year spends more on the training of foreigners than has the Rockefeller Foundation in a half-century of what it thought was a vigorous program of foreign fellowships. Yet who can measure or compare these actions? If in the molding of a new regional or world order layers of responsibility are only formally established and are not rooted in private individuals and groups, only disaster can be the result—as history has shown before, and as the future will certainly demonstrate again.

Thus at the point of life and death, of survival of values born in trial and error and ultimately of civilization itself, philosophy, diplomacy, and politics merge. The burdens and necessity of preserving life on this planet cry for insights and

---

[29] Nitze, *op. cit.*, p. 25.

resources too varied for but one approach to carry. The annals of American diplomacy are bereft of final answers to any simple relationship among the three, but if we pause in considering the ideas, institutions, and practice that have carried us forward in great moments of history, we may find examples of fruitful partnership. If this goal is kept in view, our subsequent discussion of the relationship between living ideas and emerging institutions may have more lasting value.

2

The Uniqueness of American Professionalism

ITS BREADTH AND DIVERSITY

*"A government that has at its command a sound tradition,
carried on by experienced men, is on the right track."*
HUGH GIBSON

TWO FACTORS converge in determining the importance of
a responsible and professional American diplomacy: the
nature of the diplomatic process and the present crisis. Both
call for reflection and analysis, involving as they do the processes and the problems, respectively, of our foreign relations.
Someone has suggested that foreign policy is not like an eight-
day clock that can be wound up and then forgotten. Its implementation depends on diplomats who pursue their task
from day to day. The processes of diplomacy have evolved over
centuries of experience of nations doing business with one another. Diplomacy is a laborious and serious affair, lacking
both the evil and mysterious features the public sometimes
ascribes to it.

The nature of the present crisis has made more urgent the
achievement of a wise and prudent diplomacy. Not only world
communism which threatens peace and stability, but America's
position in the world becomes important. Toward the end of
the eighteenth century, Edmund Burke wrote: "I dread our
being too much dreaded. We may say that we shall not abuse

this astonishing and hitherto unheard-of power. But every other nation will think we shall abuse it." Britain's problem in the late eighteenth and early nineteenth centuries is *a fortiori* the problem of United States diplomacy today. However pure our intentions and virtuous our approaches, we are likely to be misunderstood either by allies in western Europe, friends among new independent states, or the so-called uncommitted nations.

Not only America's position in the world, however, as a great power, alternately feared and respected, but also the nature of the struggle between East and West increases the importance of diplomacy. Diplomacy operates within a vast area between the play of imposed force and war, on one side, and the security of law, on the other. Where law is fragile and war is terrifyingly dangerous, diplomacy comes to include nearly the entire range of relations, as in the cold war. If diplomacy was once secondary to military or commercial relations, it has, within recent decades, succeeded to a paramount role. The gap between the essential functions of diplomacy and public awareness and understanding becomes, under circumstances of the cold war, more critical than in the past. Diplomacy suffers from an incurable remoteness from popular understanding, as American history testifies with compelling force.

It is ironic that however important the style and technique of a country's diplomacy may be, the very practice of diplomacy inevitably is looked upon with deep suspicion and sometimes fear. For example, the clarity and decisiveness of a small country's diplomacy has sometimes made it great, but the people have stood in judgment on the very elements that made for greatness, whether with the Venetian city-state, or Switzerland, or Sweden in more recent times. A public figure declared some years ago: "If every diplomat could spend a day or two on some fighting front, the whole unhappy spectacle of international conflict would be removed." The limited and painful achievements of diplomacy are contrasted unfavorably with the prompt and spectacular deeds of executives or men of action. To most nations, foreign relations are a nuisance filled with anxieties and frustrations and few visible achievements.

In part, the opposition to professional diplomacy may stem from the fact that the diplomat's role is unique and distinct from almost every other professional activity, including that of the military planner and the domestic political leader. Stated in the bluntest, perhaps exaggerated, terms, the aim of the diplomat is to get as much as he can for his country while giving as little as he can. His unfailing courtesy in this process is not the result of a spineless desire to make himself agreeable to foreigners or to bargain away his country's good name for good will. It is rather grounded upon a mutual recognition that current negotiation is a mere incident in a continuing relationship, that both parties will have an unending series of matters to settle in the future, and that any agreement will be facilitated through maintenance of objectivity, good will, and good temper. The process of diplomacy calls for gifts that are as seemingly incongruous as cynicism and courtesy, sophistication and sincerity, and decisiveness and patience. The diplomat is the bearer of a view of the outside world which his fellow citizens cannot entirely follow or accept.

Further, the diplomat is obliged to focus attention narrowly and sharply on concrete problems, even when he has a preference for broad philosophical issues. One authority writes: "The task of peace-making demands the intellectual gift of seeing all around a problem, leaving no element out of account, and estimating all the elements in their relative proportions, and the moral gift of an aptitude for cautious conservatism, ripe deliberation, taking long views and working for distant ends." The military profession, which in other respects has much in common with diplomacy, is oriented along fundamentally opposing lines. Men who excel in the organization of victory are often blind to the special demands of writing the peace. One of the tragedies of international policy following each war is the continuation in power of military men who have gained the victory and with it the prestige to pursue the peace. This is not to suggest that an efficient diplomacy is possible without military leaders being on tap. Nor is it to say that all diplomatists are by nature inherently wiser than military men. Indeed, part of the deterioration in recent diplomacy results from the decline in the intellectual and political qualities of diplomats. Discriminate judgments are often lacking. Issues relentlessly pose the unending choice between holding the line or conciliation, between approaches to the adversary and holding an alliance intact. Henry Wriston notes: The diplomat's "left hand works against his right. If he does not reduce tensions he is hostile to peace; if he relieves strain the strength of the alliance is correspondingly endangered." [1] There is a time to be firm and a time to negotiate, but which is it? Poincaré was as harsh to the Weimar Republic as he would have been to Kaiser Wilhelm II; Chamberlain urged negotiations with Hitler's Germany; Churchill, who opposed concessions to the Nazis, called for a political understanding with Stalin's Russia. His approach contrasts most unfavorably with Bismarck's attempt to give greater prestige to the Third Republic in France, even by allowing it to pursue its relatively "harmless African adventures." But who is right at a given moment—a De Gaulle who holds firm or a Macmillan who conciliates? Where is the course of wisdom on Berlin, Laos, or nuclear testing?

Moreover, the requirements of the diplomat carried to excess contain seeds of self-destruction. Mere cleverness and grace are seldom assets in and of themselves. Halifax was disposed to think he could charm the most "outlandish and exotic foreigners," whether Hitler or Gandhi. He felt he could tame them through the force of "noble virtue." There were some in the British Cabinet who observed that both leaders were nondrinkers, nonsmokers, and nonmeat-eaters, and through some mental twist imagined they could be equated and, with proper precautions, would thereby serve the peace.

---

[1] Henry M. Wriston, *Diplomacy in a Democracy* (New York: Harper & Bros., 1956), p. 15.

1. An Historical Note: The Origins of Professional Diplomacy in the West

IN effect, professional diplomats have long been considered a special breed of men. This was as true in the days when the Ottoman Empire enlisted the services of Greek Christians as in the present era. The historical patterns or configurations of diplomacy are many and varied, but a broad historical review suggests the ever-expanding scope of activity of the diplomatic profession. The Homeric heralds were the accredited agents of negotiation who managed the royal household, maintained order at assemblies, and conducted religious rites. As Greek civilization developed, it found that needs and requirements went beyond the functions of heralds, whose principal attributes were robust voices and retentive memories. It was not enough then—nor is it today—for ambassadors to master forensic skills and to plead the cause of their city-states in the presence of public assemblies, including those of foreign leagues and cities, although Thucydides reports that long speeches continued for some time as a function of Greek diplomacy. History may repeat itself as public diplomacy reaches its outer limits in our day. By the fifth century, Greece evolved a more continuous system of diplomatic relationships, including diplomatic missions enjoying status and immunity. Greek classics like the *Iliad* record the actions of shrewd if unscrupulous envoys like Ulysses. In Roman civilization, more noted for law than diplomatic negotiation, a profession of archivists sprang up who were skilled authorities on diplomatic precedence and procedures. The Vicar of Christ—the Pope—as the peacemaker of the Christian family of nations, may have been the creator of the first organized diplomatic service. It remained for Byzantine envoys to extend the diplomat's functions as an observer of local internal conditions in the countries to which he was assigned. The qualities of sound judgment and responsible observation gradually superseded those of persuasive oratory.

Modern diplomacy has its roots in the forms and relationships established among Italian city-states of the thirteenth and fourteenth centuries. In 1479, Venice sent an ambassador to the court of France. Governments, princes, and rulers appointed semipermanent ambassadors, and the vocabulary of interstate politics was developed. The custom of permanent embassies spread rapidly toward the end of the fifteenth century. However, the status and rules of the profession were not fully codified until 1815. According to Edmund Burke, diplomacy as the management of international relations rather than the study of archives has its origins around 1796, but not before the Congress of Vienna was diplomacy recognized as a profession separate and apart from the politician or statesman. Earlier usage had stressed the maintenance of archives, the analysis of treaties, and the scrutiny of international negotiations. This rigorous and scientific approach continues into the present era but is no longer the exclusive feature of the work of a foreign office. The Italian city-states are the birthplace of professional diplomacy, for their position outside the mainstream of feudalism, building upon mutual interests and common objectives, provided the framework within which treaties and understandings could be negotiated and observed.

Throughout the Middle Ages, legatees, orators, nuncios, procurators, and agents all assumed varying diplomatic roles. Gradually, however, two major forms of diplomatic representation developed. The ambassador became the personal representative of the head of state; while semiofficial agents carried on *ad hoc* and specific functions required by the changing requirements of foreign relationships. Later the Congress of Vienna, particularly in its *reglement* of March 19, 1815, specified four categories of diplomatic representative: 1] ambassadors, papal legatees, papal nuncios; 2] envoys extraordinary and ministers plenipotentiary; 3] ministers resident;

and 4] chargés d'affaires. Precedence was given priority of appointment rather than relative status, and the senior ambassador in a capital was the *doyen* or dean of the corps of diplomatic representatives. By 1815, the diplomatic service had its own hierarchy and rules of appointment and procedure and was organized as a distinct branch of the public service of each country. Diplomatic protocol has remained substantially unchanged since the Congress of Vienna.

As popular government and public interest in diplomacy grew and expanded, the first demands were voiced for a more rational and moral approach to the conduct of international diplomacy. By the second half of the eighteenth century, the spirit of criticism against institutions of the *ancien régime* reached out to include the customary methods of handling foreign relations. In the beginning, the target of the mid-eighteenth century philosophers and literary reformers was the conduct of domestic policy. But with the Peace of Utrecht ending a long period of wars and conflict, the foundations of a new international political system were laid. Treaties formerly restricted to the European world were extended to the non-European states. An astounding growth of economic interdependence developed with trade—sugar in the West Indies, tea in China, and coffee and chocolate in Africa and Latin America—binding together the European and non-European societies. The phrase, "the family of nations," received increasingly frequent use. International relations became identified with the interest of the human race conceived on what then seemed a universal basis. The emergence of common economic interests provided a framework for a world in which the evolution of international peace and stability was possible.

The main thesis of reformist thought in late eighteenth century writing was that foreign policy as it had evolved was the fundamental evil of an earlier age. The *philosophes* in particular launched a frontal attack on the traditional viewpoint that foreign policy was primary and was the center and culmination of political activities. They directed their sharpest criticisms against the methods of traditional diplomacy, and the symbol and object of their attack was the balance of power. Far from preserving peace, it was singled out as the principal cause of war. Alliances designed to assure the maintenance of the balance of power were, in fact, preparations for treason and conflict, and the conquests which earlier people considered heroic were identified as the arch crimes of the past. The legacy of diplomacy as a remnant of absolute monarchies with their extravagant pomp and ceremony persisted. The citizens of the American Republic had successfully resisted royal oppression on a new continent and few were prepared to accept institutions that might restore any facet of the *ancien régime*. Writers of the day pointed out that diplomacy had become a system of double dealing and deceit justified and defended by cloaking itself in a mystique of secrecy. Le Trosne spoke of diplomacy as "an obscure art which hides itself in the folds of deceit, which fears to let itself be seen and believes it can exist only in the darkness of mystery." [2] Secrecy, therefore, is not, as the diplomats pretend, necessary for the efficient day-by-day fulfillment of functions, but is rather a means whereby diplomats as conspirators plot their nefarious conduct. Reform can be brought about, not by correcting this abuse or that stratagem of the diplomat, but only by a wholesale overhauling of the entire political system. The criminal manner in which foreign affairs were conducted was evidence that politics lacked moral principles and opposed the rule of reason.

Eighteenth century thinkers called, therefore, for the application of the rule of reason to the interests of states. If the petty interests of states were measured by reason, the rulers of the separate states would find that their goals were compatible and complementary. Economic interests and the goals of domestic policy, since they were paramount, would bring states together. The natural interests of sovereign states would lead to the unrestricted exchange of goods and services; the

[2] Le Trosne, *De l'ordre social* (Paris, 1777), p. 395.

laws of international trade would inevitably teach statesmen and leaders that increase in one nation's wealth led irresistibly to increase in the wealth of all. Hence, there was no advantage in seeking expansion of one's boundaries and coming into conflict with a neighbor.

A concomitant belief in eighteenth century *philosophes*, and in particular of men like Condorcet, was that popular participation in foreign relations would best assure the common recognition of mutual economic and moral ties. If the people, not rulers, acted for their countries, conflicts would disappear. Condorcet urged not only that national governments through their popular assemblies, but individual regions or districts, should ratify political treaties between states. The principle of ratification by legislative bodies of treaties arrived at in negotiation with others received increasing emphasis. Moreover, if a legislature approved the declaration of war by a state, an immediate election should be called giving the people an opportunity to vote for or against the war. This method, it was argued, would lead to the abolition of alliances which are "the means by which rulers . . . precipitate the people into wars." The new form of international relations would thus rest solely upon moral laws. The behavior of both states and individuals was subject to the same laws. Diplomacy would be frank and open. Wars had resulted because princes and rulers had followed false ideas and selfish principles. In the new world, reformed by reason and morality, there would be no need for diplomacy and foreign policy as traditionally practiced.

The American and French Revolutions were at one level deliberate and self-conscious attempts to put into practice the trend of thought which had its roots in the second half of the eighteenth century.

The American Revolution provides graphic illustrations of this in the debates between reformers and traditionalists. On June 7, 1776, R. H. Lee introduced a resolution into the Congress calling for independence, separation from the British crown, the severing of all political connections abroad, and a confederation of the American colonies. Conscious of the need for trade, he added, "It is expedient forthwith to take the most effectual measures for forming foreign alliances." The economic necessities of the new commonwealth required ties abroad. The colonies had been grievously damaged by the cessation of all export and import trade imposed in the autumn of 1775. The economic blockade against Britain had done more damage to the colonies than to Britain. Faced with rising prices and a surplus of staple commodities, such as tobacco and indigo, the colonies recognized the need for new trade relationships if economic stability was to be attained. On April 6, 1776, Congress had ordered the reestablishment of trade with all nations except Great Britain. The supremacy of the British Navy and the weakness of American naval power required some form of guarantees through treaty relationships between ourselves and our friends abroad. Lee's resolution calling for foreign alliances was motivated by economic interests. The meaning of the term "alliance" was dictated by economic needs. John Adams declared that "we should calculate all our measures . . . as to avoid a too great dependence upon any power of Europe . . . that the business of America with Europe was commerce, not politics or war." [3] This viewpoint made scant allowance for establishing political bonds.

In the debate over the question of opening the American ports for trade with countries other than Great Britain, it was argued by the majority that the benefits of trade were a sufficient basis for Europe to respond to a request for a reestablishment of connections. Benjamin Franklin spoke of exchanging "commerce for friendship." The debate over Lee's resolution was conducted largely in the spirit of eighteenth century Enlightenment thought. John Adams, who drafted the model treaty for trade with France, reiterated that there should be no political or military connections but purely commercial ones. He declared, "I wish for nothing but commerce, a mere marine

---

[3] John Adams to Secretary E. Livingston, February 5, 1783, *Works of John Adams*, ed. Charles Francis Adams (Boston, 1853), VIII, 35.

treaty with them." France, rather than England, was to protect American ships, particularly against attacks by the Barbary States. The only concession envisaged was France's right to conquests in the West Indies, while she was expected to give up all claims to territory on the North American continent.

The question of common action in war and peace was not directly faced. The colonies, in fact, hoped for involvement of France in the war against England, but held this objective in the background. They went no further than saying that if trade relationships with the colonies should involve France in war with England, the United States agreed not to assist England in the struggle. It is striking how little was offered by the colonials for the cooperation they sought, but this was consistent with the formula "commerce for friendship." Some members of the Congress were willing to offer more in return for French help. While their approach was rejected, negotiators with the French were instructed that the United States could, if necessary, give assurances that the ties with Great Britain would not be reestablished and that no rights or privileges would be offered to any other state which had not been accorded to France. Thus the majority in the Congress held to the view that a political alliance with mutual assurances was not required even in the face of dire need of military and economic aid. The colonists acted in accord with the prevailing eighteenth century view that politics should be subordinated to commerce and that relations with foreign countries should not be cast in the historic mold of firm political or military alliances.

If the political thought of the Enlightenment provides the intellectual and philosophical framework for early American diplomacy, practical political forces on the international scene are also significant. The nature of international relations and current rivalries made it imperative, particularly during the nineteenth century, that the United States isolate the Western Hemisphere from the political and military policies of non-American nations. The interference of these nations in the affairs of the Western Hemisphere, especially through the acquisition of territory, was the only way by which the security and predominance of the United States could be challenged as it gradually emerged as the major force on the continent. Hence the United States was committed, with the exception of the War of 1812, to the maintenance of a balance of power in Europe, and to policies which assured that no European power grew strong enough to make intervention feasible. It stood to benefit from "our detached and ancient situation." The followers of Washington could well ask, "Why forego the advantages of so peculiar a situation?" Much as the new nations today seek to limit their political commitments to East or West, the United States in its early history sought to restrict its relationships abroad. Yet trade and commerce seemingly carried no threat to the independence of the Western Hemisphere and thus the objective position of the American Republic in its early days reinforced prevailing attitudes toward foreign relations inspired by the Enlightenment.

Not alone foreign policies and objectives, however, but the institutions and machinery by which they were implemented yielded to these forces. From the American Revolution to the third decade of the nineteenth century, a remarkable succession of diplomats served their country, including four of our first six presidents.[4] Every president from Washington to Jackson had diplomatic experience; only James Madison had not held a European diplomatic post and he was Secretary of State for eight years. Historians note that the colonies had a higher proportion of men trained in the essentials of diplomacy than any other country. Notwithstanding, our early leaders demonstrated a marked preference for consular and commercial representation abroad as contrasted with diplomatic representation. As late as 1830, there were 141 American consular posts

---

[4] Diplomatic representatives in the so-called "Golden Age" of American diplomacy included Benjamin Franklin, Thomas Jefferson, John Adams, John Quincy Adams, John Jay, James Monroe, Charles C. Pinckney, and Albert Gallatin.

abroad compared with 15 diplomatic posts. In his First Inaugural Address, March 4, 1801, President Thomas Jefferson spoke of "Peace, commerce, and honest friendship with all nations, entangling alliances with none." With the development of Jacksonian democracy, the case for diplomatic specialists became increasingly more difficult to sustain. A belief in the common man included the conviction that he, more than the specialist, was likely to be honest and patriotic in representing the Republic. In his First Annual Message to Congress on December 8, 1829, President Andrew Jackson declared: "The duties of all public officers are, or at least admit of being made, so plain and simple that men of intelligence may readily qualify themselves for their performance. . . ." Moreover, because every task in government was so simple that anyone could perform it, latent interest in professionalism diminished. Therefore, while the Foreign Service through its more than 185-year history has progressed toward professional status, most of its growth has occurred in the past fifty years. As legislative participation in diplomacy increased, partly as a result of the growing demands for appropriations and funds, the skepticism about a professional foreign service did not diminish. Secretary of State Edward Livingston, in submitting comprehensive reports to President Andrew Jackson on the diplomatic and consular services in 1833, was constrained to observe: "Ministers are considered as favorites, selected to enjoy the pleasures of foreign travel at the expense of the people; their places as sinecures; and their residence abroad as a continued scene of luxurious enjoyment." [5] Any legislature is tempted to conclude that diplomatic outposts staffed by men in striped pants are an expensive luxury for a democracy. More recently, the diversification of the diplomatic functions to include economic and cultural representation has had a further mixed effect on the belief that diplomats must

---

[5] He concluded: ". . . there is scarcely an office, of which the duties, properly performed, are more arduous, more responsible, and less fairly appreciated. . . ."

possess human and professional qualities of a distinctive order.

Further, the preference for consular as distinct from diplomatic representation is reflected in the evolution of the American diplomatic service. If one traces, as qualified American scholars have done, the growth of a career service, it is revealing how often demands for personnel mobility, improved salaries, retirement benefits, security of tenure, and promotion by merit within the diplomatic service have been linked with pressures for increased recognition of the role of the consular service.

In the eighteenth century, all secretaries for service in embassies abroad were elected by members of the pre-Constitution Congresses. The role of the executive in nominating and appointing them was only gradually established. Studies show that the Congress acted with dispatch in confirming nominations, but it remained jealous of its role in the choice of secretaries. The number of secretaries appointed to foreign missions fell short of the need, and in 1833, Secretary Edward Livingston, in a report to President Jackson, noted that he was unable to discharge his duties in the absence of a qualified interpreter or secretary. Partly to ease the problem, use was made of unpaid attachés whose appointments were not subject to legislative approval. This arrangement was hardly satisfactory, however, and, in the first half of the nineteenth century, diplomatic officials proposed that these appointments be eliminated. Because of the lack of clearly defined professional status and career opportunities, a significant proportion of the early secretaries were related through blood ties or family friendships to particular ministers abroad. Neither security of tenure nor promotion by merit was recognized in nineteenth century American diplomatic service, nor did an adequate salary scale exist. The foreign service tended to be spoils-ridden and the ablest young men who might have served did not come forward as candidates for appointment.

The evidence seems unmistakable that the lack of a clear

awareness of the legitimate role of diplomatic representatives abroad was a principal cause of administrative malaise. The United States through the American Revolution had severed political connections with Europe, and in the minds of even the more responsible leaders this excused the Republic from giving priority to creation of a career service. In 1783, John Adams expressed the following view: "I confess I have sometimes thought that after a few years it will be the best thing we could do to recall every minister from Europe and send embassies only on special occasion." [6] In 1832, a House resolution called on the Committee on Foreign Affairs "to inquire into the expediency of reducing the number of our ministers, resident abroad, to three, viz: to England, France and Russia." [7] Not until 1893 did an American president appoint a diplomatic representative above the rank of minister.

Moreover, in the conduct of foreign relations on a broader front, a deep gulf appeared between thought and reality. At the same time that John Adams, Thomas Jefferson, and Charles Pinckney were asking what the colonies had to do with the affairs of the world, a succession of far-reaching diplomatic crises confronted the Republic: the War of 1812, the Russian threat to the Pacific Coast, the intrigue by European powers during the Civil War to exploit bitter division and strife within our borders and in Mexico, to say nothing of the more or less constant diplomatic negotiations with the French, Spanish, British, and the Indians. American involvement in world politics was a fact of history. In 1793, the Congress appropriated ten million dollars for public purposes, and of this one million was for "any expenses . . . incurred" in foreign relations. In 1806, one-fifth of the total authorized expenses of the whole government was for this purpose. Political leaders preferred, however, to trust affairs to the special agent, legislative commission, or "some good fellow [with] a letter of at-

[6] Adams, *op. cit.*, p. 423.
[7] House Report 180, 22d Congress, 1st Session (serial 224), pp. 1–3.

torney. . . ." All that was needed was a clever representative to negotiate a treaty or a hardheaded merchant to establish commercial ties, not a generously staffed embassy or legation. When the chief executive sought to reduce expenditures, a popular form of economy was the budget of the foreign service. In 1859, a congressman was to argue: "Here is the evil, the fungus, the excrescence, a pinchbeck imitation of the pomp and pageantry of royalty, and we should put the knife to it and cut it out."[8]

If diplomats were to go abroad for sustained service, John Quincy Adams urged they return after a few years "to be renovated by the wholesome republican atmosphere of their own country."[9] In the public mind re-Americanization has been a canon of the foreign service from earliest days. Some insisted that on their return diplomats should be quarantined for a time in much the same way as were incoming foreign goods that might spread contagious diseases. While the executive tended to expand its prerogatives at the expense of the legislature in the nineteenth century, the realm of foreign affairs administration was a noteworthy exception. The reasons are embedded in the widespread belief that a professional foreign service was unnecessary, might weaken and destroy republicanism, and could safely be trimmed through stringent economies.

In the face of so sweeping and emotional a political reaction, the growth and development of a foreign service proceeded through successive stages of advance and retreat. Strong presidents were unwilling to stand idly by but insisted on their executive prerogatives. As early as 1790, President George Washington affirmed the nation's urgent need for qualified officials abroad and "provisions" enabling him to fulfill his duties. For ten years, through the annual or biennial renewal

---

[8] *Congressional Globe*, Part 1, 35th Congress, 2d Session (January 25, 1859), p. 593.
[9] *Writings of John Quincy Adams*, ed. W. C. Ford (New York, 1913–1917), VI, 357.

of Congressional legislation, he enjoyed the authority to appoint officials for such posts as secretary of legation. Washington was able to draw upon a fund made available from duties on exports and tonnage, while his successors were to call on a specific contingency fund. From 1810–1831, the Congress extended its power over appointments by requiring detailed appropriations rather than a separate presidential fund and by denying payments to any secretary not formally confirmed by the Senate. Not until January 16, 1885, was the President's authority substantially restored, this time through overall civil service reform under the Pendleton Act. When President Lincoln in 1865 refused to redistribute diplomatic appointments, his action contributed further to the founding of a career service. In fairness, the historian must record that successive presidents, whatever the philosophy they brought to their high office, came to understand the importance of a more permanent diplomatic corps. Jeffersonians who had opposed professionalism when out of power favored it in office. Increasingly the executive resisted Congressional cutting and pruning when it threatened the attainment of an effective service, although the Jeffersonian and Federalist principle of nonpartisan appointments was periodically challenged by leaders with political debts to pay.

A further point worth making is that the growth of a professional foreign service was in no sense the product of a single administration or the result of one major, powerful philosophical trend. Classical treatises on diplomacy with which at least some of the Founding Fathers were familiar or which permeated their consciousness through practical experience stressed that because diplomats "arm or pacify nations," they require extraordinary qualities and virtues. Implicit was the concept of a profession or vocation with respect both to qualities of mind and character. May I remind you of some of the qualifications of a diplomatist enumerated in studies and guidebooks: good looks, "neither so old as to be inactive through ill health . . . nor so young as to prove immature or inconsiderate," [10] able to speak eloquently when there is need but by preference brief, encyclopedic in knowledge, an indefatigable reader, a linguist, irreproachable in morals even in countries where immorality is widely practiced, possessing tact, courage, and discretion, and deserving of respect. Prior to the twentieth century, much stress was laid on the resourcefulness of the envoy. Rousseau de Chamoy wrote in *L'idée du parfait ambassadeur* (1697): "As he is bound to know the interests of his master, the ambassador may and must make up his mind [without waiting for instructions] in accordance with events, and those are the occasions when the clever and true negotiator distinguishes himself from the common man and ordinary negotiator of no parts." His dispatches must convey bad news no less than good. In the long run, his government will thank him for this. Above all, the ambassador must study the country to which he is sent, meet personally people from all levels of society, understand trends of thought, and discover the prevailing social, political, and intellectual forces at play.

Most classical handbooks give greatest emphasis to austerity and the "solid virtues." Diplomats must avoid irritating criticism of the manners and institutions of others. Incidentally, John Quincy Adams may be the exception that proves the rule, for "his manners were stiff and disagreeable; he told the truth bluntly, whether it hurt or not, and he never took pains to conciliate anyone." [11] Because of his industry, high intelligence, and knowledge of Europe, Adams, despite a crotchety disposition, proved one of our ablest diplomats. Foreign service should be a profession of mind and character; men should master these requirements from their youth. Adams served as secretary in Paris at the age of eleven. Future secretaries must supplement what they learn in college with a

[10] J. J. Jusserand, *The School for Ambassadors and Other Essays* (New York: G. P. Putnam's Sons, 1925), p. 14.

[11] Quoted in Graham H. Stuart, *The Department of State: a History of Its Organization, Procedure and Personnel* (New York, 1949), p. 53.

knowledge of international law, diplomatic history, government, and foreign languages. Callières' ideal ambassador was a man who had traveled abroad but not in the fashion of young men limiting themselves to visits to ancient monuments in Rome or Venice. Instead, "they ought to travel when a little older and better able to meditate and to study the form of government of each country." While their learning should be substantial, they must possess it and not be possessed by it. "A man who has entered public employ must consider that his duty is to act and not to remain too long closeted in his study." [12] For other publicists and writers, diplomacy took on the attributes of a sacred calling, requiring an early discipleship. It called for severe moral and mental preparation. Diplomats must learn moderation, eschew passionate attachments and bitter antipathies, never confuse nervousness with activity, but seek personal modesty, objectivity, disinterestedness, cool judgment, and truth. The "School of the Ambassador" begins in childhood and must be sustained through a lifetime of service.

In the minds of the classical diplomatists, the grounds for professionalism rested primarily on the purpose of diplomacy. Jusserand argued: "The temper, qualities, and limitations of many a man can be divined on short acquaintance; those of a nation need a longer contact." [13] The importance of this objective has steadily increased in modern times. The root function of diplomacy, in George F. Kennan's words, is "to effect the communication between one's own government and other governments or individuals abroad and to do this with maximum accuracy, imagination, tact, and good sense." [14] "No invention, no telephone, no wireless, will ever replace the knowledge of a country and the understanding of a people's disposi-

---

[12] L. H. de Callières, *De la manière de négocier avec les souverains* (Paris, 1716), p. 99.

[13] Jusserand, *op. cit.*, p. 59.

[14] George F. Kennan, "Diplomacy as a Profession," *Foreign Service Journal,* XXXVIII, No. 5 (May 1961), 23.

tions." [15] If the function of diplomacy continued simply to be knowing and persuading a prince or ruler, temporary missions might suffice. But more than this is required and professionalism has seemed to provide the answer. It is professionalism with a difference, however, for the American diplomat must comprehend what his country stands for and must remain sensitive to the people who ultimately are his sovereign, the American public.

[15] Jusserand, *op. cit.*, p. 59.

2. The Emergence of Professionalism
in American Diplomacy

THE reform movement that sought to establish a professional foreign service in the United States was at least partially a response to such considerations.

The First Phase: 1800–1875

It had its origins in the nineteenth century in a succession of small steps and often unsuccessful efforts to build a more permanent structure. More significantly, this period was one in which domestic far surpassed foreign affairs in importance. The first stage in the development of a professional service spans nearly three-quarters of the nineteenth century; the second phase continues from the late nineteenth century to World War I; the third comprises the interwar period; and the final period begins with the Act of 1946. The early period finds expression in the extraordinary qualities of some of our earliest envoys. While they were public servants in the broadest sense and not career diplomats, they nonetheless represented American interests skillfully and responsibly for extended periods. John Quincy Adams served in four posts for a total of fifteen years and Albert Gallatin and William Pinckney in two major posts. Their experience points up the value of continuity. Benjamin Franklin is often called "the Father of the Foreign Service." He was the diplomatic agent of the colonies in England for the fifteen years preceding independence, represented the Continental Congress in England in 1774, was the first of three full-fledged diplomatic appointments of the government in 1776–1779; and continued as our first minister plenipotentiary in 1779–1785. Other early Americans, including John Adams, John Jay, and Thomas Jefferson, while serving their country abroad for shorter periods, left behind them a legacy of high intelligence and wide experience in the formative years of the Republic's history.

The demands for professionalization remained limited in the first phase of our history partly because of the modest nature of the diplomatic establishment. In the early days of Washington's administration, the United States had diplomatic representation only in France and Spain. Thomas Jefferson, in a memorandum of January 4, 1797, argued that by any reasonable set of criteria missions were necessary only in Britain, France, Spain, Portugal, and the Netherlands. Throughout this early period, little sentiment was evident in support of a career service. The growth of consular posts, which doubled from 1830 to 1860 (141 to 282), stimulated efforts at defining the role of envoys. Secretary of State Edward Livingston (1831–1833) issued the first organized and comprehensive set of instructions to consular officers. He also prepared a companion report on the diplomatic service describing existing conditions, analyzing weaknesses, and recommending substantial reforms. Indeed, the first elements of the reform movement aimed at a service with independent corporate existence under appropriate supervision from the Department of State date basically from the 1830's. Livingston sought to define by law consular and diplomatic functions, prescribe salaries and advancement rules, and eliminate abuses such as arbitrary consular fees. Livingston's reforms, when taken up in the Congress, were defeated, but his reports remained the basis for future progress. Underlying all was the fact that international subjects during much of the nineteenth century did not challenge the ablest men. The axiom applies that first-class men want to deal with first-class events.

Not until 1856 did Congress successfully enact legislation embodying these reforms. The act authorized the President to set the rates of official consular fees on the understanding these would be reported annually to the Congress and be posted prominently in the various consular offices. It established a

schedule of diplomatic salaries based upon a ranking of diplomatic missions. The top salary of $17,500 for ministers to
Great Britain and France was not to be increased until the
Foreign Service Act of 1946. A similar schedule was adopted
for consular officers with greater flexibility within the separate
ratings to the end of placing as many officers as possible on a
salary rather than a fee basis. The act brought the services
under more direct and specific administrative control and
authorized the President to provide for the current guidance
of officers through issuance of further rules and regulations.

Unfortunately, the changes foreshadowed in the Act of 1856
were never fully realized. Appointments continued to follow
domestic political considerations more often than merit, salary
schedules were not broadly applied, and specific provisions
intended to create a corps of trainees, particularly for the
consular service, were repealed. The Civil War intervened, and
while President Abraham Lincoln's diplomatic appointments
were on the whole commendable, the war years were hardly
the time for remolding the foreign service. In administrations
that followed, such as that of President Ulysses S. Grant, the
emphasis was placed upon spoils rather than merit.

By 1859, the United States maintained thirty-one diplomatic missions abroad, in contrast with two in the early years
of Washington's administration. Of this number, sixteen were
in Europe, twelve in Latin America, and three in the Pacific
and Far East. The total budget for this purpose, which in 1833
was $200,000, was by 1861 $370,000. By 1890, the number
of missions had increased to forty-one, with the major increase
coming in the Near and Far East. In 1894, the legations in
Great Britain, France, Russia, and Germany were raised to
embassies, symbolizing the growing importance of our world
role. These developments, coupled with the appearance of men
who are legitimately called the first professional diplomats,
ushered in the second stage in the history of a professional
service. Eugene Schuyler, who was appointed Consul at Moscow in 1867, was to serve until 1889 in various posts in Central

Europe and the Near East. His *American Diplomacy and the Furtherance of Commerce* (1886) is still regarded as the earliest significant treatise on the foreign service. Henry White, who began as Secretary of Legation in Vienna and concluded in 1909 his service that included appointments as Ambassador to France and to Italy, was another important proponent of diplomacy as a profession. William W. Rockhill earned the distinction of being the department's top authority on the Far East in a career beginning in 1884 and continuing for more than thirty years. These men exemplified the possibility of professionalism in foreign service but, unfortunately, they were exceptions to a general rule.

The Second Phase: 1875–1914

The keynote of the second stage of the development of a career service in the late nineteenth century was the stress placed upon professional standards. The Pendleton Civil Service Act, while stimulating interest in reform, failed to benefit the foreign service as a whole, for it exempted from its requirements direct appointments by the President made with approval of the Senate. Observers discovered a wide gulf between the successful attainment of professionalism in the armed forces, the judiciary, and other departments of government, including the consular service, as contrasted with the diplomatic service. The diplomatic correspondence of the day included dispatches such as the one from the Minister to Denmark, George H. Yeamans, to Secretary of State Seward in 1866, in which the minister wrote: "The course of our own government in this respect is in marked contrast, not only with the policy of other governments, but with its own care and solicitude to prepare young men for the Army and Navy." [16] It was noted that other countries were far in advance of the United States in evolving a foreign service, and while this was tolerated in the first half or three-quarters of the nineteenth century, it proved unaccept-

---

[16] *Foreign Relations*, Vol. I, 1867–1868, 650 (dated December 4, 1866).

able in the years that followed. An overall attack on the need for a career service was launched by the National Civil Service Reform League and journals like the *Independent, Scribner's Magazine,* and the *Nation.* Writing in the *Arena* (May 1897, p. 919), Herbert H. D. Peirce argued: "As we would not put a ship into the hands of a commander ignorant of navigation, an army under the control of a general without military training . . . so we should not put the foreign affairs of our government into the hands of men without knowledge of the various subjects which go to make up the diplomatic science."

Reformers in the successive studies and reports singled out three areas for change: the end of rotation and the substitution of an effective system of tenure, merit advancement within graded positions, and entry into the foreign service through examinations. The proposals for a threefold reform attracted considerable attention both in the legislative and executive branches of government, but on each major change extended debate ensued. For example, rotation was defended by some as a means by which officials in full accord with an administration's policies, rather than lukewarm civil servants, might carry responsibility. Similarly, the questions of the structure and content of an examination system evoked opposing points of view. The primary objective of the reformers was to eliminate the baneful influence of politics, and only gradually was an overall program for a specialized and professional service evolved. Progress reached its height in the last two decades of the nineteenth and the first decade of the twentieth century as American participation in world affairs sharply accelerated. Policy was a response to growing American influence in the Caribbean, active intervention in the Far East, and limited involvement in Europe. The Spanish-American War, the acquisition of Puerto Rico and the Philippines, the annexation of Hawaii and Samoa, and our Open Door policy in Asia signaled a new era. To meet these new responsibilities, the personnel of the Department of State was doubled between 1898 and 1908.

Yet despite the concern of presidents like Rutherford B. Hayes and Theodore Roosevelt, senators like Henry Cabot Lodge, and diplomats like Wilbur J. Carr and François Jones, specific legislative reform was slow of realization. Resolutions were introduced in the Congress, but effective legislation did not follow. Instead, reform of the consular service was given priority because powerful business groups with strong overseas interests successfully brought pressure to bear on the Congress. President Cleveland's executive order of 1895 recognized the career requirements of a responsible consular service and was an historic turning point. Consular officers were part of a service that was substantially larger than the diplomatic corps, although their number dropped from 437 in 1890 to 92 in 1921 as the work was increasingly concentrated. Some supplemented their income by levying fees on commercial interests abroad and thereby provoked criticism and complaint from the business community.

As early as 1830, Secretary of State Van Buren had been asked to report on discrepancies in consular charges and resulting controversies and embarrassment to American interests abroad. President Theodore Roosevelt, having chosen to stress reform of the consular rather than the diplomatic service, appealed for changes in his Message to Congress of December 6, 1904. When Congress initially proved unwilling or unable to act, President Roosevelt turned to the use of an executive order, not unmindful of the appeal this might have for significant groups in American life. He laid the foundations for the merit system both in the consular and diplomatic service through executive orders of 1906 and 1909, and by statute in 1906, requiring application of the merit system to consular appointments and all diplomatic positions below the grade of minister. Appointments to the posts of secretary of embassy or legation were to be filled either by transfer or promotion or selection based upon a written and oral examination. Meanwhile, Congress passed legislation embodying many of the changes requested for the consular service. When the consular and diplomatic services were merged in 1924, the former had enjoyed the benefits of career development for nearly a quarter of a century. Critics suggested that the reform was not thoroughgoing enough, however, because the President alone was subject to the order and was personally responsible for the selection of those who administered the examination. Nevertheless, historians agree that a new phase in the history of a professional service was reached in the era of Theodore Roosevelt. His Secretary of State, Elihu Root, created an examining board to consider candidates for appointment and organized written and oral examinations covering subjects like international law, modern languages, and diplomatic practice. Indeed Root, and a successor, Knox, may deserve much of the credit for reforms attributed to Presidents like Roosevelt and Taft.

In effect, the first Roosevelt administration extended the classified civil service to the Department of State, and it is noteworthy that only 27 percent of the secretaries of embassies or legations were dropped during his first year in office. President William McKinley, by contrast, had transferred or dismissed 40 percent of the secretaries he inherited. Increasingly, a larger number of ministers were selected from men who had formerly been secretaries. The total number of secretaries increased from 24 to 122 in the twenty-year period following 1898, and this increase was matched by a growing esprit de corps in the ranks. If Theodore Roosevelt was not as sweeping in these reforms as some had hoped, he explained his reluctance by noting that there was a high proportion of poorly qualified people in the service and he was unwilling to preserve deadwood by assuring security of tenure to all. Furthermore, in the end, political and geographical considerations influenced the administration in the choice of the increasing number of first and second secretaries newly appointed. By 1906, the United States could point to a total of nine ambassadorial posts upgraded despite the historic American preference for lower ranking representatives—a tradition going back to President Washington's selection exclusively of chargés d'affaires. Gradually, in the nineteenth century, key diplomatic appointments were raised to the level of minister resident, somewhat later to minister plenipotentiary and, as defined in the legislation of 1893, to ambassador when the representative of a foreign country in the United States held this title. The new prestige and rank of diplomatic appointments made selection more attractive to men of influence and standing, as did increasing salary scales. From 1790 to 1865, the maximum salary for ministers was $9,000 a year. By the Act of 1865, it was increased to $12,000 (for Great Britain and France the level was raised to $17,500), but not until 1946 had it reached $25,000. Incidentally, not until 1911, with the passage of the Lowden Act, were provisions made for the purchase of suitable embassy and legation buildings in foreign countries, and major steps in this direction awaited World War II.

President William Howard Taft continued the prevailing emphasis of the Roosevelt administration, urging that higher salaries be established and civil service provisions be made permanent both for the consular and diplomatic service, including all ranks below that of minister. He did for a part of the diplomatic service what Cleveland's executive order had done for the consular service. President Taft was reasonably successful in promoting men from lower ranks to ministerial appointments, directing the secretary of state to call his attention to professionals who merited promotion to chief of mission. In consequence, 35 percent of the ministers in his administration had previously served as secretaries; appointments at the executive level in the department reflected a similar emphasis. Taft's approach led to the creation of efficiency records in the Department of State which were to furnish a rational basis for promotions from one grade to the next or for "selection out" from the service. His executive order was to receive statutory form in 1915 and was refined and elaborated in the years that followed. During this period, written and oral examinations were improved to test for resourcefulness, judgment, and general knowledge, as well as detailed information.

President Woodrow Wilson was a lifelong friend of civil service reform, but his Secretary of State, William Jennings Bryan, was decidedly hostile. The Democratic party, particularly in the South, looked to Bryan as its natural leader, capable of restoring the spoils system and rewarding the party faithful. Bryan maintained that ministers and ambassadors should be exempt from civil service. The secretary's influence was reduced by the support President Wilson received from Colonel House, but except for the consular service and the subordinate diplomatic appointments in which Wilson prevailed, the Bryan era is hardly noted for great advances in the development of a professional diplomatic service. Bryan's insistence on withholding key appointments for "deserving Democrats" is a classic case of the patronage approach.

Moreover, Wilson in a letter of September 17, 1913, to President Charles W. Eliot of Harvard explained: "We are following the merit system in the consular service more strictly even than either of the preceding administrations. . . . In the matter of the diplomatic service . . . we find that those who have been occupying the legations and embassies have been habituated to a point of view which is very different, indeed, from the point of view of the present administration. They have had the material interests of individuals in the United States very much more in mind than the moral and public considerations which . . . ought to control." [17] This belief proved another limiting factor for Wilson in consolidating the gains that had been made in building a career service.

The Third Phase: 1914–1946

The years from 1914–1918, which launched a new phase in our history, found the United States heavily engaged in war and the preparation for war and in increased diplomatic activity in behalf of the belligerents during the period of our neutrality. These years had a lasting effect on the organization

[17] Arthur Walworth, *Woodrow Wilson* (New York: Longmans, 1958), I, 346.

of the diplomatic service and the outlook of its members; it ushered in an era in the history of American professionalism extending to World War II. A shortage of personnel threatened the efficiency of the service, but one fortunate consequence of the emergency resulted from the wartime necessity of transferring personnel from one mission to another. The war found certain embassies and legations considerably overstaffed, while others were woefully lacking in personnel. The so-called Stone-Flood Act provided that secretaries were to be appointed to grade rather than to a particular embassy or legation, making it possible, through authority granted by Congress, to move officials freely from one embassy to another. The wartime period thus established the principle that men of competence were capable of serving their country in successive missions abroad.

A second development in the wartime period was the rather substantial increase in the number of secretaryships, expanding from 70 in 1914 to 122 in 1918. Secretary Robert Lansing was able to show that the United States, which had six more foreign missions than Britain, had 19 fewer secretaries. On the strength of this evidence, Lansing succeeded in enlisting support in the Congress for personnel expansion. The policy of William Jennings Bryan toward the career service became an election issue, and *The New York Times,* in an editorial of February 27, 1916 (Section I, page 16), asserted: "One Bryan in the State Department can do more harm in a brief period to upset any plans for the improvement of our diplomatic service . . . than three administrations can do to build up an intelligently devised system." As the war continued, proposals multiplied for strengthening the career aspects of the service, increasing the numbers of qualified officials, developing specialized training programs, making it more democratic, and improving the salary scale.

Following World War I, the problems of writing the peace and of reestablishing diplomatic missions in the countries with which we had been at war increased the burdens of our foreign policy, and further expansion was authorized by the Congress through provision for twenty-five new secretaryships. The career principle gained wider acceptance when President Harding took office, and all the chief officials in the Department of State save the secretary were professionals. At about this time, Congressman John Jacob Rogers from Massachusetts launched his famous campaign for a more effective professional service. Significantly, the Rogers Act was passed at a time when the United States had refused membership both in the League of Nations and the World Court. On January 16, 1919, Rogers introduced legislation "to provide a system of promotion of efficient secretaries in the diplomatic service to vacancies arising in the rank of minister." He incorporated in his bill the concept of an independent board which, from time to time, would recommend to the President secretaries for promotion to the rank of minister. While Congressman Rogers failed to achieve immediate approval for his bill, both diplomatic and consular officials, sensing the political nature of many appointments at the ministerial level, were generally sympathetic. One legislative action was particularly important in broadening the base of the service. The fact that Congress in 1919 enabled the government, at the discretion of the secretary of state, to assume responsibility for the transportation expenses of secretaries and their families traveling to a foreign post helped to assure appointment of career officers from all occupations and social classes.

In the following Congress, Rogers reintroduced his bill and added to its provisions an arrangement by which consuls-general could be appointed at the ministerial level. At a time when the diplomatic corps was striving to improve its status, further pressure was being exerted for merging the diplomatic and consular services. Most of the reform proposals called for combining the two, although some of the professional diplomatists urged that fusion not take place until the position of the diplomatic corps was more firmly established. A certain jealousy and rivalry continued throughout these years. From 1778, when Benjamin Franklin and John Adams urged the Congress to appoint full-fledged consuls to relieve our envoys of non-diplomatic functions, to the twentieth century, some of our most experienced diplomats have advocated a clear-cut separation of functions. However, the close relations between international economic and political problems has tended to break down the watertight separation that once existed. Representative Rogers, in a speech in Congress, declared, "Today every question of international politics involves a question of business, a question of expanding or protecting trade." [18] While there was opposition to merger, those who favored it could point to the need for training programs combining economics and diplomacy and a common service for those who were our representatives abroad.

The Rogers Act of 1924, not surprisingly, therefore, sought greater uniformity for consular and diplomatic officers. It provided for retirement and disability pay, the establishment of a Foreign Service school, and promotion of exceptional Foreign Service officers to the grade of minister without loss of benefits. It specified that wage scales and promotion arrangements should apply interchangeably to both groups. They were, however, to be treated as separate units or organizations and a new officer was to be assigned specifically to one or the other. Separate commissions were issued for appointments as secretaries or consular officers. Thus, while the Rogers Act sought to bring the two groups together, the viewpoint of career diplomats tended to prevail, temporarily at least. They had insisted and continued to insist that the functions of diplomatic and consular services were sufficiently distinct that a merging of the two would be unfortunate. They suggested that the personal and professional functions of the diplomat involving negotiations on delicate political problems required qualities of mind and character distinct from those of the consular officer. It must be added that an independent esprit de corps prevailed

---

[18] *Congressional Record*, LXB, 68th Congress, 1st session (April 30, 1924), 7634.

in the two bodies, and particularly the diplomatists were not anxious to be placed on an equal plane with consular officers.

The interpretations given to the Rogers Act by the professional diplomats aroused complaints and criticism from the consular service. Charges of favoritism followed, and it was said that young diplomatic officers recently appointed to their posts were treated more generously than senior consular officers. The special target was the separate promotions scale under which boards of examiners selected men for promotion to higher grades in the service; diplomats, as the dominant members of boards, tended to be judges in their own cause. This practice was later ruled contrary to the Rogers Act and abandoned. The consular service found formidable allies in the Congress, which by preference and interest was more favorably disposed to business representation abroad. Congress took action to encourage the fusion of the two services, and on February 23, 1931, under the Hoover administration, the barriers that had existed to a closer merger of the two services were finally eliminated. From that date until World War II, young men were appointed to dual commissions in both consular and diplomatic offices. This trend was to continue despite the views of diplomatic personnel and is the forerunner of the subsequent reforms leading to a unified Foreign Service.

The gains which had been made through the Rogers Act were partially lost in the depression years. In 1924, the new combined Foreign Service Officer Corps numbered 633 men and by 1945 it had increased only to 792, including 114 absorbed from the Agriculture and Commerce Departments. From 1932 until 1936, no competitive examinations for appointments in the Foreign Service were held. The pool of recent appointees fell off sharply. The prime factor accountable for this may have been the sharp drop in congressional appropriations for the Foreign Service, leading to the cutting back on salaries and promotions. The service was essentially starved by the suspension of admissions for years on end and "selec-

tion out" of incompetents made impossible by the shortage
of personnel.

With the outbreak of World War II in September 1939,
history repeated itself. American representatives abroad were
called upon not only to serve American interests, but also to
represent foreign missions to belligerent countries in World
War II. The American ambassador in Berlin in 1940 carried
on diplomatic relations in behalf of eight additional nations.
With the entry of the United States into the war, ambassadors
became involved in a wide range of wartime duties, including
stockpiling of vital materials and a myriad of relief and rehabilitation programs. The numbers of Foreign Service officers
dwindled, and at one time or another approximately 350 American diplomatic and consular officers were interned in enemy
countries. As had been true in World War I, wartime experiences highlighted the need for drastic changes in the Foreign
Service. President Roosevelt's tendency of reducing the Department of State to a "cipher" and the failures of Secretaries
Hull and Stettinius to view the needs of the department as a
whole were further sources of weakness. (I have, throughout,
drawn heavily on Warren F. Ilchman's monumental study,
Professional Diplomacy in the United States, 1779–1939.)

The Fourth Phase: 1946–

The events of World War II led to the Foreign Service Act
of 1946 and the final act in the drama of our diplomatic service. This measure raised salary levels to a maximum of $25,000
a year for our top ambassadors and brought salaries for all
grades to a point more in keeping with opportunities outside
the service. The new law further provided that a professional
Foreign Service officer could become a minister or ambassador
without losing his career status. If with a new administration
coming to power he should be passed over for an equivalent
appointment, he could be selected as counsel of embassy or
consul-general. An amendment to the Act, not approved until

August 5, 1955, established a new post of career ambassador, to which four distinguished American diplomats were appointed on April 9, 1956. Those appointed were James Clement Dunn, Loy W. Henderson, H. Freeman Matthews, and Robert D. Murphy.

The net effect of the various stages in the development of a career Foreign Service was the establishment of a cadre of professionally qualified officers capable of serving in various posts abroad. The trend following World War I, even in the appointment of ambassadors, has been in the direction of appointing professional diplomats. In 1914, not a single one of our missions in the great capitals could boast a professional as its head. By 1939, twenty-five of our fifty-one chiefs of missions were drawn from the career Foreign Service. By December 1956, the ratio had increased to forty-eight out of seventy-five, and by March 1960, to seventy-four out of ninety-seven. Seventy percent of the chiefs of mission in the Kennedy administration are career Foreign Service officers, and of President Kennedy's twenty-eight political appointees, one-half came from education, law, or journalism and nine from other government jobs. This change in a little over four decades has been little short of breath-taking. It is well to remember this when, looking back, we are tempted to say of the early days, "there were giants in the earth in those days."

The concept of a public servant with wide experience and deep awareness of foreign relations problems, capable of administering and coordinating the machinery of an embassy or mission abroad, whether in Europe, Asia, or Africa, became more widely accepted. Secretary Dean Rusk's directive of February 20, 1961, was the logical culmination of this trend when he announced: "The Ambassador is to take charge overseas. This does not mean in a purely bureaucratic sense, but in an active, operational, interested, responsible fashion. He is expected to know about what is going on among the representatives of other agencies who are stationed in his country. He is expected to supervise, to encourage, to direct, to assist in any way he can." While recognition has necessarily been given to the knowledge a diplomat may have of a particular foreign area, our leaders have emphasized no less the importance of overall administrative and diplomatic skills transferable from one area to another. At one and the same time, knowledge of particular foreign areas, their languages, customs, and practices has been given attention along with stress on an understanding of diplomacy as such. The Foreign Service has drawn on these two companion principles in developing men capable of effective leadership and representation in a growing number of foreign outposts of the United States. The need for skilled ambassadors has increased with each passing year. At the end of World War II, there were four independent states in Africa; today there are twenty-nine, with five more about to be born. Five years ago the United States had seventy-six embassies and three legations to staff. Today the number is ninety-nine embassies and four legations. Their staffing has called for a growing number of able and dedicated leaders capable of speaking in a responsible way to uphold the interests and objectives that this country would project in other parts of the world.

3. The Argument for the Amateur

THROUGHOUT American history the case for a professional Foreign Service has confronted an opposing point of view. This viewpoint has been grounded in the belief that outstanding American citizens with wide public and private experience and with close and intimate ties to a particular responsible administration had much to contribute to American foreign relations. Under the American system, it is the President who makes central decisions in foreign policy. More frequently than not, the President succeeds to his office following an administration which may embrace conflicting views of politics and foreign relations. If an ambassador who has served in a previous administration and has been associated with another philosophy of government is asked to serve an executive with conflicting beliefs, the consequences for effective policy may be unfortunate. Therefore, those who hold to the viewpoint of rotation in office, including high diplomatic positions, argue that a president must have the right to replace top diplomatic officials much as he chooses the members of a new cabinet.

A further argument in support of an "amateur" Foreign Service is that any bureaucracy runs the risk of atrophy. It moves, whether consciously or not, toward rules of procedure and routine responses that make its task more manageable and efficient. Thus an organized Foreign Service becomes the focus of a conservative, standpat approach to foreign policy. Only through the introduction of fresh thinking and strong vigorous leadership drawn from the outside can it rise above this inherent tendency. There is continual need for strong and independent thinking and for new leadership at home and abroad willing and able to stand against the tide. Any bureaucracy is likely to become a creature of the past. It is forever disposed to hold to past policies and approaches. The amateur is a healthy corrective and antidote to this force within the Foreign Service of any country. Some go so far as to urge that all assistant secretaries be chosen from outside the career service.

An additional argument for the amateur derives from the possibility of attracting men of outstanding talent. The early revolutionary and postindependence diplomats in this country were, with few exceptions, colonial leaders. They were men tested in the political arena, well versed in the theory and practice of government. Many of them were, at least until the time of President Andrew Jackson, primarily nonpolitical appointees. They looked on the service as a temporary vocation with the beneficial and adverse effects this outlook entails. From a positive standpoint, they saw the Foreign Service as a public trust. From a negative standpoint, particularly in the consular service, they viewed their work abroad as an adjunct to private commercial careers.

The first diplomatic agents chosen by the Continental Congress are the forerunners of our diplomatic and consular service. They include men like Arthur Lee of Virginia who was a physician and lawyer and who, while living in England for ten years before his appointment, had been an ardent supporter of the American cause. Another diplomatic agent was the international lawyer and linguist, Charles W. F. Dumas, a native of Switzerland who had lived in the Netherlands for many years. It is interesting to note that with his letter of appointment Dumas received the munificent payment of £100 for his work. The others included Silas Deane, Benjamin Franklin, John Jay, and John Adams. The place of Franklin in European diplomatic circles is one which no ordinary Foreign Service officer could have filled. One authority says of Franklin: "His patriarchal appearance, his simple and unostentatious manners, his benevolent but shrewd countenance, and his homely wit and wisdom all appealed to the French, to whom he became an object of unmeasured adulation." [19] To the French, Franklin was the living embodiment of the best in the Age of the Enlightenment and in a new frontier state.

The appointment of distinguished citizens permitted American presidents to use their executive prerogatives free of congressional interference. For example, President George Washington informed the Congress on February 14, 1791, that he had been employing the first executive agent, Gouverneur Morris, to confer with the British on a possible commercial treaty and the unfulfilled articles of the peace treaty of 1783. Washington read to the Congress Morris's instructions as well as communications he had sent to the President. Four days later, Washington advised the Congress he had sent Colonel David Humphreys to Madrid and Lisbon on a similar mission. Other executive agents went out to principal areas of Spanish America to study possible colonial revolts against the hegemony of Spain. In 1810, President James Madison sent Joel Roberts Poinsett of South Carolina on a confidential mission to South America. He concluded a commercial treaty with a new revolutionary government in Buenos Aires in February 1811, went on to Chile, then at war with Peru, to urge its independence and to assist Chile in the framing of a constitution. Other distinguished Americans were sent as special agents to Cuba, Mexico, and Venezuela.

Early American diplomatic history offers many such examples. The best known may be John Jay's mission to Great Britain leading to the Jay Treaty. Thomas Pinckney negotiated early treaty arrangements with Spain, and toward the end of the eighteenth century two successive missions sought to end the crisis in Franco-American relations. These missions and the work of Charles Pinckney, Elbridge Gerry, John Marshall, William V. Murray, William R. Davie, and Chief

[19] William Barnes and John Heath Morgan, *The Foreign Service of the United States* (Washington, D.C.: Historical Office, Department of State, 1961), p. 15.

Justice Oliver Ellsworth culminated in the Convention of September 30, 1800, between France and the United States. Without capable diplomats drawn from the mainstream of American life who were able to grasp the broad currents of European relations, the American Republic might never have succeeded in maintaining its independence. This early generation of American diplomats is rightly called "the old masters."

In the years that followed, American presidents were to draw on other strata of American life for our representatives abroad. Ambassadors, ministers, and diplomatic agents have included journalists and editors, philosophers and university presidents, men of letters and businessmen, and a broad group drawn from dozens of other trades and professions. The editors include Dabney Smith-Carr, the founder of the *Baltimore Republican and Commercial Advertiser*, who served for six years as Minister Resident in Turkey; John Moncure Daniel, editor of the *Richmond Examiner*, who was Minister Resident in Sardinia on the eve of Italian unification; Carl Schurz, editor of the *Detroit Post*, the German language *Westliche Post*, and the *New York Evening Post*, who was Minister to Spain; and Walter Hines Page of the *New York World*, *Atlantic Monthly*, and *World's Work*, who served as Ambassador to London. Some historians maintain that Josephus Daniels of the *Raleigh News and Observer*, who was appointed Ambassador to Mexico at seventy-one years of age, remains the most remarkable of all American journalist-diplomats. The test of Daniels' success in Mexico may have been the firm Mexican action in 1940–1941 in aligning itself with the Allies against the Axis powers and in 1942 declaring war on all three of the Axis states. The same country that in 1917 had shown little concern for the Allied cause joined with free nations to resist German expansion in World War II.

The annals of American diplomacy have also numbered a fair share of scholar-diplomats. These included Paul Barlow, Washington Irving, William Dean Howells, James Russell Lowell, Lew Wallace, and William E. Dodd. Not all of them were successful in foreign relations, but some at least, like Howells, Lowell, and Barlow, could point to significant achievements.

It is surprising that so few outstanding diplomats have been drawn from the realm of university presidents. It would seem that ambassadors and college presidents had much in common. Both have responsibility for determining and executing policy. Both become all too familiar with the mass of routine, if not trivia, in which high policy is so often submerged. Both should be experienced, versatile, and able negotiators. The roster of those who were drawn to foreign relations following university presidencies includes Edward Everett, President of Harvard and Unitarian minister, who was appointed Minister to Great Britain in 1841; Andrew D. White, founder and first President of Cornell, who served as Minister to Germany and Russia; Jacob Gould Schurman, Cornell's outstanding President, who served in three widely dispersed diplomatic posts in appointments totaling nearly a decade; James B. Angell, President of the University of Michigan, who was Minister to China and Turkey; David J. Hill, President of Rochester and Bucknell, who served in Switzerland and Holland; Horace A. Hildreth, President of Bucknell, who was Ambassador to Pakistan during the Eisenhower Administration; and James D. Conant, Ambassador to Germany, who was another Eisenhower appointee. It is symbolic of the expanding character of America's foreign relations that only the earlier of these officials continued their scholarly work while serving abroad. David J. Hill completed a *History of Diplomacy in the International Development of Europe,* and literary figures like Barlow, Hawthorne, Lowell, and Irving wrote while serving abroad. With the passage of time and the growing complexity of our foreign relations, a combination of scholarly and diplomatic work became difficult if not impossible.

If history is past politics and diplomacy, historians should stand in the front rank of American diplomats. Indeed, by any standard, the list of our professional historians who have carried responsibility abroad is impressive. It includes George Bancroft, John Lothrop Motley, Andrew D. White, Claude G. Bowers, Carlton J. H. Hayes, and William E. Dodd. Their numbers increase if diplomats turned amateur historians are added. Firsthand accounts, however personal, are grist for the mill of the diplomatic historian, and some envoys have recorded their experiences with deep insight and considerable intellectual power. They include men like Joseph C. Grew for his *Ten Years in Japan* and John Bigelow for *France and the Confederate Navy.* In less hurried, more tranquil days, some ministers, particularly in minor posts, found time to pursue long-standing intellectual concerns. For Hugh S. Legaré in Belgium this led to the publication of *Constitutional History of Greece,* for Washington Irving in Madrid a life of Columbus, and for Henry Wheaton in Berlin his *Elements of International Law* and *History of the Law of Nations.* Not all amateur historians rank with the foremost American diplomats, but a few, such as Charles Francis Adams and John Hay, earned universal and well-deserved acclaim. Of Adams it is said that no less than the generalship of Grant and Sherman his diplomacy preserved the Union by forestalling any move by the British Navy to throw its full weight to the Confederate side.

If historians as a group have showed any weakness, it has been in accepting and operating within the limitations of their role of representatives and spokesmen for an American administration. For some, discretion and self-restraint have proven too painful a burden to bear. William E. Dodd because of his prophetic appraisal and righteous hatred of Hitler destroyed his lines of contact and thereby his usefulness in Berlin. So deep was George Bancroft's dislike of British aristocracy that when asked why American ministers appeared at court "all dressed in black," he responded that they were merely paying homage to "the burial of monarchy." John Lothrop Motley fell out of grace with President Andrew Johnson and Secretary Seward when he was Minister to Vienna, and with President Ulysses S. Grant and Secretary Fish when

Minister to London. He is probably better known in the annals of diplomacy for completion of his *Rise of the Dutch Republic* than for success in his several diplomatic posts—with the possible exception of his diplomatic reports on European reactions to the Civil War.

The rich diversity of American representation is illustrated by reviewing the myriad sectors of American life from which successive presidents have called ministers and ambassadors. They include politicians like William O'Dwyer and Sherman Cooper; business and financial leaders like Albert Gallatin, Andrew Mellon, Dwight Morrow, Joseph Patrick Kennedy, and C. Douglas Dillon; and scores of military men, missionaries, lawyers, small merchants, and labor specialists. American presidents have chosen "playboys and socialists, poets, Negro abolitionists and passionate defenders of slavery, brokers and women's wear manufacturers, rose fanciers and polo players, missionaries and ex-Presidents, dozens of bankers and industrialists, baker's dozens of teachers, and countless lawyers and politicians." [20] More than two thousand ambassadors, ministers, and chargés d'affaires have served their country in a little more than a century and a half. Few observers could have foreseen the achievements or failures of individual ambassadors in advance. While all would agree that the times are too serious to send innocents abroad, the requisite qualities of the successful envoy are difficult to assay in advance.

Although the present administration has stressed the appointment of career diplomats, President John F. Kennedy has been unwilling to exclude highly qualified amateurs from key outposts. He has made appointments to sixty-eight of our ninety-nine ambassadorial posts. He has chosen historians like Edwin O. Reischauer (Tokyo) and Charles W. Cole (Santiago); economists like John K. Galbraith (New Delhi), Lincoln Gordon (Brazil), and Philip M. Kaiser (Dakar); miltary men like General James M. Gavin (Paris); and educators like John

[20] E. Wilder Spaulding, *Ambassadors Ordinary and Extraordinary* (Washington, D.C.: Public Affairs Press, 1961), p. 206.

S. Badeau (Cairo). No reasonable student of foreign policy would claim that this group of envoys surpasses in talent professional diplomats like David E. K. Bruce (London), Llewellyn E. Thompson or Foy Kohler (Moscow), George F. Kennan (Belgrade), or Walter C. Dowling (Bonn). Yet any government so hemmed in by a creed of professionalism that it felt obliged to pass over leaders in foreign relations like Ambassadors Gordon or Reischauer would be the poorer. The goal of the Republic has become professionalism within a broad and inclusive definition that recognizes excellence and capacity as manifested within and outside the Foreign Service.

4. The Road to a Professional Service

THE maintenance of a large measure of flexibility in building an effective Foreign Service should not obscure the long and successful struggle of the Foreign Service to establish a hard core of genuinely professional officials. Those Foreign Service officers who were appointed ambassadors have, up to the present, been restricted more often than not to so-called "hardship posts." As late as the outbreak of World War I, with but one exception, no American envoy to any important European state could boast prior diplomatic experience or service of more than a year abroad. The British and French representatives in key European countries were able to point to twenty-seven and twenty-three years of experience, respectively, and the French Ambassador in Washington, Jules Jusserand, combined twenty-six years of prior service with twelve years in the United States. Wartime expansion from 1939 to 1944 was a response to a further crisis, but, significantly, 90 percent of the increase in civilian officer personnel occurred outside the Foreign Service. A Foreign Service auxiliary, while useful, was hardly the answer to long-term needs.

The key to the problem seemed to be a unified professional service. The Foreign Service Act of 1946, discussed above, sought to provide stronger administrative direction, a new classification and promotions system, improved provisions for retirement and other benefits, and a more far-reaching in-service training system. Yet these advances, while desirable, were insufficient, and a whole succession of commissions recommended further changes. The Hoover Commission urged the establishment of a single Foreign Service after having noted that at least forty-five executive agencies, in addition to the Department of State, were involved in foreign affairs. Of the

128,500 civilian employees serving their government abroad in 1948, no more than 11 percent were part of the Foreign Service and the Department of State. The Hoover Commission proposed that the department not take over the operating functions of these far-flung groups but concentrate rather on providing central direction, supervision, and coordination.

Other studies followed, including that of the Rowe Committee, and a further independent survey of departmental and Foreign Service personnel. These inquiries culminated in the now famous Wriston Report under the chairmanship of Henry M. Wriston, then President of Brown University. The Wriston Report recommended, first, integration of the personnel of the Department of State and the Foreign Service "where their official functions converge" into a single career Foreign Service. While earlier reforms had stressed unification of diplomatic and consular services, "Wristonization" was aimed at uniting our representatives abroad and civil servants in the Department of State. Moreover, integration was to be achieved not gradually as in the past, but "with all possible dispatch, and certainly within two years." All previous committees had recommended integration but none had attacked the problem with the vigor and decisiveness of the Wriston Committee. It was argued that once a single personnel system was created, a sounder basis would exist for an interchangeable professional group, and specialists required by the modern problems of foreign affairs could more effectively be brought within the service. Following careful study, a total of 3,689 positions—1,450 in the department and 2,239 in overseas posts—were identified and designated Foreign Service officer positions. While departmental officers who refused FSO appointments had initially been slated for transfer or dismissal, the department found it necessary to designate 300 positions in the department as non-Foreign Service posts whose occupants were unwilling or unable to accept overseas appointments. For Foreign Service officers in general, the new system provided that during the first fifteen years of service they be assigned to the United States for not less than three years. The forces which brought the Wriston reforms into being were multiple. While State Department officers in Washington had been free to accept overseas assignments, fewer than fifty took occasion to go abroad in the eight years preceding the report. Thus Foreign Service officers were deprived of tours of duty in the United States if requirements of overseas representation were to be met. A survey in 1954 revealed that 40 percent had only one year's experience in Washington and one quarter of our Foreign Service officers with twenty years' service had returned for two years or less during their tenure. The hoped-for re-Americanization for which presidents since Jefferson had called was impossible. Hence officers abroad ran the risk of a loss of contact with the civilization they served and State Department officials with little sense of realities in the field became increasingly alienated from ministers and ambassadors. Moreover, the division between "generalists" abroad and specialists at home persisted at a time when the nature of foreign service was becoming ever more many-sided. Prior to the Wriston Report, the possibility of lateral entry had been frustrated. Of two thousand departmental officers who applied for commissions as Foreign Service officers in 1951, no more than twenty-five were appointed in a period of approximately four years. An almost unbridgeable barrier developed between what amounted to two separate services in much the same way the Foreign Office in Britain had been plagued by division some thirty-five years before and the French diplomatic service has suffered more recently.

The quality of our representatives in foreign capitals takes on increased importance if it is realized that the business of a large-scale embassy today is greater than that of the Department of State before World War II. Foreign Service officers have all too frequently lacked the administrative experience essential to their task; and the substitution of men who have had practical experience in private business misconceives the nature of the diplomatic function. The responsibility of our officials at the United Nations, the Coal and Steel Community, or NATO is specialized to the point where separate ambassadors with particular skills are needed. An experienced observer has noted that $2,000,000 to permit experienced officials to serve as envoys in high-cost posts such as Paris or London would carry a value many times over the cost. While these reforms were not fully expressed in the Wriston Report, President Kennedy early in his administration moved to respond to the needs by requesting a larger appropriation for what congressmen sometimes describe as "whiskey allowances" and by appointing distinguished Americans like Governor Stevenson to specialized ambassadorial roles.

The Wriston program represents the most far-reaching attempt to professionalize and strengthen the Department of State and the Foreign Service. Both in terms of morale and numbers, the Foreign Service had declined. Through putting stress on lateral entry and more effective recruitment at all levels, the committee endeavored to meet future needs. One major criticism of "Wristonization" has been that it deprecates the role of the generalist. Its aim has been to find better means of enlisting nonpolitical specialists. Modern diplomacy requires the know-how of economists and communication and intelligence specialists. Yet if these goals are stressed at the expense of diplomatic know-how, the advance will have been nugatory. Charles E. Bohlen has argued:

It is, of course, true that in the modern world our relations with any given country involve many factors other than the direct dealings between governments, and an effective and competent diplomat, whatever his rank, must be prepared and equipped to deal with these nongovernmental aspects of his work. But, however much we recognize the importance of the public relations aspect of a diplomat's profession, however much importance we attach to aid programs, getting in touch with the people of the country in which he is stationed—these modern developments in international relations should not cause us to forget that the chief purpose of the diplomat is the transaction of business for his country with the government to which he is credited. The success or failure of a given diplomatic mission in any country will, in the last analysis, come down to the degree of success it has achieved with the government of that country. The settlement of disputes that inevitably arise between countries, as between individuals, the ability to influence without improper interference the course of the foreign country's action in a direction which would serve the overall objectives of our foreign policy—these are the real business of diplomacy, to which all other aspects are supporting and subsidiary.[21]

This statement of the paramount role of the American diplomat suggests that changing patterns of foreign relations have left one requirement unchanged. The diplomat today no less than yesterday must be a man of extraordinary human resources. Harold Nicolson has written:

These then are the qualities of my ideal diplomat. Truth, accuracy, calm, patience, good temper, modesty and loyalty. They are all the qualities of an ideal diplomacy.

"But," the reader may object, "you have forgotten intelligence, knowledge, discernment, prudence, hospitality, charm, industry, courage and even tact." I have not forgotten them. I have taken them for granted.[22]

If improvement of the structure of the Foreign Service can better assure the discovery of the ideal diplomat, we must continue unremittingly to strengthen all its aspects.

Yet it is barely possible that so exclusive an emphasis on personnel administration may miss the central point. Most contemporary writers from John Bassett Moore to Graham Stuart, in contrast to classical scholars like Jusserand and Nicolson, say less about human qualities than about recruitment, in-service training, and integration. There is a wider

[21] Charles E. Bohlen, *The Foreign Service and the Panorama of Change* (Washington, D.C.: Department of State, 1961), pp. 3–4.

[22] Harold Nicolson, *Diplomacy* (London: Oxford University Press, 1952), p. 126.

danger that when our society indulges itself in periodic waves of anti-intellectualism it may, at the same time, grant to those with but narrow claims to expertise influence that would have been inconceivable to the founders of the Republic. More than specialization, should we not ask of a diplomat what intellectual and moral resources he brings to his task and to what ends they are directed? Are not his realism, benevolence, and judgment more basic than his specialty? Perhaps in this circumstance the uniqueness of American professionalism is the best antidote against too narrow an approach to the Foreign Service. For the blending of talents and resources drawn from the broadest possible spectrum of American life may enhance the prospect of human excellence. While professionalism is and must be a fundamental goal for the establishment of a viable and successful Foreign Service, it ought not to be an absolute. We may have more to teach nations just approaching the creation of their foreign services if we hold firmly to the lessons of our own experience. As they call on journalists, teachers, and revolutionary leaders, we have moved ahead through a professionalism broadly defined. If all we have to offer our friends in the new nations are tables of organization, revised examinations, and in-service training programs, our lessons may fall on barren ground. The uniqueness of American professionalism is its breadth, and the richness and diversity of a whole society contributing to the attack on the great issues of war and peace is a legacy we need not hesitate to share with others.

3

Responsibility within a Living Constitution

THE PRESIDENT
AND THE DEPARTMENT OF STATE

"The task of a statesman consists only in listening carefully whether he can catch an echo of the strides of the Almighty through the events of this world, and then to spring forward and seize the hem of his garment."
OTTO VON BISMARCK

"THE FOREIGN POLICY of India equals Prime Minister Jawaharlal Nehru." This statement by a well-informed student of Indian foreign policy takes some of us by surprise. Yet in fact the power of the executive in the shaping of foreign policy is in practice decisive for other democracries as well. The role of the executive within the living and evolving constitution is even greater than for the written constitution. Under the American system the President makes the central decisions, and former President Harry Truman's terse comment, "The buck stops on the President's desk," applies with special force in the field of foreign relations. The President is responsible for the conduct of foreign policy and for the tasks of the commander in chief. He has the power to make treaties, by and with the consent of two-thirds of the Senate; to nominate, by and with the advice of the Senate, ambassadors, other public ministers, and counsels; and to choose all other officials of the United States whose appointments are not otherwise provided for. Through the power of entering into diplomatic relations with other nations by treaties and the exchange of envoys, the President can grant recognition to governments and receive or ask for the recall of foreign diplomats, even without consulting Congress, as in President Washington's request for Citizen Genet's recall. Mr. Truman's claim that "The President makes foreign policy" while not the full story describes an essential truth. His powers in foreign relations as in other spheres derive from the broad provisions of Article II, considered by constitutional lawyers the most loosely drawn and by implication the most inclusive of chapters in the Constitution.

1. The Constitutional and Historical Basis

of Executive Power

CONSTITUTIONAL lawyers have long stressed the primary, exclusive, and residual character of executive power. From it, according to the mythology of government, derive legislative and judicial powers, which were established as monarchs or rulers marked out functions that could be defined, divided, and shared with others. Thus a legendary king in some primeval forest created court and council but kept for himself all powers not delegated to them. Throughout our history, strong presidents have had recourse to a broad category of executive power. The American Constitution, far from being a closed system, fairly "bristles with alternatives," and nowhere is this more conspicuous than with the executive. The uncertainties of the Constitution invite debate, and if the functions and methods of courts and legislatures can be made reasonably explicit, those of the executive remain indefinite, plastic, and ever responsive to personality and circumstance. For political and legal philosophers like Locke, Montesquieu, and Blackstone, who helped form the minds of the Founding Fathers, the executive enjoyed broad, discretionary, and residual power making him capable of response to any emergency. The Supreme Court spoke of his authority as being "plenary and exclusive." Gouverneur Morris warned: "We must either then renounce the blessings of the Union, or provide an Executive with sufficient vigor to pervade every part of it." [1] The President came to represent the people and the nation as a whole as symbol, spokesman, and guardian.

A major controversy throughout the history of the presidency centers on the scope and limitations of executive power. For some, the constitutional provisions are an explicit grant

[1] Max Farrand, *Records of the Federal Convention* (New Haven, 1911), II, 52–53.

of powers inclusive in the authority they describe. Others speak of presidential prerogatives, denoting by this a broad range of implicit executive power. The presidency, according to its more extravagant defenders, was patterned directly on the British monarchy of George III, "with the corruption left out." The first two Federalist presidents, George Washington and John Adams, viewed the office as the "dignified element of government" and went so far as to invest it with certain "trappings of monarchy." For example, President Washington appeared in person before the legislature to deliver his annual address, questioned the place of political "factions," and asserted his independent right to remove executive officers, even those whose appointments were approved by the Senate. President Thomas Jefferson, by contrast, was to substitute for the concept of a quasi-monarchical "Chief Executive" the principle of "the party leader." He drew his strength in policy-making from the party caucus, and his successors, Presidents James Madison and James Monroe, were nominated for the presidency by "the Congressional Caucus." Andrew Jackson reshaped the office by appealing to the people over the heads of legislators, but from the end of the Mexican War to 1861, the presidency was subservient to the Congress which became the prime forum for compromise and negotiation on issues of the "impending conflict." If American constitutional history is a record of the ebb and flow of executive power, it reached its nadir during this period.

President Abraham Lincoln by temperament and circumstance was constrained to call upon the full resources of his executive office in order to preserve the Union. The enlargement of the scope of his authority depended in part upon the vagueness of the constitutional mandate. Writing in 1840 of the Constitutional Convention, Abel Upshur could say: "The Convention appears to have studiously selected such loose and general expressions, as would enable the President, by implication and construction either to neglect his duties or to enlarge his powers." [2] Mr. Lincoln's response took the form of interpreting the "Commander in Chief" clause and his responsibility to "take care that the laws" Congress enacts are "faithfully executed" to affirm the "war powers" as primarily the President's prerogative. He could say: "I conceive that I may in an emergency do things on military grounds which cannot constitutionally be done by Congress." [3] In the ten-week period from the fall of Fort Sumter to the special session of Congress convened on July 4, 1861, Lincoln called up 40,000 volunteers, enlisted 23,000 additional Regular Army and 18,000 Regular Navy men, expended unappropriated funds, suspended the writ of habeas corpus, proclaimed a blockade of southern ports, detained those who were said to be contemplating "treasonable practices," established new passport regulations, and acted against "treasonable correspondence" through the mails. He took these steps to preserve a nation in dissolution, asking, for example, respecting habeas corpus, whether all the laws but one were to go unexecuted. The consequences reached far beyond the present danger of the emergency, for when in 1863 the Supreme Court in the Prize Cases confirmed his authority, Lincoln had succeeded in laying to rest the doctrine that the executive always must be subordinate to the legislature. In the struggle that continues down to the present, Lincoln's conception persists that the executive, within "generous limits," should be paramount, autonomous, and self-directing. Jackson had proclaimed that the President's powers were autonomous. Lincoln proceeded to demonstrate Jackson's brave affirmation.

This brief review may serve to illustrate the changing drama in which force of character and constitutional principle interact. However, a third factor must be added to complete

[2] Abel Upshur, *A Brief Inquiry into the True Nature and Character of Our Federal Government* (1840), pp. 116–17.
[3] Nathaniel W. Stephenson, *Abraham Lincoln and the Union* (New Haven: Yale University Press, 1921), p. 353.

the equation: the impact of the internal and external world. The American presidency in the twentieth century reflects the rise of the United States as a world power and a radical shift in outlook on the purpose and extent of governmental power. The changing circumstances of modern economic life necessitate positive government. Public authorities and constitutional restraints had for the first century of our history protected the individual against the state. The first ten amendments to the Constitution were the prime source for implementing individual rights. At the turn of the century, the concentration of power had shifted to holders of private authority and this time governmental power was thrown into the balance to secure the individual in the name of the state. An active reformist political regime supplanted a laissez-faire order; the spearhead of the war against social abuse and economic inequality was more often than not the executive.

Yet the rise of the United States as a world power may have been even more fundamental in accounting for the expansion of executive authority. It was the Spanish-American War that catapulted the Republic onto the world stage. In 1885, Woodrow Wilson was impelled to write of the executive office: "It has fallen from its first estate of dignity because its power has waned; and its power has waned because the power of Congress has become predominant." [4] In 1900, in his preface to the fifteenth printing of *Congressional Government*, Wilson amended this view: "Much the most important change to be noticed is the result of the war with Spain upon the lodgment and exercise of power within our federal system: the greatly increased power and opportunity for constructive statemanship given the President, by the plunge into international politics. . . ." In the same preface, Wilson observed:

When foreign affairs play a prominent part in the politics and policy of a nation, its Executive must of necessity be its guide: must utter every initial judgment, take every first step of action, supply the information upon which it is to act, suggest and in large measure control

　　[4] Woodrow Wilson, *Congressional Government* (New York: Meridian Books, 1956), p. 48.

its conduct. The President of the United States is now . . . at the front of affairs, as no President, except Lincoln, has been since the first quarter of the nineteenth century. . . .[5]

Between 1885 and 1900, the center of federal power had moved from one end of Pennsylvania Avenue to the other. Grover Cleveland had arrested the trend of declining presidential power that Wilson had observed in Andrew Johnson, General Grant, and Rutherford B. Hayes. In 1908, assessing the presidency in *Constitutional Government in the United States*, Wilson declared: "His is the only national voice in affairs. Let him once win the admiration and confidence of the country, and no other single force can withstand him, no combination of forces will easily overpower him. . . . His office is anything he has the sagacity and force to make it." [6] Because the congressional form of government is a living system shaped and influenced by the force of events, the political regime in 1908 was not the same as that in 1884. With Wilson and continuing through Franklin D. Roosevelt, political practice tends to confirm Wilson's theory. The growing importance of prompt initiative in foreign affairs heightens the necessity of active executive leadership.

Following Woodrow Wilson, another far-reaching development in the external world sharpened still further the urgent need for decisive presidential leadership. The western democracies in the aftermath of World War I confronted the rise of totalitarian regimes relentlessly mobilizing the total resources of a whole people at the point of a dictator's ambition. A single unscrupulous leader in control of an authoritarian regime and bent on imperial design could incite his nation to arms, issue threats and ultimata, cajole or extract concessions, and annex hapless neighbors while its adversary, committed to the democratic process, sought painfully to resolve its collective will. National socialism in Germany and

[5] *Ibid.*, p. 22.
[6] Woodrow Wilson, *Constitutional Government in the United States* (New York: Columbia University Press, 1908), pp. 67 ff.

fascism in Italy spurred the democracies to reassess the implications of legislative supremacy. In Professor Louis Koenig's words, the period between the wars was "an era in which executive powers underwent a remarkable expansion not only in countries having the revolutionary dictatorships, but also in the democracies, which, in the severity of the times . . . relied considerably upon executive action." [7] Within a continuing framework of representative government, countries like Great Britain, France, and the United States sought through orderly means to equip their executives to meet problems with dispatch. Through the varied sources of constitutional and statutory authority, the American presidency was geared to the demands of crisis government. President Franklin D. Roosevelt by executive order authorized an increase in the enlisted strength of the Army, Navy, and Marine Corps; recommissioned ancient destroyers for patrol duty; prompted Congress to pass legislation amending the Neutrality Act to permit sales to belligerents for "cash on the barrel"; and on the strength of the existence of first a limited, then an unlimited national emergency called upon a rich inheritance of statutory authority from past crises to justify far-reaching measures. Theodore Roosevelt had denied that "what was imperatively necessary for the nation could not be done by the President unless he could find some specific authorization to do it." [8] Notwithstanding, both Wilson and Franklin D. Roosevelt sought a statutory basis for their acts, in contrast with Lincoln who drew on broad provisions of the Constitution. This trend and the expansion of the domain within which the executive must act has meant that the presidency, which 180 years ago was a person, has today become an institution—an institution embodied in the White House office of 400 persons and the Executive Office with personnel numbering more than 2,700.

[7] Louis W. Koenig, *The Presidency and the Crisis* (New York: King's Crown Press, 1944), p. 1.

[8] *Ibid.*, p. 16.

2. Congress and the President

YET any review which by tracing the growth of executive power in foreign relations left the impression that his constitutional authority was unequivocal and supreme would be misleading. Professor Corwin writes: "the Constitution, considered only for its affirmative grants of powers . . . is an invitation to struggle for the privilege of directing American foreign policy." [9] Authority for external affairs is divided, with the President enjoying a favored position where initiative, dispatch, and unity of action are called for but with the Congress being favored by its control over treaties and appropriations.

Both the President and Congress draw their powers in foreign relations not alone from the Constitution but from the inherent rights of a sovereign state under international law. Justice Sutherland argued in 1936 in *The United States vs. Curtiss-Wright* that sovereignty passed directly from the English crown to the United States of America as early as the Continental Congress. National power in foreign relations is exclusive and plenary for reasons more fundamental than any explicit grant of power by the Constitution. To quote Justice Sutherland's opinion in the Curtiss-Wright case: "The powers to declare and wage war, to conclude peace, to make treaties, to maintain diplomatic relations . . . if they had never been mentioned in the Constitution, would have been vested in the Federal government as necessary concomitants of nationality."

The presidency more than any other organ of government expresses and symbolizes national sovereignty. Jefferson's dictum is significant in light of his commitment to legislative

[9] Edward S. Corwin, *The President: Office and Powers* (New York: New York University Press, 1948), p. 208.

111

supremacy: "The transaction of business with foreign nations is executive altogether." In 1897, a Senate Foreign Relations Committee report reaffirmed that: "The executive is the sole mouthpiece of the nation in communication with foreign sovereignties." [10] Professor Corwin observes: "there is no more securely established principle of constitutional practice than the exclusive right of the President to be the nation's intermediary in its dealing with other nations." [11] So far-reaching is this function that the President by his actions can confront the Congress and the people on almost any issue with a *fait accompli* even on critical matters decisive to war and peace. He can recognize or refuse to recognize a foreign government, issue major declarations that "revolutionize" policy, as with the Monroe or Truman Doctrines, engage in negotiations that lead to far-reaching formal or informal obligations, and order the armed forces of his country to remote parts of the world, sometimes committing the nation thereby to hostile acts short of war. The President by his actions can so shape the course of American action as to eliminate for all practical purposes the determining role of the Congress despite its "power of the purse" and capacity to declare war.

Yet the relation between President and the Congress in foreign relations unfolds within a framework of government by consent. The living Constitution decrees that executive-legislative association can never be one of repose. In the words of the late Justice Brandeis: "The doctrine of the separation of powers was adopted by the Convention of 1787, not to promote efficiency, but to preclude the exercise of arbitrary power. The purpose was not to avoid friction, but, by means of the inevitable friction incident to the distribution of the governmental powers . . . to save the people from autocracy." [12] The President must rally support for his policies not through

---

[10] *Senate Documents*, No. 56, p. 30.

[11] Corwin, *op. cit.*, p. 224.

[12] Justice Brandeis' dissent in *Myers vs. United States*, 272 U.S. 52, 293 (1926).

the control of a tightly disciplined party as in Great Britain; he must build consensus across party lines on the basis of well-understood goals and purposes. His task has been compared to that of a sheep dog rounding up stragglers. If presidents since Lincoln have frequently had recourse to their Constitutional responsibility to "take care that the Laws be faithfully executed (Art. II, Sec. 3)," Congress must also assure through observation, investigation, and criticism that the laws it enacts are administered. Its more than two hundred committees guarantee that it will not view this obligation lightly.

The most continuous involvement of the Congress is in the appropriations process. The point at which executive and legislative confront one another is within congressional committees. The several committees and subcommittees are at work around the calendar preparing and enacting annual appropriations acts. The practice of detailed appropriations initiated by Congress in 1862 "minutely specifying the uses to be made of the funds appropriated" involves present-day congressmen in debates over the military plans of NATO, agricultural equipment for India, or the selection of books or paintings to be sent abroad. Different committees of Congress participate in approving annual authorization legislation as well as appropriations. For example, during the lifetime of the Lend Lease Program and the Marshall Plan, the Foreign Affairs Committee of the House, and Foreign Relations Committee of the Senate annually reported out legislation authorizing another year's activity and setting a ceiling for appropriations. Subsequently, appropriations committees in both Houses specified in detail the purposes for which the appropriations could be used. As each year's legislation was completed, the committees began work on measures for the following year.

Thus Congress has emerged as an indispensable partner in the conduct of foreign relations. Together the President and the Congress have all the power necessary to formulate policy. Our wisest students of government maintain that Congress must not be regarded as an unfortunate nuisance even though friction between the executive and legislature is probably inevitable. Relations are not designed to be restful; as power strikes power and is restrained, sparks are inevitable. The central issue is not whether Congress or the President is stronger, but rather how both can be strengthened to carry their joint burdens. More often than not, claims or counterclaims that the legislature or the executive has encroached on the other's prerogative are polemics intended to advance a point of view. In the fluid and changing interplay of forces in government, the exercise of power depends on circumstance and in the end is a political question, although each side seeks justification on constitutional grounds by transforming it into a judicial question.

Those who insist that the executive is the sole organ of government in foreign relations probably misread the Constitution. Beyond this, they underrate the sense of confidence the Congress has earned from executive officers and the informed citizenry. Officials with long experience in testifying before congressional committees have difficulty in recalling discussions in which partisan considerations were dominant. Only in a congressman's constituency where politics count do the sharp edges of party rivalry appear. Students of the Congress note a high degree of expertise and skill in key committees and an esprit de corps and self-consciousness that leads to impatience when new and junior executive officers are sent up to "the Hill" to testify. On the great issues of war and peace, relations across the aisle in committees are more relaxed than the outsider popularly imagines. Congressmen maintain that local, not international issues determine elections. We recall the formula of more than one hard-pressed legislator that to be a liberal senator, you must start by being a senator. Senators seek help back home to achieve freedom of action in the foreign affairs sphere. They ask the President to give them something to support, to take the lead in a realm where they can lead only if they have a program to support. By rallying around a policy, they emerge as influential legislative leaders. The administration helps them to build a record that will strengthen them at the hustings. Indeed, this is undoubtedly the most compelling reason for a top-ranking official to appear in turn before successive committees. If he were to send a junior official, the effect for legislators seeking to build a record would not be the same.

Since Congress and the President share in the formulation of foreign policy, proposals are occasionally advanced for more intimate and continuous collaboration. The need, of course, is obvious for both sides to work together in a great variety of ways. Presidents more than once have invited leaders of the opposition party to serve on American delegations to important conferences. Recently, one American senator has proposed that a procedure be evolved whereby policy-makers and the chairmen and ranking members of the respective Senate and House committees dealing with foreign policy meet informally at a weekly luncheon for easy and relaxed consultation. Both proposals and others like them raise complex constitutional issues. Congressmen are reluctant to participate in international negotiations for which they carry no official responsibility. They insist that involvement without accompanying constitutional responsibility places them in an equivocal position as the leaders of the opposition. Similarly, any administration is understandably resistant to influences that may result from a high-level bull session where freewheeling legislators try out their favorite views of how the country should proceed without accepting responsibility for the consequences. As American constitutional history makes clear, the division of responsibility between the separate branches of government rests on solid and objective foundations. Officials and elected representatives of government can never forget, even in moments of apparent harmony and personal good will, that their constitutional functions are quite separate and distinct.

Another area in which Congress influences foreign policy sometimes by breaching the principle of constitutional limitations and restraint, relates to congressional sessions before major diplomatic and economic conferences. Individual congressmen are wont to go on record before rather than after international congresses. They may wish to establish a political base line from which subsequent criticism may be leveled, or they may imagine that what they resolve may shape the conduct of negotiations. Whatever their purpose, the effects of legislative intervention at the outset of delicate and uncertain international discussions is almost bound to be unfortunate. By throwing the spotlight of public attention on American negotiators at the preparatory stage in their work, legislators destroy freedom of maneuver and the prospects for a successful outcome of negotiations. By forcing our diplomats to outline in advance both minimum and maximum positions, the Congress makes of the forthcoming conference table a forum for reiterating fixed positions, not an instrument for reconciling differences. Once positions are publicly announced and all possibilities laid bare before Congress and the public, genuine negotiations based on responsible give and take and the skillful modification of positions to meet changes initiated by the other party become difficult, if not impossible. Worse still, rancorous debate and deep public division may compromise a negotiator's position even before he reaches the conference table. In the wake of the type of congressional debate that surrounded the Paris Peace Conference or preceded some of the periodic conferences of foreign ministers in the Truman-Acheson regime, the American representative cannot but appear as a symbol of disunity and discord, not of a united people. To make this point is not to apportion credit or blame, but the consequences of such a sequence of events should be plain for all to see.

The hazards and pitfalls of executive-legislative relations need not obscure their creative possibilities. If historians can point to debacles, they also acknowledge the landmarks to which free men must have reference if democratic foreign policy is to succeed. Few historians will be able to isolate the elements that comprise successful bipartisan foreign policy. No simple formula can embrace this elusive process, perhaps because it is secreted in the qualities of individual men and experiences. Secretary Root's relations with Congress were exemplary. The anatomy of effective cooperation includes certain elemental factors. On the side of the administration, it requires a spokesman trusted by colleagues and political rivals alike. He must find points of contact within major congressional committees that assure frank and continuous association on difficult issues with individual legislators. In short, bipartisanship requires responsible political leadership of a high order within the Congress and the executive.

Secretary of State Cordell Hull gave leadership of this character in combination with the Committee of Eight, a special Senate committee which, beginning on April 25, 1944, undertook the preparations for a more stable postwar world. This remarkable body made up of a powerful group of senators from both sides of the aisle—Connally, Barkley, George, Gillette, Vandenberg, La Follette, White, and Austin—met on at least four occasions with Secretary Hull, prior to Dumbarton Oaks, to discuss proposed drafts of a charter for a new international organization. Mr. Hull subsequently continued consultation with the so-called B2H2 group—Senators Ball, Burton, Hatch, and Hill—and with Speaker Rayburn, Majority Leader McCormack, Minority Leader Martin, and the Chairman and ranking minority member of the House Foreign Affairs Committee, Mr. Bloom and Mr. Eaton, as well as Representatives Ramspeck and Arends. Secretary Hull was successful in calling upon his experience in the Congress to rally this body in support of the charter. He drew upon his experience with the major political parties to write into their platforms proposals that endorsed the concept of an international organization in much the same way he worked successfully with legislative leaders on reciprocal trade legislation. If this success is measured against Senator Vandenberg's initial vigorous opposition to a proposed agreement enabling the President to contribute funds appropriated by the Congress for the relief and rehabilitation of war-ravaged countries, the "triumph" of bipartisanship becomes apparent. Yet the same Senator Vandenberg, after first denouncing the "executive dictatorship" inherent in an "illimitable scheme for relief and rehabilitation all around the world" concocted by New Deal crystal gazers, became the chief advocate of UNRRA, thanks to his satisfying consultation with Secretary Hull and Dean Acheson. His support on other matters of international cooperation followed a similar course of initial staunch resistance, a period of gestation, an estimate of domestic and international political consequences, and finally commitment.

An effective congressional leader in the realm of foreign policy while serving the national interest must likewise protect the interests of his party and limit the political benefits that may accrue to the opposing party. He may do this by exacting as the price of his support concessions, as did Senator Vandenberg when he insisted that the Marshall Plan be administered by an independent agency under but not directly responsive to the president. Whether the Senate leader is the chairman of a key committee like Foreign Relations or the senior minority member, he must retain the respect and trust of his own party. He must, in a word, remain a politician. He must be confident that what he is committed to support will have party backing when the voting begins and must hold a favored position in the club or the inner circle of the Senate.

The "golden age" of executive-legislative relations, then, involved Senator Vandenberg, who performed "the service of bringing together in support of a foreign policy, dictated by the necessity of events, an administration which could carry it out and an opposition which could have prevented it from doing so." [13] In 1948, the United States faced perhaps its greatest challenge. It had demobilized in haste and deeply injured thereby its capacity to implement foreign policy. In 1947, the nation was unable to muster a single combat division. The initial response to Prime Minister Churchill's warning at

[13] Dean Acheson, *Sketches from Life* (New York: Harper & Bros., 1961), p. 146.

Fulton, Missouri, of a growing Soviet threat was one of surprise, resentment, and dismay. Yet Secretary of State George Catlett Marshall and President Harry S. Truman were confident that once the nature of the threat was made clear the people would respond. Their success was to demonstrate that the president must consider not only what the public will do before but after leadership has been exerted. The country's leadership was moved by the confident hope that the American people would act when the facts were laid before them. Yet the key to support for a $20,000,000,000 program for European recovery and the establishment of a $10,000,000,000 annual national defense program is found in the extraordinary dedication and skill of Senator Vandenberg, then Chairman of the Foreign Relations Committee and Republican spokesman on foreign affairs, and Undersecretary of State Robert Lovett. By mastery of every detail in the extraordinarily complicated programs and through the trust and affection they enjoyed, Vandenberg and Lovett achieved together what neither could have accomplished alone. These men understood the anatomy of executive-legislative relations, the structure of leadership within the American system, and the enormous resources and vitality of a free people. Their work must forever remain a landmark of achievement in democratic foreign policy.

3. The President and the Department of State

THE growing complexity and the expanding character of our foreign relations has made of the President's role an almost impossible one. One presidential commission noted in another connection: "The President needs help." Yet however extensive his duties, the President cannot delegate his responsibility to the point of sharing it beyond recovery with others. The President, and he alone, is responsible for the conduct of foreign relations, the direction of departments and agencies, and decisions on the executive budget. Responsibility in other realms of American life can be divided and subdivided. A university president can carve out some part of his function to assign to others. The chairman of a board or commission can specify the responsibility of his colleagues. Under the Constitution, however, the President in a critical way is the holder of prerogatives that in the end no one can share with him, except perhaps in that ancient and prehistoric myth of the all-powerful monarch of the forest who, in founding a government, devolved upon courts and councils a portion of the functions of government.

The President's chief agent in the foreign relations field is his Secretary of State. From time to time and increasingly in recent years, proposals have been made to interpose a still higher official between the President and the secretary. Former President Herbert Hoover, Governor Nelson Rockefeller, and former President Eisenhower's Advisory Committee on Government Operations have in turn recommended creation of a new high-ranking office. More specifically, these proposals include suggestions for a vice-president for foreign affairs or a first secretary of government for foreign affairs. Some urge that the President devolve responsibility for all or part of foreign policy on "super-cabinet" officers or a "super-cabinet" staff. Yet constitutional lawyers and students of American government have largely opposed a plan whereby some third official would assume part or all of the role of the Secretary or the President. Secretary John Foster Dulles once contemplated for himself a cabinet office without portfolio with headquarters in the White House where he could think about and plan foreign policy. On examining this alternative more fully, he concluded it constituted an impractical and untenable arrangement. A recent Senate study concludes: "such novel additions to the policy process, far from reducing the President's burdens, would in all likelihood increase them. . . . In the American system, there is no satisfactory alternative to primary reliance on the great departments . . . as instruments for policy development and execution." [14] The President cannot delegate his ultimate responsibility for the conduct of foreign policy nor can he effectively turn over to a "super-cabinet" officer responsibility for the work of a department if he is removed from the context of the ongoing work of the department.

The President can afford to delegate some functions involved in the execution of foreign policy to the secretary. In part he can do this because the Secretary occupies an appointive office and is seldom if ever an independent force politically capable of rivaling the President. For the President to delegate duties to an elective office would introduce confusion in the public mind as between the responsibilities of two elected officials chosen for different reasons. The strength of the Secretary of State's position stems both from his intimate relationship to the President and his contact with the daily flow of business of foreign affairs. He maintains a constant, informed, and detailed watch over the realm of foreign affairs in order to provide the President with information, counsel, and recommendations on the momentous decisions

[14] Study by the Subcommittee on National Policy Machinery for the Committee on Government Operations of the U.S. Senate, January 28, 1961, p. 2.

that he must make. While the Secretary's task is to execute policy, the formulation of high policy is often indivisible from its execution. Because policy is the result of men working in the context of daily events, the secretary and the Department of State are both an arm of the executive and an independent source of influence on the formation of policy.

At the heart of questions such as the relationship between the President, the Secretary of State, and some other official, whether a vice-president for foreign affairs or a cabinet officer in the White House without portfolio, are fundamental issues of government and public administration. They cluster around the overriding problem of fixing the proper level of decisions in government. From the standpoint of the President, the great risk in locating responsibility is that of delegating down to a point in the administrative hierarchy where responsibility and power are divorced. If the point of decision sinks low enough in the hierarchy, those who think and recommend may be those who carry no responsibility. The temptation at this level to speculate, philosophize, and suspend judgment, or alternatively to recommend without counting the consequences, is great. Throughout public life and much of private affairs the separation of responsibility and power leads to procrastination and delay.

This is part of the continuing problem of foreign policy. In an earlier and simpler day the point of decision could readily be identified. Outsiders knew who made decisions and could hold individuals responsible. Today, the problem is one of identifying in the vast maze of a bureaucracy the point at which decisions are actually being made. The President is responsible for the great bulk of foreign policy decisions, and yet he cannot give attention to much of the evidence on which decisions must be based. Unwilling or anxious subordinates who lack the desire and the responsibility for action may frustrate prompt response at the level of responsibility. The struggle for power among office holders is true only in the formal bureaucratic sense. Power gravitates to those who are prepared to use it, and within government, for reasons of fear and insecurity, there is also a struggle to diffuse responsibility. Advancement as often depends on freedom from failure as initiative for success. If the President cannot "pass the buck," government is populated by others who find in this posture a safeguard against the worst hazards of organizational life. Former Harvard President James B. Conant's motto, "Behold the turtle; he makes progress only when his neck is out," sometimes is honored more in the breach than the observance.

The committee system contributes still further to this problem. Much of the interdepartmental machinery through which the affairs of various departments are conducted is designed primarily for kibitzing on individual secretaries or executives. Reluctance to accept personal responsibility is one reason— although not the only one—for the current jungle of committees within government. There is no existing administrative device for replacing the ultimate locating of responsibility for decisions at some identifiable point. Committee action often becomes a lowest common denominator in which initiative and innovation have no place. By the time the committee paper reaches the top, it reflects more often than not a pallid compromise, in which real issues and viewpoints are concealed and solutions are so diluted as to be meaningless. The growth of interdepartmental committees harks back to wartime experiences within the "Grand Alliance" when British and American colleagues in particular found short cuts to the time-consuming process of collecting initials on working papers by bringing their problems before a committee and obtaining agreement the same day.

Following the war, this approach gathered adherents both within the complex committee structure of the National Security Council and in the many formal coordinating groups operating outside the council framework. Moreover, foreign policy from the standpoint of objectives, formulation, and execution was forced increasingly into interdepartmental molds. Diplomatic goals and techniques, while still central to foreign policy, were merged with economic and military aid, scientific aid and technical assistance, information programs, plans for distributing surplus food, and educational and cultural exchange. The Department of State shared the spotlight with Defense, Agriculture, Treasury, Interior, Commerce, the Export-Import Bank, and a score of sister agencies, now partners in activities abroad. Representatives from these and other departments and groups, each with their own distinct missions, staked their claims for some part of the authority of decision-making without assuming a commensurate share of responsibility. At last count, there were some one hundred and sixty formal interdepartmental and interagency committees in international affairs. Mr. Robert Lovett in commenting on this trend observes: ". . . the idea seems to have got around that just because some decision may affect your activities, you automatically have a right to take part in making it . . . there is some reason to feel that the doctrine may be getting out of hand and that what was designed to act as a policeman may, in fact, become a jailor." [15] In tallying up the heavy price of the committee approach to foreign policy, critics stress the loss of individual responsibility, administrative sluggishness, and loss of flexibility and responsiveness.

The committee system has exaggerated the inherent difficulties of democratic foreign policy. Recent history has shown, as in the Korean and Lebanese crises, that swift and decisive action and mobility and initiative in foreign policy were entirely compatible with the democratic process. By contrast, the cumbersome committee procedure has led to delay, uncertainty, and indecisiveness. It has led as well to the emasculation of personal responsibility. Personal initiative is eliminated when government requires each agency and its representatives with distant and peripheral interests to agree before a policy can be put into effect. A determined minority of one member of a committee is capable of forestalling action or diluting the

[15] Quoted in the Report of the Subcommittee on National Policy Machinery, January 28, 1961, *op. cit.*, p. 1.

content of any action. Facing this barrier to initiative and innovation, a member of the executive branch of government is tempted to retreat to time-honored routines rather than proposing bold new initiatives. It is safer and easier in the committee system to pursue policies which a group can recognize as having been successful ten years before than to respond to recent events through novel and possibly risky programs. Decisiveness under such a system falls victim to the cross-purposes of the many associated agencies which can make a more or less plausible case for their participation in the making of foreign policy. The struggle between the separate agencies is if anything intensified by this process, for each acquires a vested interest in protecting its own viewpoint and program. In the end, the struggle is interrupted at best by some form of truce embodied in a formula which is acceptable because it offends fewer parties than any other statement. It leaves the determination of foreign policy itself to another committee or agency which must strive to give living content to an essentially bloodless formula.

The committee system also encourages narrow and parochial outlooks in contrast to broad perspectives on policies that might serve the national interests. The problem of developing a cadre of public servants who withstand local, departmental, or bureau interests is undoubtedly more fundamental than the issues raised by the committee system. However, an approach in which members of committees serve as representatives or ambassadors of departments and agencies makes more difficult the growth of a body of officials who view national requirements as a whole. Any administration that would be successful must give first attention to the reform of this aspect of the machinery of government if it would restore its capacity for vigorous and dynamic leadership. Not surprisingly, the Kennedy administration undertook this task early in its tenure through pledging itself to a continued effort, in Secretary Dean Rusk's words, by "freeing the national policy machinery from overdependence on committees, with their attendant dulling of issues and reduction of decisions to a least common denominator." [16] The Subcommittee on National Policy in discussing this effort notes: "Committee-killing, not creating more committees, remains the important job."

Yet even if this present weakness is cured, basic and fundamental problems would remain. Partly they result from the great expansion in the role of the Department of State in modern times. The scope and character of foreign relations has been radically transformed. From a profession launched on November 29, 1775, when the Congress resolved "that a Committee of Five be appointed for the sole purpose of corresponding with our friends in Great Britain, Ireland and other parts of the world," a machinery of government has evolved that is intricate, extensive, and sometimes virtually unmanageable. A former secretary is reported to have said that no secretary has held the Department of State under control in the last 150 years. The department has at its call personnel numbering 23,-000, plus 11,000 in USIA, and 15,000 in agencies like the Peace Corps and Disarmament Agency. This phenomenal expansion has occurred at a breathtaking and dizzying pace. As recently as 1941, the Department of State's roster approached 1,000 employees, and in 1909 the number was 209; in 1870, 52; and in 1833, 22. While its outposts today span the globe, this, too, is of recent origin. In 1823, John Quincy Adams established our tenth diplomatic mission, and not until a century later did Charles Evans Hughes announce the fifteenth. Yet by the end of Christian Herter's service, the hundredth mission had been created—nearly a sevenfold increase in some forty years. More than forty major units report directly to the secretary. In the wider framework of a career service, at least four separate personnel categories continue, even after the Wriston Report, with different terms of tenure, pay, and retirement: the foreign

---

[16] Testimony before the Subcommittee on National Policy Machinery of the Committee on Government Operations, U.S. Senate, 87th Congress, 1st Session, Part IX, August 24, 1961, p. 1280.

service, the foreign service reserve, the foreign service staff, and the civil service. During an average day, the secretary approves, disapproves, or modifies no less than twenty major proposals calling for urgent action. Their substance is likely to run the gamut from Alaskan fisheries to Sputnik. In the course of a year the department exchanges thousands of cables with missions in foreign capitals, and the daily volume exceeds the combined total of the Associated Press and United Press International offices in Washington.

The first Secretary of Foreign Affairs, Mr. R. R. Livingston, noted in a letter to the president of the Congress on January 25, 1782: "Congress having vested me with the power of appointing clerks I have appointed two Gentlemen in whose integrity and Abilities I can confide, these are barely sufficient to do the running business of the office which is much greater than I imagined it would be . . ." [17] Secretary of State Jefferson spoke of the need for a staff sufficiently large to assure that someone would be available when colleagues went to lunch. Not only the scope, however, but also the pace and timing of foreign policy has been revolutionized. In 1807, an official of the Department of State sent instructions to the consul at La Guaira, Venezuela, stating: "Not a single communication has been received from you, as appears from the files of this office, since your appointment [seven years ago] in the year 1800, have induced a revocation of your appointment as consul." A secretary of state in our early days was able to combine the conduct of foreign policy with part-time legal practice. As late as 1818, John Quincy Adams could write that he found his duties "more than I can perform. Some of them, therefore, are not performed." A recent study notes: "Washington and Jefferson dealt with information on a few handwritten sheets of paper from limited sources, in contrast with machine-tabulated, mass-produced data, assembled almost instantaneously by

[17] Gaillard Hunt, *The Department of State of the U.S.: Its History and Functions* (Washington, D.C.: Department of State, 1893), p. 23.

mechanized media from literally multitudinous sources, private as well as public.[18] When Thomas Jefferson was Secretary of State, it was his custom to consult the President frequently on much of his diplomatic correspondence. Thus on April 5, 1790, he wrote: "Mr. Jefferson has the honour of enclosing for the perusal of the President, rough draughts of the letters he supposes it proper to send to the court of France on the present occasion. He will have that [pleasure] of waiting on him in person immediately to make any changes in them the President will be so good as to direct. . . ."[19] Today, most of the diplomatic correspondence is signed neither by the secretary nor the President but by subordinates operating within an agreed upon departmental policy and framework. Until recently, a separate operations center under a senior Foreign Service officer operated within the secretary's office for coping with around-the-clock crises in foreign relations.

At the center of this network of confusing and baffling problems, calling for the capacity of reading minds half a world away, stand the President and the Secretary of State. The secretary is unique within the American system in that he is the ranking member of the cabinet for purposes of protocol. He is first among equals within the administration he serves. Only the secretary among cabinet members is primarily charged with viewing the nation as a whole in relation to the outside world. The secretary, if he succeeds, must develop an attitude or viewpoint that conceives foreign policy on a global basis. Former Secretary of State Dean Acheson has noted that: "Foreign policy is the whole of national policy looked at from the point of view of the exigencies created by 'the vast external realm' beyond our borders. It is not a 'jurisdiction.' It is an orientation, a point of view, a measurement of values—today, perhaps, the most important one for national survival."[20]

---

[18] Field Haviland, Jr., *et al.*, *The Formulation and Administration of United States Foreign Policy* (Washington, D.C.: The Brookings Institution, 1960), p. 41.

[19] Hunt, *op. cit.*, p. 65.

[20] *The Secretary of State*, ed. Don K. Price (Englewood Cliffs, N.J.: Prentice-Hall, Inc., 1960), p. 38.

Much as the President is the ultimate repository of executive responsibility for the national interest, the secretary as the agent and principal adviser on foreign relations to the President joins him as the guardian of this responsibility. The recent Eighteenth American Assembly in describing the duties of the Secretary concluded:

—he must bear major responsibility for the formulation of all aspects of national policy bearing on our international interests and security;
—he must take the lead in integrating our military, economic, and cultural programs with our diplomatic efforts into a coherent foreign policy, and coordinate it with activities of other nations;
—he must help inform the Congress, and develop the public consensus that must sustain and direct our public policies.[21]

A job specification of the qualities and capabilities for this awesome and demanding office is probably of limited value. For any given President the choice depends less on abstractions than on context and personality. Mr. Acheson reminisces about a board meeting convened to decide on an important appointment to the firm. He notes: "It was suggested that we first agree on the qualifications for the position before discussing individuals. I asked my neighbor what he thought of this logical procedure, to which he replied, 'Nothing matters till we start to vote.' "[22]

Perhaps the two most crucial requirements for the effective conduct of foreign relations are that the President and secretary remember who is President and who is secretary. Only a President of infinite patience, such as Abraham Lincoln, could have controlled and used a secretary like Seward, who wrote: "It seems to me that if I am absent but three days this Administration, the Congress, and the District fall into consternation and despair. I am the only hopeful, calm, conciliatory person here."[23] This same secretary confided to a colleague in New

[21] *Ibid.*, p. 192.
[22] *The Secretary of State, op. cit.*, p. 35.
[23] *Ibid.*, p. 31.

York that Mr. Lincoln wished him to serve as prime minister and explained to a European envoy, "There is no difference between an elected president of the United States and an hereditary monarch. . . . The actual direction of public affairs belongs to the leader of the ruling party. . . ." [24]

The secretary draws his political strength and authority from the President and is dependent upon the President's confidence and reliance on him. A secretary should never harbor or foster the illusion that he and not the President represents the people and makes the great life and death decisions on which war and peace depend. For the President to delegate the functions of understanding and deciding is to delegate in effect his office. A few secretaries have been tactless but wise enough to say bluntly to the President that he must do his homework if he is to be the President. The double risk in relationships between the President and the secretary is the risk that the President may delegate too great a part of his own work to the secretary or, alternatively, may fail to use the secretary in a creative and significant way. Franklin D. Roosevelt may have presumed too much in assuming he could be his own secretary, and Dwight D. Eisenhower, at the opposite extreme, may have delegated a larger part of his burdens to John Foster Dulles than was justified. The relation between the President and his secretary must be one of total and instinctive confidence. They must share one another's assumptions and convictions and, in practice, anticipate each other's responses. Secretary Stimson was a fighter and an advocate; President Hoover was a great organizer and manager. Their working habits were radically at odds. Might history have been different if they had been more alike? The President and secretary must hold to the same philosophy of government and foreign policy to a degree that will sustain them over frustrating, unpleasant, and distasteful matters which are inevitably a part of their responsibility. The secretary of state has the makings of an unwelcome visitor, and,

[24] *Ibid.*, pp. 31–32.

therefore, the President must share with him those convictions and outlooks that will carry them over a common life of crisis and painful choices. The President inevitably will be disappointed if he imagines that a secretary with political stature as great as his own will help in the augmentation of his own power. The classic case is that of Wilson and Bryan. A poor guide is the aphorism that a rival will "do less harm inside than outside." The chief requirement for the President must be that the secretary sees the world much as he himself does, thus enabling him to help more than others could in dealing with the great problems that lie ahead.

From his standpoint, the secretary faces a difficult and unhappy choice. He will be tempted, particularly in achieving his mission of informing the public on foreign policy, to make himself the chief spokesman on foreign policy and an independent political force. For *two reasons* he should think twice before following this course. *First,* his strength in cooperating with the Congress depends on the maintenance of some measure of nonpartisanship. *Secondly,* he depends for his political influence on the power of the President, and only at great risk can he afford to detract from the primacy of this power. The secretary must work with both parties in the Congress and if he becomes a "political lightning rod" the prospect of success in this function diminishes. Recent secretaries of state in their conduct of the office illustrate a variety of possible approaches. Secretary of State Dean Acheson considered that he was the servant of the chief executive. At the same time, his own fund of practical experience in dealing with Congress and his intellectual versatility, coupled with the circumstances under which he administered his office, led him into the political arena. John Foster Dulles, on assuming his office, observed that he had learned an important lesson from the experiences of Mr. Acheson. Mr. Dulles pointed out that Mr. Acheson, in spite of his remarkable experience and unrivaled intellectual endowments, failed because he was vulnerable at the point of his political flank. Dulles vowed that he would protect himself by neutralizing the forces of criticism, particularly from the extreme right. The conviction that Acheson and Dulles held in common was that the secretary could not escape the task of consolidating his political position through active steps he might take that affected political groups. Both secretaries assumed there were independent measures a secretary could take to protect and strengthen his position in the political sphere. Ironically, Secretary Acheson in particular held in theory to a more modest role of the secretary's political function. In discussing the view that heads of departments are obliged to participate in congressional discussion and debate to advance the public welfare, Acheson notes: "At one time I thought this proposal had more merit than I do now." [25] He goes on to say: "A Secretary who developed a capacity for Congressional debate might well be in trouble on two sides. On one side he would be rivaling and diminishing the position of the chairman of the committee concerned. . . . The other hazard . . . would be the development by cabinet officers of a status and interests independent of the President. . . ." [26]

The theory that men best qualified for the conduct of foreign policy are necessarily well qualified for public debate or the defense within Congress and out of national policy has been shaken by recent history. If the secretary becomes a political lightning rod against which the storms of politics beat, his capacity for leadership in foreign policy is weakened, even destroyed. For the secretary to persist in his central constitutional task of administering the Department of State, assisting and advising the President, and ordering and guiding the efforts of the manifold departments and agencies whose interests intertwine in the network of American foreign relations, calls for moral courage and will power to an extraordinary degree. The American press in particular and the public in general expect their officials to be oracles on each successive issue—and or-

[25] Acheson, *op. cit.*, p. 79.
[26] *Ibid.*

acles several times over as a crisis unfolds. When the secretary is succeeding in his task of minimizing conflicts within and between governments, the work load of the press is also minimized. Crises and conflicts make news and the press and the people call upon the secretary to speak in resounding tones as each stage of a conflict moves through a succeeding one. Yet as the secretary holds to a central task of exercising leadership within the government across a broad spectrum of agencies and departments and in relationship to the legislature, he can as a rule ill afford to be involved continuously in *ad hoc* commentaries or issue a stream of curbstone opinions.

Yet because the executive and the legislature share responsibility for foreign policy and the secretary is the executive officer primarily concerned with the implementation of policy, he must maintain close contact with the Congress as well as the administrative branch of government. On November 29, 1955, Secretary Dulles explained that during his tenure of office he had already met more than 100 times with bipartisan congressional groups, and Secretary Rusk acknowledged on August 24, 1961, that he had already appeared 20 times before some congressional body. In the four years that Mr. Acheson served as Secretary of State he met with congressional groups on 214 occasions. Inasmuch as many of the meetings occupied at least half a day and preparation made similar inroads on his time, Acheson estimates that something in the neighborhood of one-sixth of his working days in Washington were spent in meetings or preparations for meetings with the Congress. If to this is added the heavy burden of travel and representation abroad, the secretary is left with but a fraction of the time he needs to achieve his central constitutional task.

If President Kennedy's intention "to use freely the diplomatic channel for informal as well as formal consultations and discussions with other governments" is realized, this may reduce somewhat the magnetic pull drawing the secretary away from Washington, but even then new ways must be found to relieve the secretary from at least some of the burdens of travel and negotiation which, coupled with his responsibilities of serving the executive in relations with the Congress, drain away a heavy part of his strength and energy. One suggestion has been that a new position of "Secretary of Foreign Affairs" be established. In justification of the new post, authorities like Robert Lovett have argued that anyone representing the secretary or the government in high-level negotiations must carry the full credentials of a high executive office. They insist that to appoint an ambassador-at-large or to delegate responsibility to an undersecretary raises sensitive issues of protocol and prestige. Experience to this point would indicate a reluctance on the part of other governments to accept in lieu of the secretary an official of the United States government carrying less prestige and less authority. Particularly when heads of state and foreign ministers of other governments are involved, participation by a subordinate American official is likely to obstruct or impair efficient negotiation. Mr. Lovett and others have viewed the secretary of foreign affairs as an official who would be responsible to the secretary and through him to the President, whose cardinal task would be to represent the secretary and the President in international negotiations, particularly where they involved protracted absences from Washington. The need for adjusting the written Constitution to the living realities of foreign relations commends some innovation and reform. But change in the American system goes on within certain established constitutional restraints. The President must remain the prime source of authority and responsibility in the conduct of foreign policy. The secretary must continue to be his chief lieutenant. If the prospects for this relationship are complicated or made impossible by the creation of a new office, this is no satisfactory substitute for effective constitutional government. Moreover, change in the American system can hardly be unilateral; it is dependent upon similar adaptation in the machinery of other governments. The proposal for an international conference, therefore, to update protocol regulations, especially those regarding the level of representation at international meetings, should be linked with the proposed appointment of a secretary of foreign affairs. An international conference might conclude through a working agreement that undersecretaries and assistant secretaries of state, ambassadors-at-large, or other junior representatives meeting with their foreign counterparts should play an increasing role in serving their nations at high-level meetings. Or they might propose upgrading the role of ambassadors. Or they might accept the model of a Secretary for Foreign Affairs. Our British and French allies are reluctant to accept any form of "deputy" in the Secretary's stead. Such arrangements and understandings achieved on a multilateral plane could relieve the pressures that exist within a national framework. They might also free the secretary of state, second only to the President, to speak out through major policy pronouncements as the nation's next most important voice on foreign affairs. Among the President's appointive officials, he is the symbol and principal representative projecting our image abroad.

Above all, the President and the secretary must be equipped to deal with what some have called "the thundering present problems" as well as those that lie ahead in the emerging future. The secretary needs help in anticipating the future. He may find in one period that a policy planning staff can provide this help, or it may be that agencies and institutions outside the government, either "Institutes of Defense Analyses" or established university programs, can provide the aid and counsel that is needed. Or it may be that task forces or a single highly qualified officer are best equipped to perform this function. Many criticisms of the Department of State and its officials for "merely reacting to events" on a short-term, pragmatic basis are unfair. It is true that "the future unfolds one day at a time." But like other wise sayings, this aphorism is something less than the sum total of wisdom. Mr. Acheson observes: "While it is true that the problems of the voyage come to the mariner day by day, it is essential to his success, and perhaps survival, that he know where he is going, keep on course, and also use all the knowledge at his disposal to learn what forces are building up around him, and to prepare as best he may for what lies ahead." [27] I recall the comment of a local dentist that each day before he began his work he reviewed the various cases with which he would have to deal, not imagining he could anticipate all the problems that would arise, but seeking to be as orderly and well prepared for the future as his knowledge and medical histories, X rays, and scientific reports permitted him to be. In much this way, a secretary facing the future must prepare as best he can. To change the metaphor, he is like a hunter who, in order to come on target, must lead the bird in flight, lest he get only tail feathers for his pains.

Foreign policy in these terms is indeed a combination of response to events and prudent anticipation. Personal qualities of leaders are no less important than the machinery of government with which they work, but the issue of men versus institutions so often raised on an either-or basis can be misleading. Both men and institutions must be chosen, developed, and organized so that the living Constitution of the American people has the best chance for survival in the future. The awesome task of presidential leadership is symbolized by the fact that the President, and he alone, holds the ultimate responsibility for pressing or not pressing the button in a thermonuclear war. No arrangements of duties as between a Secretary of State, his department, or the many departments participating in foreign relations can relieve the President of this ultimate task. The wise ordering of the duties of the secretary and his colleagues and the effective structuring of government can make it more likely that the President will make his choice on the basis of the surest and most responsible advice. The living Constitution

[27] *The Secretary of State, op. cit.,* p. 36.

must be one in which human resources are harnessed to the solution or amelioration of problems that make pygmies of us all. This is the staggering but challenging task to which any President and his Department of State must in varying ways address themselves in the conduct of foreign relations.

II

PRACTICES AND PROCEDURES

IN DIPLOMACY

INTRODUCTION

A DISCUSSION of the practice and procedures of American diplomacy requires an historical approach that spans a wider
canvas than American history. A British historian writes:
"Great events are culminations, effects of causes, which, some
immediate and some remote, are only revealed in the study of
history." [1] The forms of American diplomatic practice reflect
developing patterns elsewhere in the modern world. I propose
to approach the second part of my theme, therefore, in broadly
historical and philosophical terms, leaving for the fifth and
sixth chapters of the story a more detailed contemporary review. I believe that American diplomacy is part and parcel of
the Western world and reflects, even in reaction, forces that
have their origins outside the national boundaries. In this spirit,
I intend to go back to a much earlier era in Western civilization
to trace the beginnings of American practice and procedure.
Subsequently, I expect to look ahead to the profound transformations being wrought by the rise of new and important
states.

By tracing with a broad brush the changing context of
diplomatic practice, we may grasp more clearly the point at
which we stand in the mid-twentieth century. By sketching here
in bold relief the problems facing the Republic, we may in the
final discussion proceed directly to the most pressing and immediate issues that await amelioration, if not answers. As I
attempted in Chapter I to state the problem of relating ideas

[1] A. L. Kennedy, *Old Diplomacy and New* (London: John Murray, 1922), p. 3.

and institutions, I hope now to define, enumerate, and fence in the issues and difficulties with which diplomatic practice and procedure must cope in present-day international politics. For those who prefer that every statement of a problem be accompanied by a proposal that charts a possible way out, I beg indulgence. The issues and problems we face are too serious and the stakes too momentous to deserve anything less than full exposition. In this approach, the injunction is worth repeating that we must remember as much of the past as will make us creative in the future.

4

Tradition, Turmoil, and Transition

THE OLD AND NEW DIPLOMACY

"For it is not possible for all things to be well unless all men were good, which I think will not be yet this good many yeares."

SIR THOMAS MORE

SINCE World War I, American and Western diplomats and scholars have been preoccupied with a continuing debate over diplomatic procedure. Attention to the practice of diplomacy has, of course, been subordinate to the discussion of substantive problems. For most of us as laymen and private citizens, techniques of foreign policy often seem routine and trivial except when the call goes out for new and drastic reforms. The issue of raising the status of the United States representative at the United Nations to the level of ambassador, or of reestablishing the coordinating role of overseas ambassadors to encompass the whole of American activities in foreign capitals is less dramatic and immediate than public debate over Cuba and Berlin. Yet the passage of time makes clear that procedures are inextricably bound up with substance; resolution or amelioration of problems depends on wise diplomatic practice; and style and manner in foreign policy may oftentimes prove decisive.

Numerous proposals, hundreds of blueprints, and thousands of words have been written on approaches to diplomacy. Most of the discussion tends to praise or blame what is commonly referred to as the old and new diplomacy. More than four decades of debate have done little to alter history, nor is further discussion likely to confirm the supremacy of one or the other pattern. If the subject remains worthy of examination and study, it is at another level than advocacy or defense. Diplomacy, like government, is a proper object of scholarly inquiry as it relates to the forces that shape and in turn are shaped by it. The old and new diplomacy must be viewed in historical context. Both are the products of prevailing social, intellectual, technological, and political trends. They bear an inescapable relationship to historical antecedents; they reflect an attempt to organize, control, and change the present and thereby shape the future. They mirror the conditions of particular historical eras while providing timeless lessons on the persistent problems and enduring truths of statecraft. Seen in this light, the old and new diplomacy become a workbook for the student of foreign relations rather than an invitation to controversy and strife.

1. Tradition in Diplomacy

THE elements that comprise the tradition of the old diplomacy are commonly associated with the *ancien régime*. It is said that the tradition was the outgrowth of nondemocratic, aristocratic, and monarchical regimes. Princes and rulers shared a community of interest that bound them together more closely than they were linked to their own nations and peoples. They kept the peace because they were more conscious of dynastic rights than of popular rights.

No one would question the importance of the formative role of an aristocratic elite of rulers who spoke the same languages, preferred the same culture, and shared common values. More fundamental still, however, may have been geographical, technological, moral, and political factors and restraints. Thus the scope of military or political cooperation and conflict was invariably circumscribed by technological and geographical factors. Garrett Mattingly, in describing fifteenth century Western society, notes: ". . . Western society still lacked the resources to organize stable states on the national scale. On the scale of the Italian city-state it could do so. Internally the smaller distances to be overcome brought the problems of transport, communication, and consequently the problems of collecting taxes and maintaining the central authority, within the range of practical solution." [1] The absence of the technical preconditions for national government or for the spreading of conflict among states tended to limit and restrict the area of politics, war, and diplomacy. The historian Edward Gibbon observes that as late as the eighteenth century war and conflict affected no more than a tiny fraction of the people. Technology

[1] Garrett Mattingly, *Renaissance Diplomacy* (Boston: Houghton Mifflin Co., 1955), p. 59.

also set limits to popular participation in government, for if citizens from outlying areas could not reach the political center, they were denied an influence on government, including influence on foreign policy.

The shared values of princes and rulers of the *ancien régime* reflected a wider moral and political consensus. The birth of the modern state system and its antecedents coincides with the breakup of Western Christendom. The civilization of the Roman Empire and the early Middle Ages had been marked by a considerable measure of moral unity. The remnants of this unity were to extend into the period leading up to the Renaissance and the early centuries of the modern state system. The comparison is inevitable with today's international society rent by a deep gulf of divergent moral and political beliefs separating East and West. Words and values mean different things.

The old diplomacy functioned in a day when the residual influence of a passing moral consensus was still apparent. Men and rulers lived out their lives in two realms, the spiritual and the temporal. The spiritual realm was expressed in an ecclesiastical organization going back in origin to Constantine and allegedly separate and apart from temporal life. The temporal realm found expression sometimes in the empires of Charlemagne and Otto I, but more often in the city-states, duchies, or tiny kingdoms scarcely coequal with the spiritual regime. From the time of the passing of the Roman Empire, the political realm was limited to a small part of the civilized world. It was the church and not the empire that comprehended the majority of peoples belonging to the Western world. From the late eleventh century to the fourteenth century, the one existing international state was the church, of which the historian could write: "By the time of Innocent III [it] had everything a state had—and more." It provided a centralized organization, a universal legal order expressed in canon law, and a system of ecclesiastical courts. It performed tasks now accepted as appropriately the province of the state, including education, care of the poor, and charity. It could and did interfere in temporal life on constitutional issues, such as the succession of rulers, approval of international agreements, censure or recognition of just or unjust wars, and even intervention against unjust rulers in behalf of Christian subjects. The church was strong because ecclesiastical centralism coexisted side by side with political decentralization. At least a minimum, if fragile, consensus was possible among rulers on moral and political actions, partly because they belonged to a church that was universal, while states and empires were regional at best. Rulers were subject to the precepts of the church through a discipline expressed in effective sanctions and methods of enforcement that included excommunication and interdict. Thus moral consensus was imposed from above by a central religious authority enjoying the strengths of *respublica Christianum.* The setting of international diplomacy then differed from that prevailing today primarily in the existence of a central organ deriving its authority from a source independent of political bodies, superior in any hierarchy to particular states, and capable of influencing them through outright intervention and moral suasion.

Yet this relationship between ecclesiastical and political centers of power was bound to change. Any operative definition of the temporal and spiritual spheres was beset by two contradictory principles. The ultimate authority of a spiritual international state rested upon its reputation for impartial justice and Christian love. This seemed to argue for an avoidance of politics and for independence from the temporal sphere. But if a Christian world were to influence significantly the search for peace and order, it would have to intervene in that order. The notion of a divine law above and outside the temporal realm clashed with the necessity to act through positive law if the Christian order were to have any meaning. The development of moral and political consensus resulted from the tension between the two realms. The existence of a spiritual realm untarnished by doubtful moral choices called for continued separation of the two. Therefore, the more the church intervened in domestic and international politics, the more it endangered its standing as an ultimate arbiter embracing principles of timeless value.

As the influence of the religious world diminished with the breakup of a single unified Christian realm, the necessity for a secular substitute became evident. This substitute was provided in the seventeenth century by the great systematizers of universal natural law and international law. Writers and publicists like Grotius, the father of "the science of international law," believed that men had within them a sense of justice and of right reason. Reason is ingrained in nature and in man; hence, rulers are the guardians of reason, which is the common bond that unites men everywhere. Grotius believed that each state was justified in enforcing not only its own rights but those of others as well. States help one another because of the force of justice, not through the imperatives of an alliance. Neutrality and impartiality among states is impossible, and states that are third parties must never obstruct a just state nor aid an unjust party. Grotius went so far as to insist that citizens of one state had the right to defend subjects of another against an unjust ruler.

The fathers of international law and morality were frank to acknowledge that the law of nature, or *jus naturale*, was too lofty for the real world. The law of nations, or *jus gentium*, was a compromise with reality and a recognition of the need for consent among states. Publicists agreed that natural law is not a workable scheme for a living international order. Even wars for a just cause may be dangerous, and the interests of states must be recognized. According to this view, a state has a right, but not a duty, to join in defense of a just party to a struggle if in so doing it endangers its own interests. By the eighteenth century, nations were growing more and more suspicious of wars of punishment and of intervention, recognizing that there was hardly an existent state against which these issues could not be used as excuses for war.

The central point of the relationship between the law of nature and the law of nations was the acceptance of a linkage between higher principles and international practice. Municipal and international laws were changeable and differed, but they had to conform to the unchangeable universal standards of reason and justice. In their dealings with less civilized states, the older Christian states of Europe were expected to apply more limited and restricted moral principles. International law and diplomacy were grounded in a concept of higher law, initially enforced, interpreted, and executed by an international state, ecclesiastical in origin. Even when moral and political judgments were faulty, they were based ostensibly upon an overall conception of reason and justice. In the late Middle Ages, Western Christendom had a central organization to compel observance of "the law." In Grotius' time, the spontaneous reactions of individual states grounded in reason and conscience were the basis of law enforcement. In the absence of a common spiritual or temporal authority, the pure natural law was expected to impose itself directly on the conscience of mankind.

Until the late eighteenth or early nineteenth century, therefore, the diplomacy of the European world was in the hands of men who were Europeans first and Frenchmen, Germans, Dutchmen, or Englishmen second. They were brought up on a common cultural heritage deriving from the classics in Latin and Greek, they listened to the same music, they attended the same theaters, and they spoke the lingua franca with greater facility than their national languages. Gibbon in viewing this culture could speak of Europe as "one great republic." In 1689 the Dutch *stadtholder* became the ruler of England as well. In the coalition against Louis XIV, the Duke of Marlborough became a leading figure in Dutch domestic political life. The House of Hapsburg was not Austrian alone, nor the Romanovs Russian alone, nor the Bourbons French or Spanish. Diplomats with a common cosmopolitan background served a particular ruler even though they were nationals of another state. And underlying all, they were products of Western civilization, including that aspect which stemmed from the *corpus Christianum*.

From a moral and legal standpoint, the eighteenth and nineteenth centuries saw the disappearance of a widely accepted notion of higher natural law. In its place, positive law emerged as the product of custom and convention in international law. The idea of the *jus gentium* faded and was replaced by the legal abstraction of state personality—the sole repository of rights and duties. States were no longer bound together in a moral community, but greater stress was laid on their individualism, natural liberty, and equality. Modern Western values grew ever more varied; there was growing diversity in other cultures. Men might be pacifists, Roman Catholics, scientific humanists, or Marxists. Statesmen and publicists put less emphasis on values and more on techniques for harmonizing differences, including conferences, arbitration, and mediation. Discussion of the necessary law of nations replaced emphasis on the natural law, and men increasingly recognized that in the end the ruler would decide whether the law of nations was applicable or not. Self-preservation was the first duty of the state, and assistance to others was justifiable only if states could do so without neglect of their own security. War became an instrument of self-help, not enforcement. When the international community was required to act against a disturber of public peace and security, not all states were obliged to act, but only those who had the most direct interest in limiting the expansion and power of an aggressor state. State action was measured in terms of power and politics, partly because men recognized that reasonable and just behavior did not prevail. Positive law extended its influence, for, more than natural law, it took account of men as they were, not as they ought to be. The phrase recurs in much of nineteenth century writing that imperfections have to be endured even when not allowed. The example in point is the introduction of particularly lethal methods of warfare by one belligerent justifying their use by others.

Thus the nature, extent, and character of moral and legal unity in the West changed fundamentally, beginning in the late eighteenth century. An increasingly sharp distinction was made between national and international law. National law reflects the authority of the sovereign over individuals within his jurisdiction; the law of nations is law between sovereign states, not a judgment from above them as from a sacred or secular international organization. Only states can create precepts and rules of international law, and only they are subjects with rights and duties. If the subject of one state is wronged abroad, a state may use limited methods, like reprisal or retorsion, to defend his interests, and even intervention and war when necessary. But little attempt is made to distinguish between the sources and conditions of a just and unjust war. By the rule of *rebus sic stantibus*, when an international treaty stands in the way of a state's necessary development, the treaty must yield. This is almost the direct opposite of the rule *pacta sunt servanda*, requiring that all treaties, if they are just, must be observed.

The nineteenth century was to emphasize the political nature of international relations. Legal writers and publicists recognized that the great powers could play a constructive role in building an international order. Their leadership is not incompatible with the equality of small states if those states accept it. Indeed, some international lawyers identify all progress in the evolution of a law of nations with the great powers. Law depends on an equilibrium among states, and if the great powers cannot keep one another in check, no rule of law will have any force, since every powerful state will naturally try to act according to its interests and discretion, thus disobeying the law.

The controlling character of the nineteenth century was the fact that it more nearly identified power and responsibility than any international system in modern history. Nations with the greatest stake and the broadest experience in preserving peace conferred together when threats to the peace arose. Their leaders made up an aristocratic elite who shared a common interest in avoiding violence and destruction. Austria, France, Russia, Spain, and England had achieved such influence in the European sphere that there was common agreement among them that more would be lost than could be gained through a disturbance of the status quo. The "European System" was the pattern of international order that prevailed from 1815 to 1914. In the democratic West, we have in recent times sedulously cultivated the illusion that it was the most disastrous of world systems. Oftentimes it is dismissed as anarchical, lawless, and antidemocratic. Yet one major student of diplomatic history, Professor R. B. Mowat, maintains that this system succeeded in preventing at least seven great European wars between 1871 and 1914. The most peaceful of modern centuries, as it has been called, achieved security through the informal but effective instrument of the Concert of Europe. Moreover, it should be noted that peace was achieved in an era when war was still recognized and accepted as a legitimate and appropriate instrument of national policy.

The European System in the nineteenth century had less moral foundation than the late medieval and early modern period, less legal foundation than the seventeenth and eighteenth centuries, and less constitutional foundation than the twentieth century. Indeed, almost the sole basis of the European System was its achievement of a wise merger of force with interests, since the nations who stood to profit most from preserving the peace were also the nations powerful enough to exert pressure to dissuade those who would disturb it. War was opposed not on moral grounds or legal principles, but in terms of enlightened self-interest. War's uncertainty, wastefulness, and heavy burdens, especially for advanced nations, were the prevailing reasons for limiting its occurrence. The

European System was a child of necessity and, to the extent that it succeeded at all, it was effective because it responded to genuine needs and problems. Apart from the Crimean War —which has been called a more or less colonial event— England, France, Prussia, Austria, Italy, and Russia engaged in war with one another for a period totaling only eighteen months. The previous two centuries showed an average of sixty to seventy years of major wars among the principal powers.

The operation of the balance of power, the influence of British naval power, the growth of a network of mutual interests in international trade, and the emergence of an international peace interest, all combined to bring about the so-called "one hundred years of peace." The nascent economies of Europe, with fresh memories of the ferocity of revolutionary warfare and with a glimpse of the prosperity which peace and order could bring, called for peace before liberty or patriotism. The bearers of the new interest in peace were those within each state most likely to benefit from the rising tide of the industrial revolution and the maintenance of stability. Thus Europeans acquired a stake in peace and order both within the separate nation-states and in the relationships existing among them. The European System lacked the "hierarchies of blood and grace" of dynasties and the church which had knit together the earlier systems of international order. It was at best a loose federation, meeting only rarely at the behest of individual powers. It had little organization for effective joint military action, and yet the pragmatic interests of the various states in maintaining a system of international order within which industrialization could go forward, enabled the shadowy entity called the European System to maintain peace with much less frequent and oppressive use of overt force than had earlier or succeeding systems.

For Americans, until the time of World War II, the world was stable and predictable. If war was not unthinkable, there were numerous avenues by which it could be checked and eliminated. The breath-taking success of leaders of industry and government in the rapid development of a modern state engendered faith in progress and reason. If Victor Hugo could write: "In the twentieth century war will be dead," Andrew Carnegie was constrained to advise the trustees of the Carnegie Endowment that they should turn their attention to the problem of war until the problem was solved, and after that they might turn to other problems. Yet at the moment of greatest faith in economic and technological progress and in the growing incidence of peace, the world order of the nineteenth century was already beginning to collapse. That order had been governed by the seven great empires of Europe—the Austro-Hungarian, German, Ottoman, Czarist Russian, British, French, and Italian. The first four were swept away by World War I and the supremacy of the last three was destroyed in World War II and during the years following that struggle. Twenty-two smaller powers joined the five Allied and Associated Powers at the Paris Peace Conference. The center of power in Europe, which throughout the nineteenth century had been maintained in France, whether through the power of Louis XIV or Napoleon, or the remarkable diplomacy of Talleyrand, shifted eastward to Germany and then yet farther east to the Soviet Union. On the opposite scale of the balance of world power was the might of a second great power, the United States, which acceded to a position of world leadership it had not sought. The moral and political unity of the European System within which past rivalries and conflicts had been waged, was supplanted by two great international systems, one in the East and the other in the West.

The international system in the East from the revolution of 1917 to the present was dedicated to extending its form of international order until it engulfed the rest of the world. Its system was one that gave a central place to doctrines of coercion and control beyond any earlier tyrannical system. The mutual interaction and checks and balances historically operative in the Western world—whether between church and state, empire and papacy, or among mutually independent and interdependent sovereign states—are absent in international communism. The state is the church, serving as the repository of the sacred texts and dogmas and the exclusive instrument of social justice. The faithful within the Communist world are strengthened by the knowledge that for them faith is confirmed by science and reason. Coercion, the liquidation of opposition, deviationists, or kulaks, and wars of national liberation are justified by a revolutionary system of justice and by intrinsic rational and scientific principles. Liberal democratic principles of government which placed the stress on compromise in politics had generally kept zealots in check in Western society, with such notable exceptions as the Crusades. No limiting or restraining force can check a Communist zealot, since any conduct is explained as serving the ultimate Communist purpose established by science and philosophy. Therefore, if rules of decency, ethical restraints, fair treatment of the opposition, or the judgment of an international organization run afoul of Communist ambitions, leaders have at hand a ready-made rationalization for actions of revolt, violence, and abuse. The Communist design permits its leaders to sow seeds of disorder in the name of Communist order, touch off local warfare as a step toward colonial emancipation, and employ force and violence in overthrowing existing governments. Communists face no moral conflict in their dedication to the overthrow of international order because seen in the light of doctrine it has no legitimacy. When Russian leaders say there are no neutrals between the Communist and free worlds, they affirm that their international order of coercion must prevail over any competing order of freedom. A distinguished Australian international lawyer, Professor Julius Stone, has identified certain minimal ethical convictions and rules of decency within a community as underlying any system of law and order. Those who exercise power in behalf of the community must be faithful to those convictions. He notes that a statute enacted by law providing for the liquidation of an opposition would violate the rule of law, not because it wasn't law, but because it "wasn't cricket." The great gulf that separates East and West and that shapes the functions of present-day diplomats, distinguishing the tasks of the new from the old diplomacy, relates to this point. Whether the student is devoted to the ancient past or fervently committed to the present international order, he must at least accept the fundamental differences by which the two can be compared.

2. Turmoil in Diplomacy

IT would be misleading, however, to associate the changes in present-day diplomacy too narrowly with the rise of world communism. These changes relate as well to three more fundamental revolutions: technological, political, and ideological. The technological revolution has altered the tempo and character of diplomacy through an amazing acceleration of the means of communication and transportation. In an easier, slower-moving age, international tensions at least seemed less severe. Today, modern diplomats operate in an era of triphammer diplomacy. Speed itself sometimes generates friction. Modern communications have brought peoples and nations more tightly together, and some among us have taken comfort from the view that new forms of interdependence will assure international peace. Men have found, however, that propinquity does not invariably make for peace, as even the most happy husband and wife can testify. Men and nations in close relationship with one another recognize and respond to tensions more readily.

The communication revolution has also engaged the public more frequently in the business of foreign relations. Sometimes officials weigh public reactions to a diplomat's functions as carefully as diplomatic solutions. The technological revolution can scarcely be said to have created the public's role in diplomacy. It has, however, stimulated and fed it and kept public interest in diplomatic problems at a white heat. The American Ambassador at the United Nations or the Secretary of State representing us abroad can overnight become public figures and radio-television personalities. The press officer of the Department of State can easily become its principal diplomatic spokesman—a function unknown before the technological revolution. In the late nineteenth century, Lord Lyons, of whom Lord Newton could write "there is a total absence of any straining after effect . . . of personal animosity . . . or of any desire to gain his ends by intrigue or trickery," was for five years British Ambassador to Washington without ever making a public speech. Before the twentieth century, ministers with their experts planned diplomatic measures with some thought for the legislative assembly, little for the people, and none at all for Gallup polls. It is no longer enough to know what a handful of leaders think, for today the whole nation counts. In present-day diplomacy, nearly every official must see his problems in relation to their impact upon the people. He must measure opportunities for public attention and legislative support alongside prospects of diplomatic success. Some go so far as to suggest that in an era of popular diplomacy nothing is true or false until the diplomat reads the pundits or columnists whose words daily reach audiences of one to ten million people. The press officer who accompanies a foreign minister to a major capital abroad is likely to be more closely in touch with him than is a particular ambassador. What the diplomat accomplishes in the conference room may have to compete in importance with what a press officer reports about the proceedings. The officer is continually tempted to engage in "press brinkmanship" by friends and former colleagues who knew him best as a reporter and who urge him to share with them the inside story of serious conferences and negotiations. Members of a major delegation may also become fair game to reporters.

The technological revolution may lead to the downgrading of the role of our overseas ambassadors. A foreign minister can fly the Atlantic or Pacific today in less time than an ambassador or envoy required to reach the court of a neighboring monarch. With peripatetic foreign ministers flying in and departing by jets, the ambassador runs the risk of becoming merely the person on the receiving end of a cable. There are risks that his independence may disappear along with his capacity to shape foreign policy. He may also be limited in function to channeling policy to the secretary or the government in Washington. The ambassador receives instructions almost instantaneously with their formulation in Washington, and his area of discretion therefore is considerably reduced. Today, vital decisions tend to be made in Washington and transmitted to emissaries abroad. A secretary within a twenty-four-hour period can and does confer personally on the ground with ambassadors in Tokyo, Seoul, and Manila, and from Washington he can in a morning talk by trans-Atlantic telephone with six or seven ambassadors.

Evidence of an opposing trend is clear, however, particularly in the present administration in Washington, where a serious attempt is being made to recognize the ambassador as executive head of our foreign programs. Experienced authorities argue that the ambassador must never be viewed as an errand boy. He continues to play an important role in explaining and interpreting policy, supervising American agencies and representatives (the heads of AID and USIA report to the ambassador), conducting sensitive negotiations, coordinating the many and varied aspects of policy, and reporting in a faithful and accurate way on the American effort abroad. The business of a large embassy in 1962 is greater than was that of the Department of State as a whole before World War II. If technology has reduced the ambassador's discretion, it has broadened the range of problems with which he must deal. While he cannot be expected to pose equally as an expert on political, economic, financial, commercial, military, and cultural questions, he must know enough to evaluate the counsel of experts in these fields. He deals with problems of which the diplomat of the seventeenth and eighteenth centuries never dreamed.

Hence, the technological revolution has required that the diplomat become a top rank executive and a jack-of-all-trades. To his negotiating responsibilities he must add a major administrative role. If experts are not available for problems involving the European Community, International Labor Organization, Food and Agriculture Organization, or International Telecommunications Union, an ambassador must serve. Even if his responsibility ends with the conduct of bilateral and multilateral negotiations in these fields, the diplomat must engage in enough preparatory work on technical problems to do them justice. One unsolved problem of American diplomacy in this regard is the blending of scientific and diplomatic competence. At a recent Geneva conference on surprise attack and on problems of underground testing, only the scientists in the delegation could claim mastery of the technical issues, yet in any negotiation there are skills which diplomats command and which scientists find difficult of attainment.

This problem is compounded by the problem of public information. At what point should the public be made privy to facts regarding, for example, United States and Canadian negotiations on an early-warning radar system in northern Canada? The old formula of the new diplomacy set forth by Woodrow Wilson of "open covenants openly arrived at" is difficult to apply. Some suggest that only the principles underlying the defense system, the cost, and the form of participation of the two countries are appropriately public knowledge. They would reserve from the public domain information about technical arrangements, location and range of installations, and other operating aspects of the warning system. Wherever one turns, the content of diplomacy has been transformed by technological factors. When conflict erupts, commissions, fact-finding agencies and specialized international bodies move to the scene to make their estimates, upon which future negotiations must be based.

A second revolution has accompanied, exploited, and reinforced the technological revolution. The political and technological revolutions are mutually supporting. In one sense, the political revolution could hardly have come about without the technological one. As late as World War I, foreign policy and diplomacy continued to be the business of professionals, and the public paid it little heed. The sovereigns of the eighteenth and nineteenth centuries had been individuals. Today, alongside national leaders are hundreds of legislators and millions of newspaper readers and radio listeners who influence the course of foreign relations. Their views and opinions are bound to affect diplomacy. It lies within their power to support or frustrate policy. Their expectations often exceed reasonable prospects of success. Their attitudes and moods can become fixed and frozen on the very issues with which diplomatists work. Their sense of the need for change may impel leaders to undertake new approaches that may sometimes, but not always, be successful.

The origins of the political revolution probably go back to certain profound social and political eruptions associated with the French Revolution, the American Revolution, and the Bolshevik Revolution. The French Revolution, like the Russian Revolution a century and a quarter later, upset and unsettled established patterns of government and international relations. The reactions to the French Revolution were many and varied, and some are less relevant than others to the changes in diplomacy. Conservatives like Burke and Hamilton stressed the threat to property and legitimacy; others found in the Revolution the dawn of a new age and the final downfall of an ancient evil. Jefferson once affirmed that with the French Revolution the long historical ordeal of humanity was over. Others argued that the guillotine was an instrument for the elimination of the absolutely wicked as a means of enthroning the absolutely good. Like the Soviet Communists thereafter, the French revolutionists pledged themselves to purge "the enemies of the people." Jefferson accepted the fact that the loss of innocent lives was a tragedy, but added that, rather than have the cause of liberty fail, "I would have seen half the earth desolated." No one who joined the procession of revolutionaries moving toward utopia foresaw Napoleon or Louis XVIII, any more than early Russian revolutionaries of 1917 envisaged Stalin and Khrushchev.

This revolutionary fervor surged across the emerging United States of America. The title "Citizen" took the place of "Mister." One American historian reports that Louis XIV was hanged in effigy twenty or thirty times each day. In this revolutionary atmosphere, President Washington and his cabinet faced the choice of aligning the newly independent state with France in the war against Britain, or alternatively, of remaining neutral. The strategic and military considerations were clear. Lacking a navy, the United States could hardly come to the aid of France. But issues of fact were soon engulfed in a wave of popular feeling engendered by the political revolution which made prudent decisions difficult to sustain. French sympathizers sang *La Marseillaise* in the streets. At a crucial moment, Citizen Genêt, the first minister of the new French Republic to the United States, arrived on American soil. His self-image was less that of an emissary than a missionary of a revolutionary creed. He presented his papers not to President Washington, but to the people of Charleston, South Carolina. Despite Washington's proclamation of neutrality, Genêt organized his country's military effort on American soil, dispatching privateers from Charleston to capture British ships even within American waters, set up prize courts to condemn them, and prepared a military expedition to conquer neighboring provinces then under the control of Spain. He recruited members for an American branch of the French Jacobin groups and marched at the head of a procession of supporters of France through the back country and on to Philadelphia, gathering force as he went. He extended a journey requiring less than a week to more than a month. When he arrived in Philadelphia, however, Washington had the courage to stand on formality and disregard him, even though a majority of the American people were siding with Genêt against their own government. According to John Adams, ten thousand people in the streets of Philadelphia threatened to drag Washington from his home and compel the American government to declare war on England in behalf of the French Revolution.

When Washington's administration called Genêt to task for disregarding the spirit of the doctrines of Grotius, Genêt responded that he knew nothing of Grotius but was guided by the doctrines of the French Revolution.

The point of this historic incident is to illustrate the vast surging power of popular feeling which revolutionary movements can engender. Fortunately for the future of the American Republic, Washington resisted popular opinion, Genêt finally overstepped all reasonable bounds, and a prudent policy and a wise solution were accepted. The famous dictum for diplomats, *Sûrtout, pas trop de zèle,* is more difficult to convey to the mass of citizens. George Catlett Marshall as Secretary of State frequently advised his colleagues that the first rule of any public servant was to keep down his emotions. As the political revolution has swept across the world, this advice has become more and more difficult to realize. We do well to remind ourselves that American envoys, at the very moment Citizen Genêt was rallying French sympathizers on American soil, were engaged in diplomacy that resembled French tactics. The American Minister to France, Gouverneur Morris, was openly hostile to the French Revolution and joined the attempt to bring about the escape of Louis XVI and other leaders of the *ancien régime.* When President Washington requested Genêt's recall, the French replied by asking for Morris' recall. Ironically, James Monroe, who followed Morris and was the champion of the doctrine of nonintervention in the Western Hemisphere, openly supported the French against the British in their European struggle.

The lasting effect of the political revolution has been to infuse diplomacy with a sense of absolute righteousness. The body politic and many of its diplomats tend to view conflicts in terms of absolute right and wrong. This attitude aggravates the sharp oscillation in public moods. In 1793, many Americans identified the cause of the French Revolution with the forward march of mankind. Yet a few short years thereafter, a reaction set in with the publication of the "XYZ" dispatches in 1798. So intense was the revulsion against France that the Treaty of 1778 was repudiated and an era of undeclared war against France ensued. The Alien and Sedition Acts expressed the full force of American feeling. Within a few years sentiments were moderated again, the pendulum returned to a more favorable attitude, and Thomas Jefferson was swept into office on the wave of strong pro-French opinion as the third President of the United States. Few would say that these reactions bore no relationship to shifts in the external world, but the sharp and pronounced swings of the pendulum can hardly be explained by the flow of events. The play of popular passions and the influence of the revolutionary tradition were unquestionably more decisive than any shift in our strategic interests.

The Bolshevik Revolution in 1917 illustrates the same profound change. While in liberal democracies the people have increasingly influenced foreign policy, in the Soviet Union the principal leaders of the proletarian revolution are the spokesmen of the so-called people's democracy. Soviet diplomacy has alternated between a complete rejection of the old diplomacy and an adaptation of its methods. In 1917 the revolutionary leadership repudiated the traditional functions of Russian diplomats and the champions of the new diplomacy welcomed the Soviets to the fold. It eliminated the rank of ambassador, substituting that of *polpred* for representatives abroad. It affirmed that its new officialdom exemplified Communist virtue as contrasted with the evils of bourgeois officials of the past. With the passing of time, more and more in form and substance Soviet diplomacy took shape along lines that resembled prewar Russian diplomacy. The Treaty of Rapallo was negotiated in secrecy; *polpreds* to Iran and China were suddenly designated ambassadors in order to signal their precedence over representatives of other nations; and diplomatic machinery that had been eliminated was restored. With occasional reversions to a sharp and doctrinaire opposition to the old diplomacy, as in the case of the purge of the Jewish diplomats in response to revolutionary anti-Semitism, Soviet foreign policy took on many of the trappings of traditional foreign policy.

With the rise of the new nations the spread of the revolutionary tradition has continued apace. The symbol of the political and diplomatic outlooks of some of the new states is found in the inscription on the statue of Prime Minister Nkrumah in Parliament Square which reads: "Seek ye first the political kingdom and all other things will be added unto you." The crusading zeal of the French, American, and Russian Revolutions continues in the revolutions of the new states. The purposes of the new revolutionary movements may well be virtuous and just. They may make possible—in the long run—a more stable international order. From the diplomat's standpoint, however, their impact has been to subject the course of diplomacy more than ever before to the controls, vagaries, and uncertainties of public opinion. In a revolutionary world, a public speech or an off-the-cuff remark of an aspiring political leader may be as important as a careful memorandum by a diplomatic representative in Washington or Moscow. Moreover, the effects of international rivalries reach far beyond national or regional boundaries. In the words of a former permanent undersecretary in the British Foreign Office: "In a world where war is everybody's tragedy and everybody's nightmare, diplomacy is everybody's business."

Anyone who follows the headlines of the daily press or reviews the news of the world feels called upon to take a stand on difficult issues of diplomatic tactics and strategy. This fact may in the end serve the cause of world peace, but it unquestionably alters the patterns of the old diplomacy. The fabric of the international order we have known is weakened by this development. The new diplomacy has extended the practice of bringing an issue to a head, of throwing a problem before the entire world community, and of raising to a white heat the emotional aspects of any rivalry. If the historian Herbert Butterfield is correct, a revolutionary atmosphere is one which heightens the sense of conflict and threat of war and weakens the coherence and unity of an established international system. It establishes the nation-state as the one political authority in immediate contact with the vital needs of a people. It leads to the weakening of the international community for reasons Judge de Visscher describes best:

If the international community . . . finds so little echo in individual consciences, this is less because power obstructs it than because the immense majority of men are still infinitely less accessible to the doubtless real but certainly remote solidarities that it invokes than to the immediate and tangible solidarities that impose themselves upon them in the framework of national life.[2]

More fundamental still, the political revolution leads to a separation of factors that historically have been interrelated. In Grotius' time, the moral, legal, and political order, in theory at least, were of a piece. Order and justice corresponded within the international system. By contrast, the overriding characteristic of revolutionary regimes is a commitment to the overthrow of the legal order—invariably in the name of justice. Unfulfilled goals and aspirations, not a congenital urge to wrongdoing or international crimes, pit revolutionary governments against the status quo. Domestically they may accept the necessity of order preceding justice, but internationally they grow impatient for national satisfaction and self-fulfillment. Thus those regimes whose claims were organized around the nationality principle in the nineteenth century rejected the European order based on legitimacy. More recently, the rising new states of Africa and Asia find they have no "stake" in the principles of international law derived from Western experience. An Indonesian diplomat observes: "Most of the existing laws between Asian and African countries and the

---

[2] Charles de Visscher, *Theory and Reality in Public International Law*, trans. P. E. Corbett (Princeton, N.J.: Princeton University Press, 1957), p. 92.

old-established Western world are more or less outmoded and should be regarded as a burden of modern life." [3]

Confronted by circumstances in which order and justice conflict, international society runs the risk of acceding to one and abandoning the other. The Congress of Vienna in 1815 restored political order but neglected the moral order embodied in rising nationalism and breached the legal order by confirming the extinction of Poland. In the case of the League of Nations, the one persuasive argument opposing the use of sanctions against Italy in 1935–1936 was the political effect of destroying an obstacle to Germany's predominance in the heart of Europe. Franklin D. Roosevelt's policies in World War II invite criticism not from the standpoint of their impact on the moral or legal order, but as they led to the derangement of the European balance of power. The United Nations with its predominance of Afro-Asian members may be predisposed to assume responsibility for creating moral order based on the justice of national self-determination without paying equal heed to conditions of political and economic viability. If loyalties of new states disturb calm reflection on this problem, observers need only reflect on the consequences of the Balkanization of West Africa. The moral of the story for old and new states alike is the price historically of separation of the moral, legal, and political requirements of international order —a problem aggravated, not ameliorated, in an era of political revolution. Reinhold Niebuhr enunciates a principle with relevance for the ages when he writes: "Order precedes justice in the strategy of government; but only an order which implicates justice can achieve a stable peace." [4] The prime question of the age is whether the emerging international order can be infused with enough justice to insure its survival.

[3] Remarks by Mr. Abdulgani, the representative of Indonesia at the first Suez Conference in London on August 16, 1956. Quoted in *The Review of Politics*, XIX, No. 4 (October 1957), 442.

[4] Reinhold Niebuhr, *The Children of Light and the Children of Darkness* (New York: Charles Scribner's Sons, 1944), p. 123.

The new diplomacy is influenced by a third profound and far-reaching event, the ideological revolution. In an earlier age, particularly in the eighteenth and nineteenth centuries, the fostering of internal social and political change within neighboring jurisdictions was subordinated to the maintenance of international peace and order. Examples at random illustrate the point. Charles VIII intervened in Italy in 1494; Russia, Germany, and France by the Triple Intervention in 1895 compelled Japan to relinquish the Liaotung Peninsula which she sought to annex from China; in 1849 the Hapsburg government invited Russian intervention in Hungary; and in American foreign policy, the Mexican War was fought primarily for reasons of national security. These examples of intervention rested on the objective of preserving or reestablishing a balance of power in Europe and Asia. They were seldom if ever evoked for primarily ideological reasons. When a government felt it was losing its capacity for effective control, or a faction out of power sought help in gaining power, it called for external assistance. Jurists who espoused the positivist approach to international law denied that internal disturbances alone provided grounds for intervention unless, like the French Revolution, they threatened to lead to conquest or subversion abroad. Foreign policy was separated from domestic affairs and unless interests affecting the former were engaged, encroachment on another's territory was prohibited.

The ideological revolution has wrought a far-reaching and basic transformation in this pattern. The long-standing distinction between domestic and foreign affairs shows signs of disappearing. Soviet Communist leaders astride a world revolutionary movement conduct foreign relations alternately through embassies and national parties, through diplomats and party functionaries. Moreover, Soviet diplomacy is part of an unrelenting war against capitalism. While it employs tactics of advance and retreat, intensifying and then relaxing tensions, its ultimate objective indisputably is world domination. It seeks to impose its will on other nations through active intervention by threats and cajolery, subversion and blackmail, promises and pressures, propaganda and provocation, or by spreading chaos and aiding and abetting *coups d'état.* Its armory of weapons includes talk of hostages, threats of violence, persecution of oppositions, political infiltrations, and, in certain cases, war itself. In its doctrines regarding the use of force and the conduct of war, it is neither as romantic as the Fascists nor as pacifist as American isolationists. Professor Hugh Seton-Watson in his study, *Neither War nor Peace,* asserts:

Secret diplomacy, propaganda by mass media . . . [or] international conference, espionage, subversion, economic aid, the granting or withholding of foreign trade, guerrilla war, the threat of war, war with conventional forces and war with atomic weapons are all potential instruments of policy, to be used in accordance with the need of the moment, the chances and the cost of success.[5]

Soviet diplomats view their task within a far broader framework. They cannot accept the continuing pragmatic assumptions of traditional diplomacy as primarily the search for a durable political settlement or a lasting armistice in the struggle for power. Because nations reflect the class struggle and play out the roles assigned to them by the dialectic of history, their struggle must go on until Soviet communism prevails. Class contradictions cannot be erased through a political *détente* with capitalist states; nothing short of "unconditional surrender" by the opponent can assure peace and justice. Even in a period of so-called peaceful coexistence, according to the party journal *Kommunist:* "The class war in the international arena continues, but the forms of that war are different—economic competition and an ideological fight in place of war." [6] The Soviet negotiator at the conference table is no different from other envoys in seeking the most he can get for his country. The point at which he differs is in the com-

---

[5] Quoted in *The Listener,* LXVI, No. 1702 (November 9, 1961), 755.
[6] *Ibid.*

pulsion he feels to prevail, to triumph over an adversary, to bury an opponent. And what is more serious, the wellsprings of his conduct are doctrinal, not personal; ideological, not political; and strategic, not tactical. Since he and all those who march in the vanguard of the proletariat are servants and not masters of the Communist's apocalypse carried along day by day by historical determinism, their approach is impenetrable to the influence of fact or logic.

The cold war is in effect a contest between two conflicting political orders. Within less than fifty years, one-third of the world's population has fallen under the domination or ideological sway of the Communist order with its peculiar sense of justice and vision of the future. Even if its successes are exaggerated and its failures too often discounted, the Communist world shows little sign of abandoning its ideological commitment. Within the Communist code, the end quite explicitly justifies the means, and the end remains a utopia founded not upon a consensus among divergent views but upon total victory of the Communist creed. A just war is one that hastens this process; successful negotiations are a means to the end. To see in this approach the basis for a working framework of common ideas and values with the West—what Callières in his day called the "commerce d'avis réciproque"—is to invite illusion and despair. So long as Communists uphold their basic ideological position, mutual hostility, suspicion, and perhaps overt conflict are more likely than peaceful accommodation.

Yet even if there were no Soviet threat and if the Communist ideology remained for the future, the international order would be in upheaval and turmoil. States face one another across a further deep ideological divide. The present setting of world politics offers scant grounds for complacency. In the terse and cogent phraseology of President Grayson Kirk of Columbia University: "There are too many weak governments, too many inexperienced, ambitious and unseasoned political leaders, too much belligerent nationalism among too many recently liberated peoples, too many statesmen . . . in the older countries where minds have been unable to keep pace with fast-moving events."[7] Nearly a billion people have gained their independence from the Western colonial powers since World War II; eighteen African states achieved independence little more than twelve months ago. Britain, which sixteen years ago ruled 600,000,000 people, today rules 30,000,000, and of these 11,000,000 in East Africa will soon be free. Many have embarked on the trying voyage of statehood with able crew and sturdy craft that are a tribute to a colonial past. One thinks of the Indian Civil Service, the cocoa reserves of Ghana, the trained leadership of Nigeria, and the governmental and educational system of French West Africa centering in Dakar, Senegal. Roads and schools, harbors and plants, urban developments and scientific agriculture are other aspects of the legacy. However, because the virtue of the colonial powers and their officials has been fragmentary and incomplete, it can scarcely obscure the taint of self-interest and self-pride that accompanies every virtuous measure. It is axiomatic that states cannot assure the good will of others merely by their good works. This is because even the best among men and nations are less virtuous than they imagine themselves to be. Measured against their claims to virtue, their performance, corrupted by human shortcomings and too much self-satisfaction, makes them easy targets for political foes.

Hence, the common interests the new states share with the West are counterbalanced by the political interests of a rising elite of revolutionary leaders who have captured power by challenging even the most benevolent colonial powers. Africa is in the grip of a revolt against the power and authority of the West. Independence offers little assurance that this rivalry will cease, for revolutionary leaders whose promises invariably exceed their achievements turn to ancient scapegoats. A perilous discrepancy yawns between the ambitions and capacity of

---

[7] Address by President Grayson Kirk at the University of the South, Sewanee, Tennessee, April 19, 1958.

many African states. If their former masters should not oblige with a concrete example of residual imperialism, nationalist leaders or their aspiring successors will not prove lacking in ingenuity. The ideology of newly independent states carries a heavy freight of nationalist protest that has served effectively in preindependence days and that hard-pressed leaders are hesitant to abandon in a new era. For another perhaps more basic reason the consensus between diplomats of the new and old states is hemmed in and restricted. It would be unfair to say that the emergent states are oblivious to the rising threat of Russian communism, but this threat seems distant and remote compared with their own immediate problems. Of the world's 40,000,000 Communist party members, authorities estimate that no more than 50,000 are in Africa—and these chiefly in the extreme north and south.

If we view the world crisis through the eyes of some African leaders, there seems little they can do to turn back the tide of world communism, whereas there is so much to be done in serving the daily needs of their people. From policies calculated on a cool appraisal of the ultimate threat to political stability and national security, these states might logically have been expected to erect barriers to the spread of international communism. In this they might have seen the West as their sole guardian against the Communist colossus, from whose "colonial" grip more than 12,000,000 people have fled since World War II, including 3,000,000 Germans and 200,-000 Hungarians. Yet Western imperialism and its memories are more immediate, vivid, and by happy experience subject to pressure, negotiation, and change. Moreover, it is tempting if misleading to believe "the enemy of my enemy is my friend." By sponsoring at little cost to herself antiimperialist policies, the Soviet Union is temporarily able to nullify the long-run common interests of Western and newly independent states. By joining with the emerging peoples in a crusade to dislodge the West from its positions in Asia and Africa, the Soviet Union, China, Egypt, and Ghana keep alive the ideology of antiimperialism, weaken the bonds that otherwise reunite men with a common vision of liberty and justice, and stimulate opposition to the embryonic international order enshrined at San Francisco. Moscow radio denounces the 5,000 American missionaries in Africa as "imperialists working in black garments to serve United States monopolies rather than God." It proclaims that "colonialism regards poverty, disease, ignorance, brutality, treachery, the bondsman's chains, and the hangman's rope as its allies in Africa." No responsible Westerner can ignore the so-called imperialism problem if the people most directly concerned insist on treating it as more momentous than all other issues combined, coloring their responses to each succeeding crisis. A lukewarm response that recites historic American resistance to imperialism and raises the specter of a new and far more sinister imperialism scarcely meets this issue at the point of its depth and persistence. An episode from the autobiography of the young Nkrumah symbolizes the problem. On arriving in England, he read a placard: "Mussolini invades Ethiopia." At that moment, he writes: "it was almost as if the whole of London had declared war on me personally. . . . I was ready to go through hell itself if need be in order to achieve my object."

3. Transition in Diplomacy

THE new diplomacy, then, was born into a world of profound disruption and social change. Its defenders and noblest spokesmen had caught a vision of a brave new world. They sensed and properly measured a part of the revolutionary change that was transforming the world. For it is true that the technological revolution has drawn men ever more closely together, replacing a large-scale map with a small-scale globe. It is true that the political revolution sounded the death knell of an era in which a handful of leaders could plot the destiny of mankind without reference to the popular will. And finally, it is true that the ideological revolution thrust the doctrines of states and societies into the forefront of international relations generating commitments to prevailing world views more powerful than "reason of state." The ideas unleashed in two thousand years of Western history spurred non-Westerners to measure Western conduct against these standards. The new diplomacy assured men everywhere of an open hearing for airing their rights, claims, hopes, and insecurities before the forum of mankind.

Two world wars and sixteen years of threats and rumors of war have deepened our understanding of the new diplomacy. The first embodiment of the new order, the League of Nations, was battered and broken by forces outside its walls more powerful than those it could rally within for peace and order. This first experiment, now but dimly a conscious factor in international planning, taught nations that unresolved conflicts between member and nonmember states could destroy an international system. It suggested that reason and persuasion were less formidable than naked power and aggression. It caused a reexamination of the notion that the world was moving decisively across the threshold of a new era in which independent national interests and autonomous foreign policies were yielding to a world view. Instead, the interwar period found "have" and "have not" nations arrayed against one another, mobilizing total resources to achieve their goals, and exploiting the limits and self-restraints of a noncoercive international system to seize new territory and power. The fond hopes that an international organization whose substantive actions required unanimity and whose authority was moral rather than military could preserve peace and order were shattered.

The years of the League of Nations revived knowledge that seventeenth century jurists had taken for granted. It made plain the fact that states still lived astride two worlds—the one a world of respect for law and justice and the requirements for peaceful change, and the other a world of force, power politics, and strident nationalism. The new diplomacy was equipped to facilitate agreement on many things. It accorded with the rise of popular governments, it brought together leaders of diverse states and cultures, and it fostered an awareness of international responsibility. But it fell prey to forces that had defined the tasks and determined in part the methods of the old diplomacy. The new diplomacy was geared to a world not fully realized; it failed because the time was not ripe for the enthronement of good will and trust among all the nations.

The United Nations was cast in a mold whose makers imagined they had profited from the League's mistakes. Its primary business was to keep the peace among the great powers who had triumphed in World War II. It struck a compromise between establishing an organization strong enough to check the collisions of middle and small powers and realistic enough to accept its limits in coercing the superpowers. It recognized from the start that peaceful settlements required serious efforts by states to achieve understandings outside as well as within the organization.

Since coercion of the superpowers was impossible, their

continual conciliation within an international framework became the central goal. Yet open diplomacy has not always served this objective; the great powers locked in a profound ideological struggle are more often impelled to score points on a wide propaganda front in United Nations debates than to harmonize outstanding differences. Lacking both the underlying consensus on which national legislatures are founded and the full panoply of informal machinery by which Congress or Parliament hammer public debates into private agreements, the United Nations has been unable to ameliorate the great world conflict. The unbridgeable ideological gulf between the Soviet Union and the United States has turned the international organization away from issues of the cold war to a related but different sphere.

In practice, the leaders of the world organization have been required to preside over the vast and turbulent changes of the revolution of rising expectations. At its founding, few architects of the United Nations could anticipate the breathtaking speed with which the colonial empires in Africa and Asia would be dissolved. Who can say that he forecast in 1945 the emergence of forty new states in the international arena? Who was convinced that in sixteen years the balance of power would shift to the more than half a hundred Afro-Asian states? Who at a time when our wisest leaders urged the building of an international system to conform to the realities of great power politics—a reality which League of Nations architects had not recognized—anticipated that their world institution would preside over the death agonies of old empires and the birth pangs of successor states? Who saw clearly that the several branches of the United Nations would become sounding boards for the complete and final liquidation of the British, French, Belgian, Dutch, Portuguese, and Spanish empires? Who supposed that eleven African states with fewer than 3,000,000 inhabitants would each have votes in the General Assembly counting for as much as those of Britain, the United States, or Russia? Who prophesied that an organization limited at birth by the supremacy of national loyalties inherent in the political revolution would suffer even greater restraints imposed by an ideological revolution which divided East and West and, in more recent days, North and South? Who had the vision and courage to predict that the world of the new diplomacy might be rent by conflicts and disputes so profound that given crises found East aligned with South or West joined with East against itself, as at Suez? The United Nations has become a bridge between North and South and the old world and the newly emergent states—nations that have ended an ancient if often beneficent imperialism only to be called by their former masters to resist a more ruthless and total imperialist threat less real to those who are schooled to associate evil with but one colonial imperialism.

Faced with the travail of an international community enjoying technological and economic foundations but lacking solid moral and political roots, the new diplomacy scarcely fulfills the design of its earliest and most fervent champions. Their prediction rings hollow that with its establishment "the old special functions of diplomacy will fall away and administrative conferences will take the place of diplomatic conversations." [8] The United Nations, far from assuring "more simple and direct dealings," [9] has demanded a more complex and intricate form of international relations. History has refuted the prognosis that the present era would be one in which society would "outgrow and transcend politics for more comprehensive, pervasive and essential principles of action." [10] The hopes following World War I that revolutionary governments with mass followings would ease international tensions are little more today than scraps of ancient folklore overthrown by events. How quaint are the words of Paul S. Reinsch written in 1922:

---

[8] Paul S. Reinsch, *Secret Diplomacy* (New York: Harcourt, Brace & Co., 1922), p. 15.
[9] *Ibid.*, p. 16.
[10] *Ibid.*, p. 13.

The Russian Soviet government in giving to the public a full knowledge of international affairs, was at first inspired primarily by a desire to discredit the old regime. But it is also undoubtedly true that the hold which this government has on the party which supports it, is in a measure due to the fact that all foreign policies and relationships are freely reported to, and discussed in, the party meetings and the Soviets.[11]

It may be true that "the old diplomacy rests entirely on skepticism as to the wisdom and self-control of the people." [12] It can be argued that "it does not provide means for a sufficient contact among the peoples of the world," [13] although I would ask whether other forms of international relations than diplomacy are not better suited to this function. It can be said that the old "diplomacy is far more eminent in autopsy than in diagnosis," [14] but what should we say of the new diplomacy? In fairness, the prophets of the new diplomacy were conscious that historically diplomatic negotiations resembled most a horse trade in which participants could hardly be expected to tell each other in advance all they might do or might accept. They knew that negotiation was similar to well-established patterns of relations between industry and labor. They found that at the peak of talk about "Open Diplomacy" the Council of Four at the Paris Peace Conference locked themselves behind closed doors to conclude a peace treaty following World War I. But such aspects of diplomacy, however deep-seated, were associated by these prophets with a particular region of the world or a certain period in history. Thus it was Europe in particular, not diplomacy in general, of which President Woodrow Wilson said: "European diplomacy works always in the dense thicket of ancient feuds, rooted, entangled and entwined. . . . I did not realize it all until the peace conference;

[11] *Ibid.*, p. 20.
[12] *Ibid.*, p. 214.
[13] *Ibid.*, p. 218.
[14] *Ibid.*, p. 177.

I did not realize how deep the roots are." [15] Or having cited
John Jay's dictum in *The Federalist Papers:* "It seldom happens in the negotiation of treaties, of whatever nature, but
that perfect secrecy and immediate dispatch are sometimes
requisite," [16] Mr. Reinsch concluded: "Jay's explanation is
dominated by the conception . . . [of] the eighteenth century." [17] And before quoting the famous speech of Balfour on
March 19, 1914, in the House of Commons, the same American
spokesman prepared the reader: "This plainly is the language
of a statesman to whom the idiosyncrasies of the European
system are so familiar that they seem to be the only natural
state of affairs." [18] Balfour had said:

How is the task of peace-maker . . . to be pursued if you shout your
grievances from the housetop whenever they occur? The only result is
that you embitter public feelings, that the differences between the two
States suddenly attain a magnitude they ought never be allowed to
approach, that the newspapers of the two countries have their passions
set on fire, and great crises arise, which may end, have ended sometimes in international catastrophes. . . . I do not hold the view that
antique methods are pursued by diplomatists which no man of common sense adopts in the ordinary work of everyday life.[19]

In the era of transition surrounding the mid-twentieth century, men of common sense have sought to evolve diplomatic
patterns that were neither wholly new nor old. If it is true that
"pain makes men think, thought makes men wise and wisdom
makes life endurable," successive crises have carried us beyond simple slogans and panaceas. We see more clearly today
than in 1919 or 1946 that we live in a world bereft of the
comforting unity of moral and political purpose. Coué's grand
illusion that man by giving thought was becoming better and
better day by day in every way, or Wilson's vision that na-

[15] *Ibid.,* quoted on p. 21.
[16] *Ibid.,* quoted on p. 150.
[17] *Ibid.*
[18] *Ibid.,* p. 161.
[19] *Ibid.,* quoted on pp. 162–63.

tionalism was dying or dead, or the dream of institutionalists, free traders, and world lawyers that their prescriptions would remove conflict and assure perpetual harmony are but empty shells. Progress is always uneven and bounded by circumstances, interests, and events. The evidence to support this is clear in the concrete event. Thus while Americans, Asians, and Africans turn increasingly to the United Nations, Europeans and the Soviet Union are reluctant to give it the support by which it must live. While those who belong to the North Atlantic Community speak of supranational unity, nationalism in Asia, Africa, and the Middle East grows more intense.

The great historical moments in American foreign policy are periods of tension between the new and the old, realism and idealism, and self-interest and enlightenment. If the practice in contrast to the theory of the new diplomacy is viewed in this light, its significance can be perceived. Within a framework of open diplomacy, a great innovator who by instinct embodied the most lasting qualities of Western civilization, a detached sense of justice and respect for freedom and human dignity, Dag Hammarskjold, joined the old with the new. Lest greatness pass again in the night, we remind ourselves that here was a man who in 1953 was hailed as the archetype of the confidential clerk. For Mr. Hammarskjold, who acted on behalf of a community of nations that has not yet achieved community, who could be gloomy but never disheartened, and who despised "diplomacy by loudspeaker," quiet diplomacy was the fusion of ancient arts with novel techniques and a marriage of the wisdom of the ages with present imperatives. He gave contemporary expression to Lord Rosebery's aphorism: "Cordiality as between nations can only rest on mutual self-respect." To accept this as he did is to perceive that realism is not cynicism, that diplomacy is not dead but must be modernized, and that the search for peace, while endless, has an ally in history. The present task is to bring techniques of accommodation into line with a transitional era in world politics rising above the harsh dogmas that divide and confuse. The subsequent discussions of parliamentary and personal diplomacy and diplomacy in a changing world may serve to illustrate this truth and to complete our account by tracing the underlying unities that modern man slowly, painfully, and not without repeated setbacks seeks to fashion under dark clouds of destructiveness more threatening than any in human history.

5

Parliamentary and Personal Diplomacy

MID-TWENTIETH CENTURY INNOVATIONS OR ENDURING INSTITUTIONS?

"The United Nations perfectly embodies in institutional form the tragic paradox of our age; it has become indispensable before it has become effective. . . . To exist at all it cannot depart very far from its present structure; to develop at all it requires the focus and drive which only a permanent and potent leader can give it."
HERBERT NICHOLAS

THE PROVERBIAL "man from Mars" thrust suddenly into the maelstrom of contemporary international politics would doubtless find diplomatic institutions novel and perplexing to assess. On returning, he would be hard pressed to explain them to fellow Martians, partly because of the wide gulf separating popular theories and practical use, and partly because of the paradox and ambivalence inherent in policies of certain major states. He would note, for example, that the United States, an early arch-defender of the new diplomacy, first rejected the international institution created as the principal embodiment of a brave new world and then, while staunchly sponsoring its successor organization, felt obliged to play upon not one but many diplomatic keyboards. If asked to describe the American approach to diplomacy, he might in summing up suggest that we combined bilateral, regional, and universal diplomacy, using ambassadors, special envoys, parliamentary, and personal diplomatic techniques. The truth is, he might be forced to say, that present-day diplomacy is in a transitional state. Old forms are passing or being absorbed by the new; and rash is he who affirms that one technique or another is assured of long life or widespread use in the years ahead. For the outsider, the point of decision in our foreign policy and the probable level at which diplomatic contact is likely to be joined remains a matter of uncertainty, inconsistency, and oftentimes of confusion.

In discussing the life expectancy of diplomatic institutions no one should ignore the play of personalities and events which at any moment in the present remain hidden from view just beyond the veil of the future. The balance will be tipped in the direction of personal, traditional, or parliamentary diplomacy by strong personalities, far-reaching national attitudes or overpowering world trends sweeping unannounced across the horizon. The role of the President, and hence of personal diplomacy, ebbs and flows with a leader's personality and conception of his office. Some American presidents, like James K. Polk, Theodore Roosevelt, Woodrow Wilson, Franklin D. Roosevelt, and apparently John F. Kennedy, strive to place their stamp on every significant external action. Others, like Ulysses S. Grant, Warren G. Harding, Calvin Coolidge, and Dwight D. Eisenhower, are content to invest a trusted secretary of state with far-reaching powers. Similarly, a Congress with majorities favoring the President and with friendly chairmen of the great committees may free him from the shackling controls of a suspicious public to make fresh diplomatic overtures abroad. Thus Congress following World War I in an era of immense prosperity and sharp domestic reaction to the intrinsic importance of foreign affairs placed restraints both on the President and his Secretary of State. By sheer personal force of character and tactical skill, an outstanding secretary like Charles Evans Hughes (1921–1925) was able to shape policy. A weaker secretary like his successor, Frank B. Kellogg, was contained partly by the force and ability of William E. Borah, Chairman of the Senate Foreign Relations Committee, and by a powerful national trend of thought.

Few would deny that national sentiments that spread like wildfire across the land or deep undertows of political animosity also shape the choice of diplomatic institutions. Secretary Hughes had assured the American people in the 1919 campaign that support of candidate Harding guaranteed American participation under "reasonable conditions" in the international diplomacy of the League of Nations. In the face of opposition from an irreconcilable body of Republican legislators, however, he abandoned his position and, subsequently, by refusing to take a position for or against the Geneva Protocol to strengthen the League in 1924–1925, helped bring about its collapse. By contrast, a powerful national viewpoint toward the outlawry of war enlisted wide popular support and, despite initial resistance within the Department of State, led to the Kellogg-Briand Pact of 1928. Although it seems clear that President Franklin D. Roosevelt was no isolationist, nevertheless, in his first term of office he felt constrained to pursue isolationist policies, prompted no doubt by the temper of the times. His preoccupation with domestic affairs, his love of analogies drawn from national experience, his natural disposition to view the world in Wilsonian terms, and the intensification of foreign problems only in later years of office delayed Roosevelt's attainment of a mature and seasoned conception of diplomacy. It is interesting, in this connection, to speculate whether John F. Kennedy, having early confronted Khrushchev, will carry into the future the same notions about personal diplomacy with Soviet dictators that President Roosevelt brought to Yalta. Timing, personality, circumstances, and events all fashion men's outlook toward avenues of discussion and negotiation.

World trends are another factor in determining diplomatic

methods. If a growing number of states associate prestige and standing in the world with participation immediately upon independence in a parliamentary diplomatic body, its status and importance are enhanced. One measure of the importance of United Nations diplomacy may be the fact that new states like Tanganyika have established their principal American diplomatic outposts in New York, not Washington. If we turn to the realm of personal diplomacy, we note that when certain powerful states persist in raising decisions and actions to the level of chief executive, others, including governments with serious reservations to personal diplomacy, may resign themselves to top-level negotiations. Or again, when security becomes an issue of worldwide concern affecting states both adjacent to and remote from a zone of dispute, they will demand and receive representation in an appropriate international body. Thus parliamentary and personal diplomacy in our day are partially, at least, the outgrowth of worldwide forces.

1. Diplomatic Techniques in a Fledgling Nation

AN observer reflecting on present-day transformations of diplomacy must begin by reminding himself that the patterns of American diplomacy inaugurated on independence were heralded then as ushering in the "new diplomacy." He may gain perspective on modern techniques by a brief survey of early American diplomatic practice. A comparison of the era of Washington and Jefferson with the present may throw light on the passing as against the enduring features of diplomacy. European envoys to the new republic had expected an American approach foreshadowed in the work of revolutionary agents abroad who had scorned and rejected time-tested precepts of protocol and etiquette. In the decade and a half that followed 1776, American diplomats, including Silas Deane and John Adams, modified their views on what they had contemptuously called the "ridiculous business of etiquette," as they perceived the importance of orderly and predictable methods for acknowledging the authority and prestige of other governments. The handicaps of conducting foreign relations by committees of secret correspondence led to the formation in 1791 of more traditional machinery for the conduct of diplomatic business. If management of foreign affairs was to achieve continuity and direction, it required more stable machinery than that provided by *ad hoc* committees of Congress or important national leaders. In describing the system of multiple diplomatic agents chosen by Congress to balance one another's political views, Benjamin Franklin could write:

. . . all the advantages in negotiation that result from secrecy of sentiment and uniformity in expressing it and in common business from dispatch are lost. . . . And where every one must be consulted on every particular . . . the difficulty of being often and long enough together, the different opinions and the time consumed in debating them . . . occasion so much postponing and delay, that correspondence languishes, occasions are lost, and the business is always behindhand.[1]

Sentiments like Franklin's led to the creation in 1781, under the Articles of Confederation, of a Department of Foreign Affairs under the leadership of a secretary of foreign affairs. The first secretary, Robert R. Livingston, became the channel for communication between American envoys abroad and the Congress, sharing with members of Congress only that portion of confidential diplomatic correspondence touching "great national objects." Livingston and his successor, John Jay, laid the foundations for a more professional, if traditional, approach to diplomacy with responsibility reserved to a small executive department rather than agents of the larger popular branch of government. Leaders concluded it was not enough to conduct relations on the assumption of a natural affinity between revolutionary peoples, for example, between France and the United States. Something more basic determined their relations, for in John Adams' words: "The circumstances of modes, language, and religion have much less influence in determining the friendship and enmity of nations than other more essential interests." [2] A corps of professionals was needed to identify and execute policies grounded in interests. Early American leaders came to see that the maintenance of freedom required an exact and continuous knowledge no less of the state of the rivalry between France and England, or the balance of power in Europe, than of the goals and slogans of the French or American Revolutions.

The early years of the American Republic found individual leaders of the highest political intelligence rediscovering a coherent system of thought and principles underlying the long-

---

[1] Benjamin Franklin to Lovell, July 22, 1778, *The Revolutionary Diplomatic Correspondence of the United States*, ed. Francis Wharton (Washington, D.C.: U.S. Superintendent of Documents, 1889), II, 658–59.

[2] John Adams to Genêt, May 17, 1780, *ibid.*, III, 687.

established practices of diplomacy. Despite the loyalties of a broad segment of the people to revolutionary concepts of politics and diplomacy, their leaders sensed, as they turned from protest to responsibility, that diplomacy was seldom a job alone for spokesmen of independence, amiable businessmen living abroad, or talented amateurs with no more than passing interest in foreign policy. The problems of foreign policy would persist and a republican form of government was no guarantee of escape from power politics and war. Alexander Hamilton, in calling for greater preparation for the difficult tasks of diplomacy, argued in *The Federalist*, No. VI:

> Have we not already seen enough of the fallacy and extravagance of those idle theories which have amused us with promises of an exemption from the imperfections, weaknesses and evils incident to society in every shape? Is it not time to awake from the deceitful dream of a golden age, and to adopt as a practical maxim for the direction of our political conduct that we, as well as the other inhabitants of the globe, are yet remote from the happy empire of perfect wisdom and perfect virtue? [3]

The first president, George Washington, during his first administration concentrated attention on domestic issues essential to the founding of a national government. Washington could look back on his first administration as giving content to the internal structure of American government and his second administration as establishing the "proper" constitutional arrangements for the management of foreign policy. The European struggle threatened to embroil the new government in conflict with England and Spain, whose colonies encircled the boundaries of an emergent United States. The United States, as we have seen, was bound both by treaty (1778) and sentiment to a French revolutionary government with possessions in the neighboring West Indies. If France were to call for the fulfillment of the commitment entered into by a revolutionary ally, or if the British blockade of France

---

[3] *The Federalist, op. cit.,* pp. 24–25.

should lead to the intolerable harassment of American trade, the United States could find itself at war under the most threatening and hazardous circumstances. To forestall this unhappy prospect, Washington issued a neutrality proclamation of friendship and impartiality to the several belligerent powers and sent an experienced and trusted envoy, John Jay, to Britain to negotiate more favorable relations. The failure of the controversial Jay Treaty of 1795 to prevent an undeclared war with France or to remove the seeds of conflict that were to result in the War of 1812 with Britain should not obscure its significance for future American diplomacy. It charted the course of American policy for decades to come, contributed specifically to the philosophy of Washington's Farewell Address, and demonstrated the government's resolve to maintain freedom of action even in the face of ideological forces that pulled in the direction of one group of European powers or another. In the Address, Washington was to warn: "Excessive partiality for one foreign nation and excessive dislike of another, cause those whom they actuate to see danger on only one side and serves to veil [sic] the other." It assured at the outset of American history that trained and experienced diplomats and calm and judicious national leaders would play as vital a role in maintaining national security as soldiers or naval leaders.

Hostility to the Jay Treaty extended to open resistance in the House to the appropriation of funds to implement its provisions. The House by opposition to the treaty-making powers ascribed to the President and the Senate may have considered that it was giving expression to popular and revolutionary principles of government, but for Washington its action brought the Constitution "to the brink of a precipice." [4] He did not hesitate, therefore, to throw his great authority and prestige into the balance in support of a national as against a factional view of foreign policy, of a broad and constructive rather than a

---

[4] Washington to Charles Carroll, May 1, 1796, *The Revolutionary Diplomatic Correspondence of the United States, op. cit.*, XXV, 30.

partisan spirit, and of a certain restraint and judiciousness in undertaking permanent as against temporary, artificial as against natural, and ideological as against political connections. For the future such an approach puts a high premium on discretion and judgment by men engaged full time in distinguishing the essential interests of their own states and those of others. The most enduring legacy of Washington's second administration and his living "political testament," the Farewell Address, provided the basis for a national approach to diplomacy.

The national outlook of American diplomacy spanning party and factional strife is reflected in the design and staffing of the principal organ of government charged with foreign affairs. The Department of State, which followed the Department of Foreign Affairs under the Confederation, was the first of the executive departments formed under the Constitution. Its authority was early extended, enabling it to serve as the keeper of the Great Seal and of the acts and records of the Congress. Its prestige is reflected in the fact that, of the first forty-two secretaries of state, six went on to become presidents of the United States. Their devotion to the peaceful settlement of disputes is perhaps symbolized by the attitude of the Secretary for Foreign Affairs of the Continental Congress, Robert R. Livingston of New York. Although Livingston was appointed along with Thomas Jefferson, John Adams, Benjamin Franklin, and Roger Sherman to draft the Declaration of Independence, his hope for a reconciliation with Great Britain went so deep that he did not favor immediate independence. His successor, John Jay, was similarly one of the last to be convinced that the colonies must be separated from the British. Both secretaries were so profoundly committed to conciliation that they favored testing to the limit the resourcefulness of the responsible executive department in the interests of peace. They contributed to the shaping of diplomatic practice in other ways. Livingston opposed the "militia diplomacy" whereby members of Congress fearful of "executivism" negotiated directly with the Minister of France; Jay opposed the policy of sending correspondence directly to the president of the Congress. Livingston urged American representatives abroad to send him directly frequent and detailed reports of political and economic developments—in an era in which six weeks to nine months were required for dispatches to reach Europe. The lasting contribution of Livingston and Jay in the preconstitutional era was to demonstrate the need for effective executive powers in foreign policy and diplomacy. Their experience laid the basis for the creation of a Department of State, and for a secretary with powers "intrusted to him by the President . . . agreeable to the Constitution, relative to correspondence, commissions, or instructions, to or with public ministers or consuls, from the United States, or to negotiations with public ministers from foreign states . . . or to such other matters respecting foreign affairs as the President of the United States shall assign to the said department. . . ." [5] During this era the powers of the President and his principal appointive officer in foreign policy were recognized and Jay's efforts toward this end were more significant than his successes as a diplomatist.

George Washington in appointing the first formally accredited Secretary of State under the Constitution turned to Thomas Jefferson with his five years of practical experience in European diplomacy and well-deserved renown as national independence and state leader. He combined a residual faith in revolutionary principles of the rights of man with a growing awareness that Europe's quarrels and the maintenance of an equilibrium of power abroad were to America's advantage. In the end, he was to ask whether the alignment of European powers and American relations to them were not more vital to security than efforts at national preparedness.

There was no question in Jefferson's mind that France, hav-

---

[5] Section One of the Act of Congress of July 27, 1789, creating the Department of State.

ing spent her energy in war and given support in peace to the new American nation, was a more trustworthy ally than Britain. When foes of Jefferson answered that gratitude to France was no basis for policy, he replied: "To say . . . that gratitude is never to enter into the motives of national conduct, is to revive a principle which has been buried for centuries with its kindred principles of the lawfulness of assassination, poison, perjury, etc." [6] In this he expressed a philosophy more in keeping with revolutionary times than the most pressing demands of early American foreign policy.

Beginning in his first administration, President Washington had recourse to a diplomatic technique that persists to the present day. He sent his personal representative, Gouverneur Morris, to Great Britain to explore the attitude of the Foreign Office to the new republic, toward the remaining outposts of British occupied territory, and to the possibility of a treaty of commerce and prospects for an exchange of ministers. Morris found the British amiable and full of good will but vague and evasive on any treaty arrangement. He discovered that British willingness to discuss occupied posts bore a direct relation to the intensity of her struggle with Spain. Incidentally, Morris between 1795–1799 regularly furnished the British Foreign Office with a digest of his European impressions—an unlikely function for the present American Ambassador to the Court of St. James. Yet his efforts were nullified by his own truculence and the British reluctance to modify an unsatisfactory state of affairs. Jefferson chose to report to the Congress on the failure of Morris' mission in December 1790, and, stimulated no doubt by his Francophile viewpoint, to launch a campaign for discrimination against British commerce and trade intended to bring them to their senses. This issue pitted Alexander Hamilton and the Federalists against Jefferson and the Republican-Democratic party; it gave fuel to the underlying con-

[6] Writings of Thomas Jefferson, ed. P. L. Ford (New York, 1892–99), V, 111.

stitutional debate over a stronger or weaker central government. And it confronted the Secretary of State with a strongly
pro-British opposition, who in Hamilton's case let it be known
that he personally would be pleased to transmit important exchanges from the British direct to President Washington. Consequently, when the first British Minister, George Hammond,
charged in 1792 that the states were obstructing the payment
of British creditors, Secretary Jefferson issued a powerful
denial in what may have been his greatest state paper. Hammond turned immediately to the Secretary of the Treasury,
who led the British minister to believe that Jefferson was not
speaking for the administration. The effect that Jefferson's
memorandum might have had was lost and with it the chance
of bringing a change in British policy toward the new republic.
This encroachment on the perogatives of the Secretary of
State was a factor in his subsequently leaving office, and it
demonstrated the importance within a national government of
locating responsibility and of a single acknowledged channel
of diplomatic communication. The difficulties in achieving this
are illustrated by the fact that Jefferson himself, despite his
unhappy experience with Hamilton, was to advise Citizen Genêt
in the early months of his mission on the political winds at
work within the American government. That neither government could accept the relationship of an envoy to the people or
a party group is suggested by the words of Genêt's superiors
reminding him of his instructions "to treat with the government
of the United States, not with a portion of the people. . . ."

Jefferson, with all his intellectual versatility and his wide
experience abroad as Secretary of State, did not resolve any
of the weighty problems of his day, whether the securing of
American territory from British or Spanish outposts or the
negotiating of treaties of commerce and trade with either
"great power." His loyalty to the goals, if not as faithfully the
practice, of the French Revolution never stampeded him into
open involvement in European struggles, but it did set him
apart from Hamilton. The calm wisdom and sage judgment of

George Washington prompted the rival leaders to seek and hold a place in the government, and the President's good judgment enabled him to draw on their talents without being misled by their errors. While remaining in the background and leaving to his secretary and envoys the complexities of day-by-day affairs, Washington molded and shaped the affairs of state. The secretary and not the President conducted negotiations with foreign ministers. In the words of Jefferson's successor, Edmund Randolph, it was "fixed usage for the Secretaries of State to seek conversations, or to continue them, with . . . every . . . diplomatic resident." [7] At the same time, Washington continued to call on the experience and resourcefulness of special envoys like Chief Justice John Jay. More often than not the secretary of state claimed the President's envoy as his choice, partly to retain a measure of control over whatever distinguished figure went abroad to negotiate American interests. Significantly, in one of Jay's missions, both Randolph and Hamilton presented to Washington drafts of possible instructions, reflecting the struggle going on within the government. Yet it was the President who arbitrated and acted and set the nation on a steady course.

Those who today in other new nations are laboring to create the basic machinery for an effective diplomacy may discover common experiences in the early developments in the American Republic—the striving for a national outlook, the search for machinery essential to the wise management of policy at home and successful representation abroad, the marriage of revolutionary ideals with response to practical necessities, the fixing of responsibility within a living Constitution, the building of consensus behind the necessary executive powers, the attempts by political factions to sway the President, the harnessing and harmonizing of varied and divergent talents within a common national approach, and the choice of selected national capitals with whom continuous relations were decisive. In the manner

[7] Quoted in *The American Secretaries of State and Their Diplomacy,* ed. Samuel Flagg Bemis (New York: Pageant Book Company, 1958), II, 108.

that, say, Tanganyika today must choose—balancing resources and interests—a limited number of embassies abroad, the major American effort was concentrated in Great Britain, France, and Spain, and to a lesser extent Portugal and the Netherlands. Many of the problems of procedure and authority that continue to plague more mature governments raised their heads. Jay, when negotiating the famous treaty that bears his name, corresponded directly with Washington and Hamilton, although he addressed and received a flow of formal notes from Secretary of State Randolph. These early years raise all the classic issues regarding the management of foreign affairs. What should we think of diplomatic arrangements in which an envoy's binding instructions are not known to his titular superior? This question was to recur in other chapters of our history. So would the issue of the sympathy and affection of envoys abroad: Jay for the British, and Monroe and Jefferson for the French. What are the limits of affection for the peoples in whose midst an envoy labors and works? What should the President do when his secretary aligns himself too fervently with one or another nation? How does the chief executive seek what is best for the nation within the welter of conflicting ambitions and partisan pressures?

These were basic problems that faced the Republic at birth. It undertook to meet them with diplomatic machinery that even to the contemporary leaders of new nations must seem incredibly sparse. Livingston succeeded in organizing a department for external affairs and training four assistants. Jay's office comprised two rooms, one a parlor and the other a workshop for the secretary and two clerks—enough of a staff to assure that one clerk would be available while the other went to lunch. When Jefferson on relinquishing his office summarized its routine business, he noted that the total expenses of maintaining his office were $9,661.67. By 1799, at the appointment of Timothy Pickering, the payroll of the department had increased to $9,800, the staff numbered six clerks and one messenger, and the only library resources were the texts of a few international lawyers like Vattel. It must, of course, be added that in these same years the national government had virtually no military force under its direct control. Its tiny army was spread out on the western frontier; its little navy was not yet prepared for active service. Thus both the political and military arms of the nation's organization for foreign relations were more symbolic than real, but its problems were also limited by comparison with any future standard.

Yet all through the founding period of the Republic, it is true that relations with other states were continuous. If Washington's Farewell Address is read as proscribing international relations, it runs in the face of the practice of his administration. The new government faced a congeries of problems involving territorial integrity, neutral rights, property compensation, indemnities, seizures, contraband goods, diplomatic immunities, and treaty negotiations. Nor did Washington flinch from the severest test of a foreign policy: preparedness to go to war as the best deterrent against war. In urging a program of national armaments in his final address to the Congress on December 7, 1796, he declared: "To secure respect to a neutral flag requires a naval force. . . . This may even prevent the necessity of going to war, by discouraging belligerent powers from committing such violations of the rights of the neutral party as may, first or last, leave no other option." [8] Washington and his successors were sensitive to the risk that partisan rancor and factional strife might plunge the fledgling state into war. They walked the knife-edge separating peace from war in an atmosphere of intense ideological rivalry that divided the nation not only into factions and parties but left succeeding governments disunited within themselves. Secretary John Marshall spoke of the wild and unreasonable construction which certain diplomatic commissioners brought to their task. There is evidence that a secretary of state was likely to be pro-French or pro-English or Jeffersonian or

[8] Quoted in *ibid.*, p. 208.

Hamiltonian, thus coloring his approach to negotiations. When the capital was moved from Philadelphia to Washington, we are told that the humid and malarial climate was less a deterrent to a calm and temperate view than the climate of opinion with its ominous portent of a deep schism in society. Political cleavage was a factor determining the outlook of President John Adams toward the cabinet inherited from George Washington, of which he wrote: "I had all the officers [Cabinet] and half the crew always ready to throw me overboard." [9] The mood of the day prompted a secretary of state to warn his secretary of legation in London:

When in the correspondence from this office, the feelings and resentments of the people of the United States are expressed in warm and indignant language, it is by no means intended that the language of such letters should be used in addressing a foreign court.[10]

He urged that passionate words yield "to mild language and firm but respectful representations; and always, where peace and friendship are the objects of pursuit, words as well as actions must be conciliatory." [11] Although the author of this advice is not famed for his diplomatic successes, Secretary Pickering's suggestions can hardly be improved upon as a rule of diplomatic behavior. His words were addressed to a day when powerful sympathies for or against the French Revolution tended to override stable judgments. Substitute communism or crusading nationalism for this early revolutionary creed, and his counsel is as fresh and contemporary as the latest essay on the pursuit of peace in the cold war.

A final word on presidential leadership in diplomacy may be in order. Not by accident, the Farewell Address is quoted as the one great "political testament" of the President on foreign policy. When Secretary Pickering urged at the height of the debate over the Jay Treaty that President Washington

[9] Quoted in *ibid.*, p. 247.
[10] Quoted in *ibid.*, p. 186.
[11] *Ibid.*

should make "a solemn, public declaration . . . of the principles of his administration . . . appealing to the train of
actions which marked his whole life . . . ," [12] this approach
was rejected as ill-befitting the dignity of the highest executive
office. John Jay objected on grounds that: "It appears to me
to be a good general rule that the President should very rarely
come forward. . . ." [13] The viewpoint that prevailed conceived the presidency as above party strife, functioning more
or less ceremonially as a king or monarch. This conception
of the presidency as little more than a nominal office gave
freedom to individual cabinet members to follow their own
consciences and politics. The Constitution had been silent
except to say that the President enjoyed the authority to "require the opinion, in writing, of the principal officer in each
of the executive departments, upon any subject relating to the
duties of their respective offices." It remained for a later period
to establish the rule that the head of an executive department
must give loyal support to the President's policies or else
resign. President John Adams in his brief period with a cabinet
inherited from Washington recognized this need, yet the dis-
tance that separates the present view of responsible executive
leadership from that of the past is illustrated by his willingness to launch his administration with his predecessor's cabinet.

What endures from this early American experience are certain perennial truths. The first is the importance a nation must
give to the organization of the government for foreign policy.
Within the meaning of the Constitution, it is the President and
his appointed officer, the secretary of state, who are responsible, and they can ill afford to suffer interlopers. The early
years of American history offer no defense of personal diplomacy, for contacts with the chief executives of other nations
awaited the technological revolution. They do support the
maxim that other executive officers must never be in doubt as
to who is the President and who the secretary of state. They

[12] Quoted in *ibid.*, p. 177.
[13] *Ibid.*

also make clear that those who defend freedom and are the children of independence are themselves subject to "general principles" and the "great rules of conduct" familiar to states through the ages. These are the facts of geography and of the endless striving for power and influence among sovereign states with which responsible nations must learn to live. Nor are democracies immune from the passions that lead to war, for as Hamilton argued: "There have been . . . almost as many popular as royal wars." [14] Washington, in counsel to the American people of "an old and affectionate friend," asked only that his words might "controul the usual currents of the passions . . . moderate the fury of party spirit . . . [and] guard against the Impostures of pretended patriotism." He warned that were the passions to govern, "real patriots, who may resist the intriegues of the favourite, are liable to become suspected and odious; while its tools and dupes usurp the applause and confidence of the people, to surrender their interests." A nation that remained united as one people, identifying and safeguarding its interests without abandoning its national goals, would be one in which diplomats serve the executive in accordance with their organic and appropriate purpose. When the goal of a nation is to achieve freedom of action with the issue of entangling relations to be determined on its merits in every case, the diplomat's role becomes more varied—if more essential—for all its complexity of professional skills. An agrarian democracy, our security depended on the freedom to complete our nationhood and by eschewing entangling alliances abroad gradually to eliminate foreign threats on this continent. The general rules that guided our diplomats arose from the facts of the case and from the luminous thought and action of a generation of political leaders who, whatever their differences, subscribed to a common philosophy, accepted the same moral code, understood men's motives in pursuing evil and virtue, and adhered to the republican theory of government. With the

---

[14] *The Federalist, op. cit.*, p. 24.

outbreak of the French Revolution, both Jefferson, who remained devoted to the French, and Hamilton, who was drawn to the British, agreed that the Republic should follow a neutral course, although Jefferson preferred a more benevolent neutrality toward the French struggle for the "rights of man." What united eighteenth century Americans and Europeans alike was a mentality that provided a workable framework for diplomacy in the late eighteenth and early nineteenth centuries as the policies of a fledgling nation unfolded.

2. Parliamentary Diplomacy in the
Mid-Twentieth Century

A century and a half and vast intellectual and political changes separate present-day diplomacy from that of George Washington, Thomas Jefferson, and John Jay. During this period more than two thousand ambassadors and lesser diplomatic officials have served their country abroad. While the budget of the Department of State at the beginning of the nineteenth century fell below $10,000, by 1929 it was approaching $10,000,000, and by 1961 it had reached $300,000,000—a 30,000-fold increase in a century and a half. The sum total of foreign aid from appropriated moneys since the end of World War II amounted to the staggering total of $84,000,000,000. The President has become his nation's chief diplomatic leader and the archprotector of the peace. The burdens of the presidency have expanded far beyond those that impelled Woodrow Wilson to say: "Men of ordinary physique and discretion cannot be Presidents and live, if the strain be not somehow relieved." Despite the fears and unrest of some American citizens that the United States would flounder and fall before totalitarian onslaughts because of presidential limitations and restraints, his capacities have proven sufficient to the task. The judgment of the President's Committee on Administrative Management in 1937 has been vindicated because history has shown that the presidency "stands across the path of those who mistakenly assert that democracy must fail because it can neither decide promptly nor act vigorously." The chief requirements of effective diplomacy—secrecy, dispatch, unity, representation, continuity, and access to information—lodge the conduct of foreign affairs ever more in the President's hands.

Moreover, the President's functions have spread to new and significant fields. His duties continue to center in the appointment of diplomatic representatives abroad, adjustment and reduction of tariff barriers, recognition of new governments and nations, communication with foreign powers, and "negotiation" of treaties and executive agreements. Beyond this, it is the President who must welcome and receive visiting executives and chiefs of state, address the General Assembly symbolizing support of the United Nations, and join in "little" and full-dress summit meetings with friendly, neutral, and rival heads of state. Read the collected speeches of recent American presidents, study their appointment calendars and briefing sessions, and review their correspondence, and the preponderance of efforts in international diplomacy becomes clear. In wartime he has the responsibility, in Lincoln's words, to take "any measure which may best subdue the enemy," and, in a world in which peacetime merges imperceptibly with strategies of warfare, he decides whether or not to develop thermonuclear weapons; whether, when, and where to use them; and whether or when to press the button launching a global war.

Yet it is a measure of the profound changes in American diplomacy that these far-reaching developments in presidential power are matched by the novel, revolutionary and worldwide institutionalizing of diplomacy. Parliamentary diplomacy was best described with characteristic clarity by Secretary of State Dean Rusk five years before assuming his present office:

What might be called parliamentary diplomacy is a type of multilateral negotiation which involves at least four factors: First, a continuing organization with interest and responsibilities which are broader than the specific items that happen to appear upon the agenda at any particular time—in other words, more than a traditional international conference called to cover specific agenda. Second, regular public debate exposed to the media of mass communication and in touch, therefore, with public opinions around the globe. Third, rules of procedure which govern the process of debate and which are themselves subject to tactical manipulation to advance or oppose a point of view. And lastly, formal conclusions, ordinarily expressed in resolution, which are reached by majority votes of some description, on a simple or two-thirds majority or based upon a financial contribution or economic stake—some with and some without a veto. Typically, we are talking about the United Nations and its related organizations, although not exclusively so, because the same type of organization is growing up in other parts of the international scene.[15]

The United Nations by now is a continuing organization with more than one hundred members including—by contrast to its predecessor, the League of Nations—all but a handful of the most important nation-states. Its existence dictates that a majority of foreign offices conduct a significant fraction of their international business within the United Nations framework. The smallest of the new states may in fact at particular moments have as many officials at work in United Nations organs and agencies as serve their governments in foreign ministries at home. Beyond this, countries like the United States annually participate in 350 to 400 international conferences with delegates instructed by their government on a long list of agenda items. In the setting of international conferences, the representative must practice the arts of both the negotiator and parliamentarian. The necessity of combining them has forced states to reconsider the qualities of their diplomats. For the Greeks, the gift of rhetoric was included among the attributes of the ideal diplomat, but with modern history this requirement largely disappeared. With the birth of parliamentary diplomacy, in Sir Harold Nicolson's tart phrase, it resumed "its clumsy place among the arts of negotiation." [16]

I would suggest with respect to public diplomacy that three distinctions must be made. First, if by rhetoric we mean "fine language without conviction," Nicolson's stricture is doubtless controlling. Yet are there not times when a diplomat by the

[15] Dean Rusk, "Parliamentary Diplomacy—Debate *vs.* Negotiation," *World Affairs Interpreter*, XXVI, No. 2 (Summer 1955), 121–22.
[16] Harold Nicolson, *The Evolution of Diplomatic Method* (New York: The Macmillan Co., 1954), p. 65.

clarity of his remarks and his evident sincerity moves fellow negotiators to accept his viewpoint? Surely we can point to such instances in "quiet" diplomacy as in Judge Philip C. Jessup's example: "I have witnessed a Secretary of State of the United States in most confidential session with a large cabinet group of a friendly power thus turn antagonism into friendliness and misunderstanding into accord." [17] John Foster Dulles observed: "The United States delegation has almost always modified its initial position after hearing the point of view of other delegations. The same can be said of most delegations." [18] Since the aim of negotiations is to harmonize the varied interests of states, evidently this requires logic and precision of thought if the reciprocal advantages of the parties are to be established. Yet threats, menaces, invective, and provocation will rarely serve this goal and the public spokesman is all too readily the victim of those techniques. Today no less than in the days of Jules Cambon: ". . . the best instrument at the disposal of a Government wishing to persuade another Government will always remain the spoken words of a decent man." [19]

Secondly, the strident and raucous exchange that marks the debate between Communist and other diplomats within international forums may excite patriotism without providing a reasonable alternative to diplomacy. Communists approach international negotiations with the grand assurance of men carried along by the dialectic of history. The open forum of the United Nations becomes a sounding board for missions and crusades. Their affirmations of faith may be more fervent in the halls of international conferences than in the suite of a rival negotiator. Of the Communists, Nicolson writes: "Their activity in foreign countries or at international conferences is formidable, disturbing, compulsive." [20] No one can afford

---

[17] Philip C. Jessup, "Parliamentary Diplomacy," *Recueil des Cours*, Academie de Droit International, I (1956), 235.

[18] *Vital Speeches of the Day*, May 15, 1949, p. 465.

[19] Quoted in Nicolson, *op. cit.*, p. 84.

[20] *Ibid.*, p. 90.

to underestimate Communist potency or danger. But neither should it be confused with diplomacy, as Premier Khrushchev learned to his dismay.

Third, those who mistake forensic propaganda for the sum total of United Nations diplomacy are in error. Parliamentary shenanigans conceal more than meets the eye. Today's international parliamentarians include men who are genuinely professional in debate and maneuver; they have mastered the rules of procedure to serve diplomatic ends. Moreover, it is broadly true that the majority of delegates are capable of distinguishing between sincerity and bombast, devotion to the Charter and pure opportunism. Leadership in multilateral diplomacy comes to the top; character is not extinguished even in harsh international debate. The General Debate and the days that follow are a time for placing before the world community the issues of greatest concern to the national interest. Painful and protracted as these statements may seem, and oftentimes tailored to the world press or an audience back home, they are the tribute men pay to their prime loyalty to the sovereign state. Yet, however responsive national leaders must be to their parochial interests, they have found that "you cannot secure the sympathetic support of the General Assembly by ignoring moral values." [21] No responsible delegate is likely to mock the high principles of the United Nations within its walls—and if he does, like the Asian diplomat who spoke of the Charter as a mass of words, he will probably amend his statement the following day.

The parliamentary forms and continuing organization of the United Nations have led to another hopeful and important development. I have suggested earlier that the moral and political consensus which linked the rulers of eighteenth century states has been gravely weakened in our day. The moral cleavage between East and West or North and South is a fact with which we must learn to live. Only the naïve or the dupes

[21] Jessup, *op. cit.*, p. 56.

expect these profound differences to erode overnight, and yet we may each of us help to remove those that rest on myth and illusion. Massive and glacial movements are after all the result of countless small shifts of particles, whether of mind or matter.

One major criticism of the itinerant international congresses of the twentieth century has been that continuous, confidential, and informed negotiations were impossible. By contrast, the traditional ambassador in a foreign capital enjoyed numerous local assets. He knew the people with whom he was expected to negotiate; was able to assess local interests, personalities, and events; could confer with the host country's foreign minister on a courteous, routine, and undramatic basis; and felt secure in interrupting and then resuming discussions without thereby dashing popular hope or arousing public clamor. In negotiations, the inevitable stages of disappointment and delay mixed with progress and understanding seldom if ever became matters of public controversy. The results and not the stages were the object of public scrutiny. Envoys had faith that confidence would not be betrayed or indiscretions committed. Negotiations were a process and not an episode conducted by a corps of professionals who shared common values, standards, and rules of the game.

The United Nations family has become a latter-day approximation of this earlier corps of diplomatists. The family is, of course, divided within itself. Yet its solidarity exists despite a pervasive disunity made tolerable by the principles of the Charter. This clash between the forces of unity and disunity is seemingly endless. Thus if the philosophy of the Charter pays tribute to freedom, respect for individual rights, and the consent of the governed, many of the peoples living under it are drawn to authoritarianism, submission to native tyrants, and the achievement of mass security and rapid economic development by means of drastically thoroughgoing state controls. New states find they require a firmer social and political discipline if they are to avoid economic and social disintegration. The problem is broader than communism. For some, anti-Americanism is the strongest unifying tie—stronger even than the Charter with its happy identity of Articles 1 and 2 and the Declaration of Independence. Yet no matter how profound and divisive the forces of national antagonism and of conflicting political philosophies, the common interest of members of national delegations, the Secretariat, and top-ranking visitors also exists. At the opening of each session of the General Assembly, ties of camaraderie unite "old friends, old enemies, all old colleagues." The bonds are not those of an ancient diplomatic elite—common language, class, and purpose—but for that reason perhaps more in keeping with the present age.

A decade and a half of experience with a world institution enables the observer to say that the restoration of some measure of consensus among men and states is under way. The struggle of community with disunity has been joined. It rests on the hope that when men work side by side, their personal friendships may help to override national differences. Edmund Burke in another era explained: "When men are not acquainted with each other's principles, not experienced in each other's talents, nor at all practiced in their mutual habitudes and dispositions by joint efforts of business; no personal confidence, no friendship, no common interest subsisting among them; it is evidently impossible that they can act a public part with uniformity, perserverance or efficacy." [22] The United Nations with its continuing organization shows signs of creating this nexus of common interests. Within its chambers, "one observes—as indeed one does so frequently in many national legislative assemblies—public denunciation and private rapprochement; speeches for the record and a quiet word for the ultimate objective." [23] Disunity in theory may be matched by unity in action—as in the rallying of United Nations members to the struggle in Korea or the common task in the Congo.

[22] Quoted in Jessup, *op cit.,* p. 237.
[23] Jessup, *op. cit.,* p. 237.

Yet this community is unlikely to grow and flourish if its sole foundations are open parliamentary debate. The test of the parliamentary approach internationally differs significantly from the measure of its success nationally. Within an organized national society, the test is lawmaking and legislation; on the world stage, the purpose is peacemaking. To assert this detracts not a whit from the search for orderly rules of procedure that are binding on the members. An international body that is more than a collection of negotiators takes on a corporate character. It resolves important questions concerning voting procedures, the role of its presiding officer, and acceptable techniques for the handling of disputes. Agreement on the rules may reduce the impact of powerful national emotions and keep to a minimum unnecessary disagreements. The constitutional practice of the United Nations and its rules of the game are probably at a crucial phase of growth or decline when the limits of majority action are unclear and the habit of majority decision still comparatively new. Parliamentary procedures "should be calculated to promote a maximum of negotiation and agreement in international discussions as contrasted with a sterile majority vote achieved by parliamentary maneuver but ineffective in practice. . . ." [24]

The late Secretary-General Dag Hammarskjold sensed this more keenly than many of his contemporaries. In a speech at Ohio University in 1958 he explained:

since the legislative processes of the United Nations do not lead to legislation, and the power of decision remains in the hands of the national government, the value of public debate can be measured only by the degree to which it contributes to the winning of agreement by the processes of diplomacy. If public debate contributes to winning consent either immediately or in the long run, it serves the purpose of peace-making. If it does not so contribute, then it may be a useless, or even harmful exercise. [25]

[24] Wilfred Jenks, "Craftsmanship in International Law," *American Journal of International Law*, L (1956), 54.

[25] Address by Dag Hammerskjold, Secretary-General of the United Nations, at Ohio University, Athens, Ohio, February 5, 1958.

If public debate sometimes serves the cause of peacemaking, it can as readily be slanted for home consumption or for waging the propaganda war. A parliamentary triumph in a national legislature leads to decisions that carry the force of law. A voting victory in the United Nations leads at best to recommendations without the force of law and at worst to a steadily declining consensus between the powers opposing one another in parliamentary debate. Dean Rusk has noted: "Success in the conduct of our foreign affairs is to be measured not in tally sheets, but by issues satisfactorily resolved, friendships consolidated, rivalries reduced or circumscribed." [26]

"It is diplomacy, not speeches and votes, that continues to have the last word in the process of peace-making." [27] In 1954, provisional settlements were reached on the Iranian, Suez, and Trieste problems, and at some stage along the way the United Nations was involved in all three. Is it crucial that the United Nations was not in on the final stages? This standard may lead to new uses of parliamentary machinery not envisaged by its framers. It calls to mind the skillful use of committees of rapporteurs under the League of Nations and the functions of the Council of Four at the Paris Peace Conference. In the late Secretary-General's words: "I think the experiences of the past twelve years have demonstrated that there is need to redress the balance between public and private procedures of the United Nations." [28] Perhaps historians will find that Mr. Hammarskjold's most enduring efforts were as innovator blending the two procedures. In this he reflected the Charter which requires prior obligation to pursue other means before bringing an issue before the United Nations (Art. 33, Par. 1). It was he who gave dignity to "quiet diplomacy" within a United Nations framework and practiced it himself with consummate skill. He preferred confidential dealings with leaders and would have accepted Dean Rusk's pungent phrase: "There is

[26] Rusk, *op. cit.,* p. 137.
[27] Hammarskjold, *op. cit.*
[28] *Ibid.*

utility in tedium, and I suspect that we could use more of it in the conduct of our foreign policy." [29] Among public officials, he had the courage to proclaim to those who viewed open diplomacy too simply: "The best results of negotiation between two parties cannot be achieved in international life, any more than in our private worlds, in the full glare of publicity with current public debate of all moves, unavoidable misunderstandings, inescapable freezing of position due to considerations of prestige, and the temptation to utilize public opinion as an element integrated in the negotiation itself." [30] What is called for is a proper perspective between secrecy in deliberations and publicity in results. It is essential that debate and voting follow careful advance preparation through available channels of negotiations. Without this it may be unproductive and even dangerous. Open diplomacy is often the last phase of negotiations.

The Secretary-General as the symbol of an international body preserving objectivity and neutrality in the great struggle is peculiarly well qualified for quiet diplomacy. In Mr. Hammarskjold's words: "He is in a position of trust vis-à-vis all the member governments. He speaks for no government. . . . He can never give away what must be considered the property of the government with whom he is working." [31] He has at his command subtle resources of power and prestige deriving in part from past successes in implementing U.N. resolutions. He and his staff keep watch over the peace 365 days of the year. He consults with permanent missions when major U.N. organs are not in session and is more continually on hand than others who serve the continuing organization. By deft reporting or a helpful remark, he can guide the negotiations of others, for as Mr. Hammarskjold once remarked: "A car can often be driven by only a light touch of the wheel."

The deep conflicts and the limits of consensus within the

[29] Rusk, *op. cit.*
[30] Hammarskjold, *op. cit.*
[31] *Ibid.*

United Nations not infrequently impel the chief bodies of the United Nations to pass broad and general resolutions calling on the secretary-general to act but providing him with few guidelines for action. The vagueness of his directives may reflect the lowest common denominator of agreement attainable for states torn by dissension or at times the bypassing of a broad area in which compromise had proven impossible. Sometimes member states prefer to escape responsibility and other times they prefer to provide the U.N. executive with the authority for urgent and necessary action—"Let Dag do it!"

From the standpoint of diplomatic techniques, the secretary-general seeks to respond through a variety of techniques. Particularly noteworthy are the advisory committees to the secretary-general whose members meet with him in private, contributing day-by-day advice on delicate problems in which they possess a vital stake and helping him to carry out his mandate. No votes are taken, but while the committee members reflect their governments' views, they show independence in discussing practical issues of the moment. Members remain in touch with their governments on details of the meetings and thus provide the secretary-general with a more secure sense that his policy is "on the rails." The secretary-general as the presiding officer guides the discussions and rallies the judgments of participating states. The Advisory Committee on Peaceful Uses of Atomic Energy is a body of seven outstanding nuclear scientists sitting as government representatives of the three major atomic powers, the U.K., U.S.S.R. and the U.S.A. Its work has paved the way for constructive agreements despite barriers of the cold war. Of the Advisory Committee on the United Nations Emergency Force in the Near East made up of smaller member states, most of whom have supplied troops to UNEF, Mr. Hammarskjold had written:

> Its work is an example of the practical value in the United Nations of a formal instrument of private diplomacy in carrying forward action once the main policy lines have been laid down by a decision of

the General Assembly. That decision, in turn, was made by the General Assembly in the public proceedings of parliamentary diplomacy only after the informal procedures of private classical diplomacy had done their work. Thus, this case is also an example of a kind of three-stage operation which is natural in the United Nations and which is capable of yielding constructive results . . . private diplomacy preceding public debate and then employed again to follow through.[32]

The Advisory Committee on the Congo met with the Secretary-General on more than fifty occasions for discussions lasting on the average of three hours. In a series of complicated and difficult meetings following the Security Council resolution of February 21, 1961, representatives of member governments who were deeply divided on the issues nevertheless in discussion enabled Mr. Hammarskjold to formulate a consensus of views, to which members might dissent, that furnished a basis for his policy in the Congo. An earlier Advisory Committee of Foreign Ministers concerned in October 1956 with the impending Suez crisis succeeded in informal and private negotiations in reaching unanimous agreement on the six principles essential to any settlement of the Suez crisis—principles that proved their worth even after fighting had broken out.

Taken together, the work of these advisory committees illustrates the resources for private diplomacy that exist in the United Nations. Their success underlies the proposal of a wise U.N. diplomatist: "Classical diplomacy continues to be usefully practiced in the old tradition on a bilateral basis. But more of it is needed now in the practices of the United Nations if we are to develop to the full the capacity of the Organization. . . ." [33] Beyond this, the U.N. may provide from time to time the one common meeting place for ambassadors and foreign ministers from more than one hundred countries. The opening of the General Assembly may even allow heads of state to contact one another for private, off-the-record talks.

[32] *Ibid.*
[33] *Ibid.*

Their physical presence in New York gives a unique opportunity for the continuing exercise of private diplomacy without the fanfare of public diplomacy or the formal procedures of "summit" diplomacy. The presence of Foreign Minister Gromyko in New York in the autumn of 1961 enabled Secretary of State Dean Rusk and President John F. Kennedy to engage him in exploratory talks on the Berlin crisis—an approach that was wholly consistent with Mr. Hammarskjold's view of parliamentary diplomacy.

Other forms and combinations of classical and parliamentary diplomacy are suggested by the Japanese Peace Conference of 1951. Following ten months of preparatory consultation, negotiation, and drafting, a treaty was sent to fifty-two interested states by the host governments, the United States and the United Kingdom. The invitation to meet in San Francisco in September 1951 stipulated that the conference would be for the purpose of signing the text of the treaty to be revised in accordance with comments from invited states sent three weeks before the meeting. The preparatory consultation and negotiations were interpreted as replacing substantive discussion at the conference and at the first plenary session, the temporary president, Secretary of State Dean Acheson, explained that since "the treaty had been negotiated by diplomatic rather than conference methods," each government was free to make a historic record of its views prior to signing. Because the treaty had been based on the broadest negotiations with large, small, and middle powers, forty-nine delegates, excluding only the Soviet, Polish, and Czech representatives, signed the accord. It remains a classic instance of a flexible approach to diplomatic method.

Underlying the procedures of parliamentary diplomacy are, of course, common interests and purposes expressed in the words of the Charter. As compromise and politics are possible within the American system because of agreement on constitutional ends, the basis of U.N. diplomatic procedure rests squarely upon the Charter. Seen through the eyes of the framers of the Charter, the United Nations is more than an international conference. It embodies historic concepts broader than any single national view concerning the equal rights of men and nations, fundamental freedoms, the creation of conditions under which justice can be preserved, international objectivity and equity, and the outlawry of force except in the common interest. The agents of parliamentary diplomacy, therefore, have a Charter and a "Constitution" to interpret and defend. While this discussion does not center on the ends of international life, we must recognize that parliamentarians live and operate within such a framework.

3. Personal Diplomacy and the Cold War

WINSTON S. CHURCHILL as early as the famed Fulton Speech on March 5, 1946, called for negotiations among the Great Powers, saying: "The supreme hope and the prime endeavor is to reach a good and faithful understanding with Soviet Russia through . . . patient perseverance and resolute endeavor." By proposing talks at the highest level, Mr. Churchill harbored no illusions that by firing men's imaginations or seeking their approval for a decisive solution, he could bring about a prompt ending of the cold war. He was persuaded, however, that free peoples must be convinced that those who lead them do not despair of peace if the nation is to take the measures which self-preservation demands if the worst should come to the worst. On February 14, 1950, at Edinburgh, he declared: "The idea appeals to me of a supreme effort to bridge the gulf between the two worlds, so that each can live their life, if not in friendship, at least without the hatreds and maneuvers of the cold war." Mr. Churchill's belief in the function of direct negotiations goes back to his wartime experiences. In one memorable exchange in the House of Commons, a member was sharply critical of his frequent travel. Sir Arthur Salter of Oxford in a stirring response declared that Churchill's willingness to travel and to meet with Soviet and American leaders had made him the true architect of Allied unity and added: "The oldest of the three, he has been the most mobile. When the President could not be there, he was there with the Marshal; when the Marshal could not be there, he was there with the President; when both were there, he was there too."

Churchill's confidence was born of his wartime discovery that issues that remained hopelessly tangled at the routine bureaucratic level often could be swiftly resolved at higher levels. Time and again in the years following World War II, he complained that the habit of easy and frequent consultation had been broken and allies caught unawares of conflicts that might have been foreseen and resolved. The French have a saying: *Les absents ont toujours tort* ("the absent are always wrong"). When nations have a stake in harmonious relations, it is wholly wrong for any one of them to forswear discussions and negotiations. Prior to the Korean War, the Labor government in England had allowed the machinery for joint military consultation with the Americans to be dissolved and this provoked Mr. Churchill's comment: "Half the misunderstandings which have been so dangerous to Anglo-American relations during the Korean War would, I believe, have been avoided had there been a regular and constant meeting, as there were in the bygone years, between our two Chiefs of Staffs Committees."

Mr. Churchill was convinced that relations had deteriorated and events been allowed to drift partly because conferences were conducted by technicians and subordinates who could hardly permit themselves the close harmony which had prevailed at the highest executive level during World War II. He was mindful that the problems of peace between East and West differed not only in degree but in kind from those of wartime allies. Yet in the first decade of the cold war, he saw three opportunities when peace might have been viewed as a whole and claims and concessions been balanced off against one another. Between 1945 and 1960, he proposed negotiations between East and West on more than forty occasions. On October 6, 1943, he reminded Mr. Anthony Eden: "At a Peace Conference the position can be viewed as a whole, and adjustments in one direction balanced by those in another. There is therefore the greatest need to reserve territorial questions for the general settlement." At a moment in World War II when the Western armies were still in Central Europe, he saw the first opportunity for a lasting settlement with the

Russians. The Western powers had not yet evacuated central and eastern Germany, and the American armies were not demobilized and dispersed. A second historic opportunity lasted until September 1949, when the West enjoyed a decisive advantage in consequence of its atomic monopoly. Third, as late as November 30, 1950, Mr. Churchill announced in the Parliament: "Now I hope that we may come to terms with them before they have so large a stockpile of those fearful agencies, in addition to vast superiority in other weapons, as to be able to terrorize the free world, if not, indeed, to destroy it." Mr. Churchill, in other words, believed that opportunities for a settlement existed in the period during which the United States retained its overall military supremacy—a period that was to end in 1955.

Personal diplomacy, then, is a response to circumstance and experience. It had served as an instrument for resolving conflicts and differences before and during World War II. Lord Hankey had written of the Council of Four (Wilson, Orlando, Clemenceau, and Lloyd George):

The proceedings . . . were quite informal and unhampered by rules or written procedure. These four men . . . were free to conduct the business in the best way they could discover. They all possessed in common the invaluable gift of humor and many a time have I seen a difficult period tided over by some sparkle of wit or the timely interpolation of a good story. . . . An atmosphere of . . . mutual respect was created in which the thorniest questions, where national or other interests appeared to clash almost irreconcilably, could be adjusted.[34]

Leaders dismayed by their failure to reach understandings at lower diplomatic levels returned to this method with the deepening cold war crisis. In Mr. Churchill's words in the House of Commons on May 11, 1953: if "there is not at the summit of the nations the will to win the greatest prize" of peace, where can men look for hope? If leaders are to parlay

[34] Lord Hankey, *Diplomacy by Conference* (New York: G. P. Putnam's Sons, 1946), p. 29.

together, the way must be prepared "by formal diplomatic processes with all their privacy and gravity." This suggests one fundamental difference between Churchill's approach to personal diplomacy and that of his successors in Britain and the United States. Classical methods, in Churchill's view, were never incompatible with the healing forces of personal diplomacy. Only the chief executive and his associates can appraise the time and place of an approach, and no one can judge in advance if a high-level meeting will succeed in removing the barriers to peace. The raw matter on which decisions are based is thrown up by working diplomats. The purposes and objectives of "summitry" vary. On occasion, for example, meetings at the summit may be used to gain time for more effective forms of peaceful relations to evolve even though the prospects for a firm agreement are not favorable.

One form of personal diplomacy within the American system is diplomatic communication with foreign governments and officials by the President. By letter or telegram, telephone or telecom, he may support a move for peace (President Jefferson's exchange with the Czar of Russia during the Napoleonic Wars or President Franklin D. Roosevelt's efforts during the Sudetenland crisis), may invite the establishment of friendly commercial relations (President Fillmore's letter of July 1853 to the Emperor of Japan delivered by Commodore Matthew C. Perry), or may offer mediation or good offices (President Theodore Roosevelt's approaches leading to the Portsmouth Conference of 1905 between Russia and Japan and to the Algeciras Conference between British, French, and German delegates in the Moroccan crisis). President Woodrow Wilson appealed through official and personal letters to most of the wartime leaders, and although presidential communication fell off in the decade after Wilson, President Franklin D. Roosevelt renewed and extended the use of this technique. President Harry S. Truman for the most part preferred more traditional diplomatic channels, but President Dwight D. Eisenhower in successive exchanges with Bulganin, Zhukov, and

Khrushchev engaged in what some have called "Correspondence Diplomacy." After repeated exchanges, President Eisenhower on February 15, 1958, expressed growing doubts as to the value of this approach in his reply to Bulganin: "I begin to wonder . . . whether we shall get anywhere by continuing to write speeches to each other. . . . I cannot avoid the feeling that if our two countries are to move ahead . . . we must find some ways other than mere prolongation of repetitive public debate. . . ." While presidential messages may occasionally pave the way for serious negotiations or may dramatize in time of crisis the gravity of a situation, the limits of this instrument of diplomacy seem clear. Responsible students of diplomacy ask if many of the topics of presidential correspondence are not more appropriately dispatched by foreign ministers or through established diplomatic channels. They question whether the temptation to strive for a favorable judgment at the bar of world opinion may not impair genuine efforts to arrive at mutually acceptable settlement.

While personal diplomacy assumes the direct involvement of the chief executive, he may also employ an alter ego as his personal diplomatic representative abroad. In the first hundred years of the Republic following independence, the President appointed more than four hundred special representatives, reposing in them varying degrees of confidence and trust. The practice has continued into the present with recent appointments including Harry Hopkins, Averell Harriman, George C. Marshall, Philip C. Jessup, John Foster Dulles, Milton Eisenhower, Senator Walter F. George, Harold Stassen, Lucius Clay, John J. McCloy, and Arthur Dean. When a president is convinced that a particular diplomatic activity can be accomplished best outside the normal diplomatic channels by a roving ambassador, personal confidant, trouble-shooter, or special assistant, or prefers that a special agent report directly to him, he has asserted this right under his essential foreign relations powers and provided for it by drawing on the President's contingency fund instead of requesting legislative appropriations. From Gouverneur Morris to Lucius Clay, the Congress, while expressing opinions about given individuals or the proportion of officials freed from senatorial confirmation, has never seriously limited or restricted the President. If the special envoy because of his stature or close ties with the President can sometimes more immediately and directly engage foreign officials, his role can also work a demoralizing effect upon the established diplomatic corps. When a nation's leaders conclude that the one broad avenue to the point of decision in American foreign policy is through the President's personal representatives, this can essentially destroy the value of the ambassador and his colleagues.

The uniqueness and the peculiarities of personal diplomacy may be obscured by speaking only of top-level military conferences or by concentrating too narrowly upon the functions of presidential envoys. To a considerable extent there is nothing unique about these diplomatic or military procedures. The novel feature of personal diplomacy is the immediate and continuous engagement of the principal executive officer who neither through state visits nor summit conferences was actually involved until fairly recent times. Not until the presidency of Theodore Roosevelt had an American president felt able to leave the territorial limits of the Republic; since World War I each successive president save Harding has been abroad during his term of office. No more than thirty top-ranking foreign leaders had visited this country throughout our history up to the end of World War I; since 1939, well over two hundred have found themselves on American soil. Nor is the phenomenon of state visits confined to the United States, for in the eighteen months from January 1955 through July 1956 no fewer than nineteen heads of state and foreign ministers visited New Delhi. During World War II and the postwar era, from the meeting of President Franklin D. Roosevelt and Prime Minister Churchill, aboard the cruiser Augusta off Newfoundland, to the summit conferences inaugurated by Dwight D. Eisenhower, the United States was involved in thirty meetings at the summit, including eighteen involving President Roosevelt, six for President Truman, and six for President Eisenhower. The postwar trend has been unmistakably toward increasing the number of formal and informal, official and unofficial, conferences and visits among chiefs of state, heads of state, and foreign ministers.

A prime factor in the growth of personal diplomacy is the steady increase in the centralization of power, even in nations of widely divergent ideologies. For all states, the dynamics of modern government combine with the methods of modern travel to raise the level of decisions in foreign policy. In relations with the Soviet Union, this demands recognition that: "If you wish to negotiate, you must talk to Mr. Khrushchev." But for others as well, power flows to the top and complex problems call for a stronger executive capable of decisive responses. The trend that Bertrand de Jouvenel calls the "monarchization" of government leads to a persistent upgrading in the titles of negotiators: ambassadors take the place of ministers and first secretaries; foreign ministers fly in by jet to negotiate for ambassadors; and heads of state replace their top appointive foreign ministers.

Another factor providing an impetus to personal diplomacy is the importance of mutual information, particularly in relations with peoples and leaders of a closed society. In his address to the nation on June 6, 1961, following talks with Premier Khrushchev, President John F. Kennedy made only one terse claim: "At least the chances of a dangerous misjudgment on either side should now be less. . . ." The risks of miscalculation touching off a Korean-type conflict are sometimes reduced by discussion at the summit. Or the President, who carries the heaviest of constitutional responsibilities, may be enabled to reach final judgments from a more intimate sense of reality. The opinions adversaries hold of one another may affect decisions. Thus the coldly grim and formidable impression left by General de Gaulle on Khrushchev before the abortive Paris summit meeting in 1960 may have tipped the balance against a Soviet move on Berlin. Or in more positive terms, negotiators may test how far significant changes are taking place in one another's policies. One objective of "summit" diplomacy is a probing operation to measure an adversary's intentions and his interest in equitable solutions. Is there a genuine thaw in cold war relations and a willingness to accept a relaxation of tensions? Does a Communist leader need progress at the summit to bring about liberal reforms within his system? Are the compulsions on both sides sufficient to yield tangible agreements—compulsions like staggering armaments burdens and the growing awareness that should the situation not improve it will almost certainly grow worse? Are there ways through which major leaders confronting one another at the highest level can improve the atmosphere of international relations, reduce apprehensions, and uncover possibilities for cooperation that had not been anticipated?

From Potsdam in 1945 to Geneva in the summer of 1955, no American president engaged in summit diplomacy. With the death of Stalin and the aftermath of the improved relations symbolized by the Austrian Peace Treaty, a series of high-level talks were initiated at Geneva, Camp David (1959), Paris (1960), and Vienna (1961). Despite the apparent relaxing of tensions, the public clamor for negotiations, and the increase in Soviet power toward a position of parity, these confrontations did little to improve relations. If they served to clarify intentions, they assuredly did not yield any miraculous results.

President Eisenhower on returning in December 1959 from travels that carried him over 22,000 miles to eleven countries on three continents explained: "My trip was not undertaken as a feature of normal diplomatic procedures. It was not my purpose either to seek specific agreements or to urge new treaty relationships. My purpose was to improve the climate in which diplomacy might work more successfully." During his administration, Mr. Eisenhower visited twenty-seven nations with what he described as "favorable results far transcending those of normal diplomatic conferences." [35] This statement introduces a philosophy and an approach by which widespread and frequent use of personal diplomacy must stand or fall. It suggests the beginnings of a magic solvent to all the intractable problems by which workaday negotiators are frustrated and perplexed. It assumes that the democracies, by throwing onto the scales the weight of a famous personality, will dissolve the troublesome issues that separate East and West. It imagines that only personal differences lie in the path of international understanding. It contrasts, as Professor Kurt Wimer has pointed out, with President Wilson's use of personal diplomacy to rally support for specific policies and objectives. I would suggest that whatever we believe regarding the bona fides of Soviet objectives, this views our own aims and vital interests—the safeguarding of which has prevented an earlier understanding with the Russians—in too frivolous and light-hearted a vein. It underestimates the risks and hazards of failure in much publicized talks. Where negotiations fail, the layman is tempted to say "a plague on both your houses." Yet whenever issues that divide East and West have yielded to understanding, it has been as a result of long, tedious, and persevering conversations among officials with full powers and ample preparation for their seemingly unending task. In the words of one articulate critic:

A summit conference combines the risk of such misunderstandings as are likely to arise between people who are meeting for the first or second time and have only a few hours in which to discuss weighty and often appalling problems through interpreters, with the most sensational publicity. It is a cross between secret and open diplomacy, and ends by accumulating the drawbacks of both. Either it creates the short-lived allusion of an easing of tension, as at Geneva and Camp David, or it aggravates the antagonism, as in Paris and Vienna.[36]

[35] *The New York Times*, June 28, 1960.
[36] Domenico Bartoli, "Are Summits Necessary?," *NATO Letter*, IX, No. 12 (December 1961), 12.

The arguments against personal diplomacy, then, are tactical, constitutional, procedural and philosophical. Tactically, the defense of personal diplomacy which is grounded on the locus of the power of decision at the top within the Soviet system scarcely resolves the question "where and when and on what issues are Western negotiators most likely to reach a modus vivendi with the Russians?" If participants at the summit possess the authority to settle disputes, they are also capable of deciding that their brief talks have reached a dead end and plunge the whole world into deeper despair. Whether we speak of the climate of world opinion or of more specific points of dispute—which incidentally give form and content to the international atmosphere—the tactical question persists: Can a handful of busy leaders, harassed by a thousand pressing concerns, settle in a few days problems that have escaped resolution by the most skillful negotiators for over a decade and a half?

For Americans, the more serious objection to personal diplomacy is constitutional in character. The President is the chief executive of a vast sprawling governmental system based on the consent of the governed. If he is away from his desk, as was President Wilson for nearly seven months during the Paris Conference, or constantly on the move, as was President Eisenhower in his last two years in office, the effective performance of government will be seriously impaired. Decisions are postponed and long-range policies become impossible. Even should high-level negotiations buy time, the likelihood is great that the time will not be wisely and constructively used. The President by prolonged absences loses touch with the pulse of his party, with congressional leaders and the public, and other responsible associates with whom he must work. Thus his necessary sources of power dry up before he can succeed in his mission abroad.

More significant still may be the procedural issue, for the signs are not lacking that "summitry" is an awkward and unwieldy instrument for the recording of lasting agreements. The public business of foreign policy and its overall direction and supervision is difficult enough for the busy chief executive. Diplomatic negotiations place demands upon him the mastery of which lies always just beyond reach. Where is he to find the time to prepare himself for the complexities of sustained consultations without neglecting his continuing and inescapable political and constitutional duties? How is he to understand "the full scope of the issues and their innermost details"? What will be the effect of his being called away at the crucial stage of discussions? How is he to explain failure or affirm success without needlessly complicating the future of ongoing relations for sensitive states jealous and fearful of one another's power and status? How can he be confident about all the details and implications of nuclear testing, cultural exchange, or arms control, and if he restricts himself to agreements in principle, what should he say of Secretary George C. Marshall's statement: "Don't ask me to agree in principle; that just means we haven't agreed yet"? And if he reviews the high-water marks of successful negotiations with the Russians, what should he make of the fact that procedurally they were not the result of top-level personal diplomacy? They were, rather, the work of Ambassador Llewellyn Thompson through more than three hundred days of negotiations leading to the Austrian Peace Treaty, of Ambassador John Foster Dulles in consultation with more than forty states that were to become signatories to the Japanese Peace Treaty, and of Ambassador Philip C. Jessup, who within and outside the formal organs of the United Nations found a solution to the first Berlin blockade.

Finally, those who evaluate personal diplomacy must face a difficult philosophical issue. What are we to say of the nature of a more prudent diplomacy? Is more to be gained in harmonizing differences from the overflow of popular ovations accorded presidential negotiators abroad than from craftsmen at work on the knotty edges of outstanding diplomatic problems? How does the student measure the possible risks and dividends of a court of last resort in which leaders confront one another in deliberations that must yield answers of "yes" or "no"? How calculate the gamble that personal affection may lead to a concert of views against the heavy risks that personal impulse or animosity may override the dictates of common interest? Is the personal rapport or healthy dislike of heads of state a sufficient basis for agreements on war and peace? What happens to negotiations *ad referendum* when the President as negotiator is committed, losing his freedom of action, flexibility of approach, and the possibility of subsequent review? These issues pose questions worthy of the most prayerful reflection as men consider the function and limits of personal diplomacy, whatever one's private opinions on the problem.

No one would question, of course, that negotiations at the highest level may serve an essential purpose in ratifying agreements produced at the working diplomatic level. Nor can one deny the usefulness from time to time of broad exploratory talks that offer guidelines for more concrete and substantive deliberations. Nor can there be any argument against reopening clogged and frozen channels of communication if there is any prospect of success. Yet personal, like parliamentary, diplomacy must never be viewed as an end in itself. Both must find a proper place in the mid-twentieth century armory of diplomatic techniques. Both quite possibly are well suited to drastic changes on the world scene and both may serve men well when solid shifts in policy are contemplated. Yet both must be employed with wisdom and restraint and both must harness the insights of the past. Diplomacy in the mid-twentieth century is the public trust not alone of presidents but of international institutions. It continues in the present as in the past to require skilled professionals and ingenious amateurs who hand in hand with the diplomatic innovators of the new era— the personal and parliamentary diplomatists—must strengthen methods and procedures that can stand the test of time. The world will not survive an addiction to shining new diplomatic techniques if it thereby forgoes all that history can teach it of the role of careful, painstaking, impersonal diplomacy through normal channels. The days are too fraught with peril and opportunity to seek salvation in either the new or the old. If both are to survive and civilization with them, they must yield to the practical wisdom of modern man.

6

Diplomacy in a Changing World

"It's a complex fate, being an American. . . ."
HENRY JAMES

CHANGE is the dominant theme of contemporary world politics. Secretary of State Dean Rusk reminds us: "We are seeing a world in turmoil, reshaping itself in a way which is at least as significant as the breakdown of the Concert of Europe, or as the emergence of the national states in the Western system, or as the explosion of Europe into other continents of the world three centuries ago." [1] No one can doubt that diplomacy, which adjusted to the rise of the modern state system and the expansion of Europe, must adapt to the new order. The wind of change has awakened peoples everywhere to the promise of the twentieth century. They proclaim the right to escape the oppression and poverty to which for centuries they had been resigned. They can no longer be told that the will of God or the sovereignty of some external or local authority opposes their demands. The peoples of the world grow ever more attentive to words like those of the great South American leader, Simon Bolivar: "The veil has been torn asunder; we have seen the light; and we will not be thrust back into the darkness." With knowledge and under-

[1] Dean Rusk, "Foreign Policy and the Political Officer," *Foreign Service Journal*, XXVIII, No. 4 (April 1961), 32.

standing, men come to reject a version of life according to which misery and suffering are part of an ordained environment about which little if anything can be done. Today millions "are struggling to throw off the bonds of hunger, poverty and ignorance—to affirm the hope of a better life for themselves and their children." [2] Within national boundaries, regional organizations, and the United Nations, with common purpose they seek to advance economic progress and social justice. If misery and suffering for the many was inevitable in the sixteenth century, the movement toward social and political advancement is irresistible in the twentieth century. Ironically, this worldwide commitment to progress coincides with the achievement of man's capacity to destroy himself and the planet on which he lives. It also corresponds to a period of uncertainty and flux in the attainment of moral and political consensus in the world.

Some who measure these changes ask whether the pace is too swift for human resources, the challenge beyond the wit of man, and the needs so compelling that free institutions will not suffice. Is it possible that the machinery of government, the traditional humanistic view of the world, and civilization's faith in the individual are outmoded? Can we sustain the assumption that man requires time for intelligence to take hold and for judgment to contrive workable approaches to complex moral and political problems? Or must men reach out, as it were, for radically novel forms of human relationships, for the social equivalent of penicillin or sulfa drugs to cure mankind's collective needs and national and international ills? Could the men who split the atom, if they set themselves the task, devise an ethical, political, or economic counterforce to neutralize the weapons with which man has armed his savage instincts? Or is man forever condemned to the burden and glory of building brick by brick whether or not there is time?

[2] Speech by Secretary of State Dean Rusk to the Ministers of the American States in Punta del Este, Uruguay, *The New York Times*, January 26, 1962, p. 4.

1. Political Philosophies in a Changing World

THE two prevailing worldwide political and social philosophies offer essentially conflicting answers to these questions. One philosophy assumes that change is compatible with freedom and order, that social progress is possible through discussion and consent, and that the individual need not be subjugated to the needs of the group as a whole. The other philosophy insists that the pattern of the future is clearly demarcated. Marxist-Leninist doctrine as the way and the truth provides scientific predictions of the course history will follow and moral justification for every step that might serve this end. These absolute scientific and ethical claims lie at the heart of the doctrine; they are intrinsically the outcome of the inner dialectic. Its evils are not merely the result of abuses by this leader or that national group. International communism cannot be excused for taking the route of tyranny and dictatorship because of the accident of circumstance or personality. Its ruthlessness is not explained by a simple reference to traditional Russian authoritarianism, the subservience of Chinese peasants, or the personal strategies of Stalin, Mao, or Castro. On the contrary, its brutality and reaction are the logical outgrowth of a philosophy unchecked by inner or external restraints, freed from the controls of a higher order of justice that is sensitive to the rights of society and individuals, and lacking in that wider hierarchy of values which includes both freedom and justice. Nowhere does Marxism allow for justice arising from an equilibrium of forces. It considers virtue the monopoly of a single social class, the workers. The corruption of pure Marxism-Leninism is inherent in its original design; we need not seek it in decline wrought by events. The permanent evil of communism stems from its promise of redemption from all social evil and the accompanying human sacrifices it exacts to serve its fanatical ambition and goal. Coercion is inextricably bound up with the Communist design.

From East Germany to North Vietnam the programs of communism come as no surprise to those who assess its doctrine in realistic terms. "Whatever contribution communism has appeared to make to industrial development comes only because it does what Marx charged nineteenth century capitalism with doing; that is, it grinds down the faces of the poor and forces from their postponed consumption the capital necessary for arms and industry." [3] Its failure to rally the working class around the globe testifies to growing uncertainty and doubt whether communism, particularly in developed countries, is the pathway of liberation or exploitation. Outside of China and Russia, and excluding the satellite countries in which communism was imposed by force of arms, the underdeveloped areas, as the scene of greatest turmoil and change, are the latest arena of the Communist crusade. Lenin sought world revolution through the universalist appeal to the Marxist creed to industrial workers; Stalin made Marxism a mere ideology to justify and rationalize the military might and Oriental despotism of Russian "socialism in one country." Khrushchev, in contrast to Stalin, has reasserted the worldwide triumph of communism, but less from doctrine than performance. He offers to the world a model for the achievement of rapid economic growth for those impatient with the deliberate workings of the market place. At the same time, he accounts for its successes by primary Marxist intellectual assumptions. Thus Khrushchev, the pragmatist for whom Soviet might and prestige are more essential than Marxism as instruments to transform the world, returns to its doctrines to make the transformation intelligible. Recent history suggests that both Soviet prestige and Marxist doctrine—whatever its expectations at

[3] Rusk, *op. cit*

birth—have their greatest chance in areas torn by pressures of rapid transition and far-reaching social change.

Across the whole broad spectrum of countries of rising expectations, the world and the West assess the crisis as requiring a many-faceted approach. They would afford leadership for constructive change through strengthening educational systems, economic and social improvement, modernization and widening the scope of social justice. Development plans link together programs for health, nutrition, food production, and education. Neither economic growth, family planning, nor social reform can be approached in isolation, for progress assumes advances on all fronts. Underlying these steps to social reform and giving it direction is the second great philosophy of democracy—the principal working alternative to communism for societies in the throes of change. For free men democracy is the *summum bonum* of the good life. For Europeans and Americans it expresses the highest stage of social and political development.

But men and nations around the world persistently raise two questions: Is democracy the most certain route to rapid economic development and social justice? Is it a simple and easily attainable alternative to communism for peoples at every stage of cultural growth? The answers to the first question are not yet in, but present evidence scarcely supports the darkly somber view that communism everywhere provides technically superior forms of economic growth. Those who despair of democracy should not forget that the Soviet Union, in the workings of its economy, has restored a modified price mechanism and is witnessing the rise of a new elite and the solidification of its own class structure. Or they might remember the numbers of Communist states which are abandoning or modifying experiments in collectivized agriculture. They cannot disregard the straws in the wind that bespeak communism's failures in famine on mainland China, hunger in North Vietnam, and drab stagnation in eastern Europe, contrasting vividly with the thriving postwar economic growth of western Europe. For minds not yet closed to the truth, communism is far from having proven its technical superiority.

The second question poses more troublesome issues that form the central theme of many recent studies of democracy. Is democracy suited for a people shaking off the vestiges of feudalism, lacking a tradition of political responsibility, and bereft of the educational base on which popular government rests? Is democracy attainable when these factors are lacking, and if not, is communism as dictatorship by a tightly disciplined minority controlling unquestioning masses the sole alternative? If democracy rests on the consent of the governed, what are we to say of the many new nations within which no more than a tiny fraction are capable of judging their rulers? Is some measure of ethnic and linguistic unity essential to free institutions? We are told that in income and education nearly two billion peoples, most of them with yellow, black, or brown skins, fall below the minimum level of $200 a year per capita and the 50 percent adult literacy that differentiate the developed from the underdeveloped worlds. Are peoples at this level prepared for democracy? And where democracies exist, will they, as islands of freedom in troubled seas, raise other men's sights toward constitutionalism and human rights, or will the few struggling republics stagnate and disappear beneath briny waters? Is genuine democracy possible in the face of poverty, starvation, and disease? How can a people break through the fateful cycle of protein deficiency with its resulting drop in productivity that brings declining purchasing power and a further lowering of livelihood and diet? How reverse the formula "nothing fails like failure"?

Democracy, whatever its moral superiority to dictatorship or tyranny, assumes a working political system that tests to the limit the human and material resources of a people. The road to its high purposes is long and painful. Even within societies blessed by an abundance of riches, eternal and continuing vigilance has been the price of liberty. Democracy presupposes a minimum of social order if justice and freedom are to be possible. In some states the necessity of first establishing order leads to the postponement of justice. This hardly excuses the gloomy fatalism that engulfs much contemporary thinking. Surely we can distinguish, at least over time, the nation deliberately embarked on imposing a permanent, solid, monolithic order for its own sake and one that, because of residual traditions, conceives a one-party system as paving the way for freedom and justice or the ultimate attainment of free competition of social forces and "giving each man his due." The issue is not whether limited and temporary authoritarianism is sometimes necessary but how to keep tyranny in check and ultimately reduce limited and temporary authoritarianism. The trouble with most answers to the question "Is democracy possible?" is their too narrow perspective. The short-run answer to the question "Are literacy, education, family planning, and economic development possible in hard-pressed fledgling nations in which every resource is in short supply?" must be negative. Not surprisingly, therefore, the short-run answer to the question "Is democracy within reach for two-thirds of the world's people?" is also negative. If development and democracy are viewed in more profound long-run terms as stages along life's way for nations that aspire to a better life, this provisional judgment is not the whole story.

The historian of social change and of the revolution of rising expectations must ask himself what is the inner structure of the worldwide revolution? If he would understand the challenge to which democracy and communism are responding, he must dissect the anatomy of this latest revolution. Does it not rest on the fact that in the long run men would rather be fed than hungry, healthy than sick, educated than ignorant, free than slaves, housed than homeless, self-respecting than self-despising, constructively and creatively employed, proud of their culture, joined with others in the quest for dignity, and committed to providing for every child a fair chance for life? Is not the nub of the revolution the resistance by all mankind to being pushed around, ground under, or deprived of essential humanity—socially, politically, and economically? Are not the ends of dignity, self-respect, constructive change, and the war against hunger and ignorance interlaced in the wrap and woof of these revolutionary claims?

If I correctly identify the goals of the great mass of mankind, what is the historian to say of their attainment? The two worldwide philosophies locked in deadly struggle for men's loyalties each offer diagnoses and prescriptions that are mutually contradictory. The one assumes that the manifold hopes of mankind lie within easy reach for those who embrace the Communist faith. The straight and narrow path to health, education, and the eradication of poverty lies along a fixed and historically predetermined route. Overthrow the capitalist exploiters and install the forerunners of the classless society and the rest will follow. Yet in the fifth decade of communism in the Soviet Union, wage differentials are greater than in free societies; production for the needs of consumers is continually postponed; the state grows ever stronger with no sign of withering away; a small, ruthless, self-perpetuating oligarchy adds year by year to its power; and the individual citizen seeks the fragile roots of his dignity and self-respect in the reflected glory of the state. The one estimate of communism no one can refute is that its doctrines bear little relationship to the course of events. Thus the wages that Marxists promise to the disinherited in accordance with their need are determined strictly by performance. Moreover, communism, while posing as the great liberating movement, intrudes on the rights of individuals and nations, disrupting the sanctity of daily lives and at the same time isolating and destroying visible forms of independence and honest difference. Therefore, those who seek economic progress and social justice in the murky shadows of this conspiratorial society are likely to suffer bondage. Those in revolt against the failures of the past will not gain their broad ends from "the scavengers of the transition from stagnation into the modern world"[4] however alluring the distant and imaginary Communist utopia. "Giving the devil his due," acknowledging the concentrated industrial expansion, breathtaking technological advances, and immense military power of the Soviet Union must never obscure its organic purpose and essential methods.

The best measure by comparison of the force and power of the democratic revolution is the implacable and unremitting efforts of communism to resist and obstruct its efforts. At far-flung points around the globe, whether in Laos, the Belgian Congo, or Berlin, Communists and their henchmen seek through subversion, guerrilla warfare, violence, and intrigue to forestall the creation of viable societies because in their hearts they fear the democratic solution once men enjoy free choice. In emergent states, communism works unflaggingly to plant seeds of chaos, disunity, and thereby subservience to Moscow. The inescapable difference between communism and democracy lies in the realm of individual responsibility. The individual Communist's responsibility is to the vague and remote ends of his creed—and even these are expected to care for themselves. Since the party and not the people guides society toward these ends, the individual is not accountable. Representative democracy, in striking contrast, involves the individual in the progress and the failures, the accomplishments and misdeeds of the government. Democracy, in Edmond Cahn's well-chosen words, implicates the citizen. "It consists in examining, judging, and assuming responsibility for what our representatives do in our name and by our authority, the unjust and evil acts as well as the beneficent and good."[5] If the hopes and aspirations of newly independent peoples are worthy of the decent respect of others, do they not owe themselves the self-respect that comes from responsibility and moral involvement? Will those who have thrown off the chains of subjugation wrought

[4] Rusk, *op. cit.*

[5] Edmond Cahn, *The Predicament of Democratic Man* (New York: The Macmillan Co., 1961), p. 29.

by a largely benevolent outside power long accept those thrown around their shoulders by far more despotic rulers—even in the name of the millenium? Democracy consists "in discounting the millenium by realizing its promise of complete freedom here and now and by compressing it into the realms of conscience, thought, belief and opinion." [6] The free play of intelligence is at once an instrument for releasing the creative processes of man's inner life and assuring the unshackled pursuit of his social transactions. It forces him to determine on a scale of values the aims he most urgently seeks and their linkage and consistency one with another. Does economic growth merit a place on his agenda above all other national goals? Or are education, better roads and houses, improved food production, or population stabilization more important? Or must free men pursue these aims concomitantly, each intertwining with the others until they are knit together in the fabric of society?

Beyond this, the democratic revolution assumes that men seek the grand purposes of society within a framework of constitutional principles that set the rules of the game. Some enjoy the blessings of written constitutions, while others are guided and restrained by tradition and an unwritten constitution. Professor Cahn has observed: "It makes a difference of substance and moment in human affairs that King John did issue the Magna Carta, that William and Mary did assent to the Settlement Act, and that the American people did adopt a written Bill of Rights." [7] These positive, recorded facts and hard historical events assure that tyranny is unlikely to go unchecked or persecution be excused in the name of the millenium. Moreover, Anglo-American constitutional history demonstrates that great ordering and enabling texts need not bind a people to the past. Indeed, constitutionalism fulfills its role only to the extent men "rescue it from the past and use it

[6] *Ibid.*, pp. 185–86.
[7] *Ibid.*, p. 33.

to grapple with the problems of the present and the conceived future." [8]

Not only does democracy respond to felt needs within well-understood and accepted rules of the game, eschewing the more arbitrary play of power, but it accepts the challenge of peoples in the grip of change whose aims are many and not one. Communism is incurably corrupted by the belief that men fundamentally seek only economic advances. Democracy, by comparison, is prepared to accept the challenge of the war against ignorance, poverty, and disease by rallying its forces along a broad and moving front. It assumes that man lives both by bread and the spirit. It is prepared to believe that both national and international assistance are necessary and possible. It looks to public and private resources in responding to successive challenges. Thus an emerging nation may turn to public sources for major capital assistance while depending for its programing on private economic consultants. A university abroad may find the United Nations Special Fund, the Agency for International Development, or the World Bank responsive to long-term building needs while drawing on private foundations or sister universities for faculty and staff. The Alliance for Progress reflects the determination of more than twenty states on a vast continent to press forward voluntarily through measures of self-help and social reform. Technical assistance or foreign aid or international trade may alternately provide the means for building roads and dams, or houses, schools, and factories. Some of the experiences of friendly nations in pretechnical circumstances may be transferable to serve requirements of education, health, and increased productivity. As neighbors aided neighbors in early American villages and towns, free men seek to unite across national frontiers in the building of strong and healthy independent societies.

In a world of change and of nearly infinite variation of

[8] *Ibid.*, p. 34.

national institutions and human resources, the United States must choose between leading or moving with the tide. The major barrier to leadership lies within free societies. In the present-day world with all its insistent demands, peoples and nations fall readily into alibis of helplessness. Since so much that occurs will not yield to the direct influence of any one of us, we ask plaintively if there is anything we can do. A former colleague who often found this question thrust upon him offered the gentle reminder that the individual is not responsible for the United States but for his part in it. To this we might add that the Republic is not responsible for all that happens in the world but for its ever more important part in it. We must all of us start from where we are, prepared for whatever may come. I am impressed that American leaders responsible for our relations with other parts of the world are never as confident about the future as when they return from touring the length and breadth of the land. Then they radiate the strength that comes from a nation getting on with the job. They speak of millions of peoples engaged in doing the things they do best: buying and selling, teaching and learning, raising families and building communities, farming and manufacturing, discussing and worshiping, and reviewing their problems and moving ahead. Surely the importance of foreign relations in no way diminishes the significance of free peoples doing what they must. My colleague went on to observe that talking up interest in world affairs should never mean talking down concern with local affairs.

The blunt truth about democracy is that what happens internally in attitudes and programs either strengthens or becomes a drag on relations with others. The foreign visitor in our midst heightens tendencies made possible by technology and communication. Fifty thousand foreign students measure conduct by the principles we have long professed. Who can assess the weight of minor incidents in the light of the next decade? Who can say what influence good schools, living expressions of equal opportunity, small acts of kindness and encouragement, or institutions functioning effectively on the basis of shared responsibilities may have on others? Or alternately, what of our Golden Ghettos, segregated lunch counters, or communities that draw too narrowly on rich and varied human resources? The nation at work in a world which, with a few glaring exceptions, is ever more an open society cannot escape these implications. It must remind itself that nationality and race are no bar to capacity and intelligence; when we look beyond the national boundaries, we are reminded that Bacon was an Englishman, Descartes a Frenchman, Spinoza a Dutchman, Picasso a Spaniard, Sibelius a Finn, Tolstoy a Russian, and Mann a German. And who would say that the nation could have done without a George Washington Carver, Booker T. Washington, or Ralph Bunche? Our nation would do well to heed the Rev. Theodore M. Hesburgh's powerful words: "Personally, I don't care if the U.S. gets the first man on the moon, if while this is happening . . . we dawdle along here on our corner of the earth, nursing our prejudices, flouting our magnificent Constitution, ignoring the central moral problem of our times, and appearing hypocrites to all the world." [9]

Democracy, then, rests on values that provide a measuring rod for what we do both at home and abroad for ourselves and for those who listen in on what we do and say. We can be judged by the number of citizens that go hungry, by children who are without shoes, by per capita income and tons of steel, and by the living conditions of working men and teachers, leaders of industry, finance, and state. Plainly these measures are not irrelevant to questions being asked around the world. However, to leave it at this is to disparage the doctrines by which we must live. Winston S. Churchill has written: "Those who are possessed of a definite body of doctrine and of deeply rooted convictions upon it will be in a much better position to deal with the shifts and surprises of daily affairs than those who are merely taking short views, and indulging their natural

[9] Father Hesburgh's separate statement attached to the Civil Rights Commission Report, *The New York Times*, November 17, 1961, p. 22.

impulses as they are evoked by what they read from day to day." [10] Even if Americans lived in a state of isolation divorced from the rest of the world, the doctrines on which the nation was founded would have relevance to the state of the union. Even if winds of change were not blowing across the world, the winds of freedom would blow within the Republic because our society is the kind of society it is.

The doctrines that guide our destiny find expression in our own revolutionary manifesto, the Declaration of Independence, and in the Constitution and the Bill of Rights. They are embodied no less in the living Constitution—the thousands of statutes and millions of decisions in courts of law. Taken together, they reflect the high value we give to government by the consent of the governed and to the rule of law. We recognize with the Athenians of the fifth century B.C. and the English of the late nineteenth century that public service can be "the exercise of vital powers along lines of excellence, in a life affording them scope." The gusts of fanaticism that drive us from this faith have never for long effaced devotion to its principles. Mr. Dean Acheson reminds us that: "Brave men are not uncommon in any system but there is a tendency in most systems to make courage and a disciplined openness of mind to the significant facts mutually exclusive. This is the immediate cause of the downfall of every ruling class. . . ." [11] Public responsibility and the exercise of vital powers within a constitutional framework is a safeguard against so fateful a division. Blind courage or bondage to the significant facts are not ends in themselves, and this lesson of free government may have meaning for friends in other lands.

For those who appraise America's position in the world or the controlling principles of its national existence, nothing would be more misleading than to underestimate the citizen's

---

[10] Winston S. Churchill, *The Second World War: The Gathering Storm* (Boston: Houghton Mifflin Co., 1948), I, 210–11.

[11] Quoted in "Dean Acheson on a Career in Government," *The New York Times*, February 2, 1958, Section 4, p. 8E.

role or, with due allowance for human failings, the high position of the public servant. The people determine the consensus
of the nation on the direction it moves. They mark out with
their leaders a broad highway of reasonably well-understood
goals and policies. This requires them to be fully informed
about the world situation and the course of action their leaders
propose in dealing with it. Leaders and not the people must
map and follow the stages along this broad route. Those who
enjoy public trust must in this respect serve the public interest,
and not merely its passing curiosity. Secretary of State Dean
Rusk defines this responsibility more clearly than any contemporary Western statesman when he explains:

> The public has a right to know, including the right to know that
> its serious business is being handled in a responsible fashion. For ex-
> ample, if there are differences between us and friendly nations about
> one or another aspect of the passing parade of events, these are more
> likely to be resolved by quiet conversation than by a public quarrel.
> If two of our friends find themselves in difficulty with each other, it is
> not always conducive to agreement for it to be publicly known that
> we have been offering friendly counsel.
> Our policies are public, our purposes are those which the nation
> itself enjoins upon its Government; in the main, our acts are public,
> because that is the way a democracy moves. But diplomacy cannot
> always be so, or else it would be little more than debate, adding its
> fuel to the very fires it hopes to quench.[12]

The rule of law internationally is a natural extension of
a nation's dedication to constitutionalism internally. The United
States, because of the doctrines to which it holds, can never
flagrantly and publicly defy the common law of international
practice. Sometimes this may seem to place us under severe
and disabling restraints in the struggle with a ruthless and
totalitarian foe. Yet this same foe, while periodically violating
the rule of law, has not seen fit to defy it publicly or denounce

---

[12] Speech by Secretary of State Dean Rusk to the National Press Club, Washington, D.C., *The New York Times*, July 11, 1961, p. 4.

it as a capitalist or reactionary device. In a revolutionary age, states must have somewhere firm ground to which they can repair. There must be some haven of impartiality in a bitterly partisan world. That there are links between the working constitutional principles of the American Republic and the fragile but emerging international order—links not vouchsafed to our rivals in the Soviet Union—is a factor of immense significance in a changing world.

All these many and varied strengths of democratic doctrine reduce anxieties and fears about its future in a changing world. Perhaps scholars and statesmen should be less defensive about its place in the modern world. From the standpoint of political practice, it has shown itself marvelously adaptive to change. Seen in respect to the manifold needs of new nations, the outsider is understandably reluctant to prescribe. Yet does not being an American involve the obligation to focus the spotlight on these core truths of democracy that a crafty foe may misrepresent, that criticism and political analysis may not fully explore, but that daily give to men dignity, hope, freedom, and the pursuit of happiness along both material and spiritual pathways?

2. Diplomatic Practice in a Changing World

THE truth that emerges most clearly, then, from any review of democratic practice is its capacity to adjust while preserving its doctrines and the rules of the game. Yet in another realm, while new international machinery for diplomacy is supplanting older political forms, no systematic review or far-reaching adaptation of diplomatic practice had been attempted for a century and a half until the recently concluded second Congress of Vienna. Its forerunner, the first Congress of Vienna of 1815 at the close of the Napoleonic Wars, codified diplomatic procedures for nineteenth century Europe. A remarkable group of European diplomats, representing the major powers of that day, provided rough guideposts that have persisted into the twentieth century. Today, increasingly, our best-informed leaders question whether diplomacy is keeping pace with the changing world. They call for a reexamination of diplomatic practice running the gamut from the more trivial rules of protocol all the way to the procedures of great international bodies and the problems of summit diplomacy. The present American Secretary of State, Dean Rusk, his immediate predecessor, and some of our ablest ambassadors exposed to a wide variation of national rules are in the forefront of those urging study and revision of protocol.

In response to these felt needs, representatives of more than eighty governments discussed and negotiated for six weeks in Vienna in the spring of 1961 a draft agreement reformulating concepts of diplomatic immunities and usages. Their understanding, before coming into effect, required ratification by twenty-two governments by March 31, 1962. The conference had received a Report of the International Law Commission, referred to it by the General Assembly of the United Nations, on the rules of diplomatic intercourse which served as the basis for its deliberations. The principal world forces dominating thinking and giving shape to the discussion were the rise of new states and the impact of the cold war. Not surprisingly, therefore, key articles in the agreement deal with the size of diplomatic missions, the right to operate radio transmitters and receivers, freedom of movement, inviolability of domiciles and archives, and immunity from arrest and local taxation. When on April 18, 1961, the conference officially terminated its discussions, participants from Communist, non-Communist, and uncommitted nations had harmonized their views on such disputed points as whether Communist states, including East Germany and Communist China, which were not members of the United Nations, were entitled to sign the agreement. Fearful of the implications, the majority of states successfully resisted Communist efforts to claim rights and privileges for "satellites" who have not undertaken responsibilities under the United Nations Charter.

Historically, diplomatic procedure with its trappings of exaggerated formality, stilted language, and grotesquely archaic patterns has rested less on private vanity or aristocratic pretension than on political necessity. It should be remembered that ceremonial rules and quarrels over rank and precedence reflect the struggle among nations for recognition and prestige. Diplomats are the symbolic representatives of the influence and status of their respective nation-states. In this role, the acts of respect or insult which they initiate or receive are initiated or received by their countries. Leaders of emergent states almost immediately upon their country's independence hasten to New York partly because—for Nigeria or the Ivory Coast—admission to the United Nations symbolizes the attainment and recognition of a new and respected status. In 1945, Churchill, Stalin, and Truman at Potsdam could not agree on who should enter the conference room first, for at a decisive moment in postwar history, when the world distribution of power was in flux, the relative prestige and power of the three nations was at stake. The issue was resolved by their entering the conference room simultaneously through separate doors. The annals of diplomatic history are replete with comparable examples of the significance of symbolic representation. In the seventeenth century, France and Spain were locked in a struggle for the domination of Europe. On one occasion in The Hague, the carriages of the French and Spanish ambassadors met on a narrow street and each refused to give way. Following a long and bitter dispute, each safeguarded its prestige by pulling down a fence alongside the road, thus allowing them to pass without yielding to one another.

The ancient and stilted practices of diplomacy serve another essential purpose. They take away the accidents of personality from interstate relations. Summit conferences and personal diplomacy, by comparison, accent the role of likes and dislikes, of health and illness, and of moods and tempers. For example, neither Secretary Dean Acheson nor Secretary John Foster Dulles got along with Anthony Eden, while Secretary George C. Marshall and Ernest Bevin were drawn together instinctively in the pursuit of a great common task. The influence of personal illness on high matters of state is difficult to measure, but one can speculate about the effects of President Franklin D. Roosevelt's health at Yalta or Mr. Dulles' before the ill-fated Suez crisis. When negotiations are raised to the highest level, conditions that should be irrelevant to the partnership or accommodation of nations may become decisive. All this in no way implies that personal qualities like intelligence, knowledge, and judgment are any less important.

Diplomacy at the working level following well-established procedures minimizes the human factor. It follows the ancient pattern of exchange of notes, preliminary soundings, repeated discussions, and slow but gradual progress toward agreements registered in hard print. A recent exchange of carefully drafted policy papers and proposals on Berlin is particularly illuminating. Ambassador Thompson in Moscow received three notes on January 12, 1961, dispatched three in reply on February 1, and acknowledged Mr. Gromyko's response on February 9. This form of diplomacy based on precisely defined policy statements is less likely, in Sir Harold Nicolson's words, "to arouse public expectation, lead to misunderstandings and create confusion." In his view, "diplomacy is not the art of conversation, it is the art of negotiating agreements in precise and ratifiable forms." The modern techniques all too frequently aim merely at creating a more favorable atmosphere and general good feeling among the parties. The hard and serious business of hammering out agreements flourishes best when personal whims and preferences are kept in the background.

Nevertheless, the fact remains that rules of protocol were fashioned in another age when the pressures and demands of statecraft were less intense. Early American secretaries of state combined responsibilities of office with other vocations, including part-time legal practice. On one occasion, Secretary Thomas Jefferson wrote that for over two years nothing had been heard from the minister in Madrid. He promised himself he would dispatch a sharp and pointed note if his reticent envoy were not heard from during the following year.

There are countless examples to show that this era with its graceful and casual attitudes has passed. Today, whereas the quaint symbolism of ambassadorial calls may have been appropriate in more leisurely times, it has become an empty ritual involving serious stress and strain for badly overworked officials. In major capitals every newly assigned ambassador must call on every other ambassador in order of seniority and await their visits in return. The question of relative rank among members of the diplomatic corps and the numerous officials of host governments becomes a recurrent source of acrimony. When there were only a few embassies and the pace of business was leisurely, visits were often helpful, but with our one hundred diplomatic outposts in capitals like Washington, wear and tear on officials far exceeds the benefits in brief human contacts and formal relationships.

Protocol further demands a round of national holidays with the inevitable full-scale receptions on our Fourth of July, Bastille Day for the French, or the Queen's Birthday for the British. Delegates at the seat of the United Nations move about from reception to reception honoring national days organized at great expense to hard-pressed national treasuries and with uncertain effects on digestion and good health. Abroad, visiting officials, tourists, and congressional committees expect entertainment, and Ambassador David Bruce reports that during a two-year assignment in Paris he succeeded in having only one meal alone with his own family. This invasion of the diplomat's schedule goes on at the expense of his most precious resource: time. He finds himself drawn away from his essential tasks at a time when other tasks and duties are multiplying nearly beyond his control.

Moreover, protocol and its reform is linked more directly than is commonly supposed with the recruitment of the best qualified ambassadors regardless of party, wealth, or sex. On July 4, 1959, the United States Ambassador to France, Mr. Amory Houghton, entertained 8,000 resident and visiting Americans at a Fourth of July party. His reception continued a tradition going back to Benjamin Franklin of looking after homesick Americans on the national holiday. Since Mr. Houghton's annual entertainment allowance was $6,000, this event illustrates the difficulty of paying for the functions of a major United States embassy, particularly in western Europe. Observers point out that, faced with these demands, no one but a man of great wealth could afford to serve in Paris, London, Bonn, Rome, Madrid, and New Delhi. They estimate that Congress by appropriating annually an overall representation fund of $5,000,000 would solve this problem and make possible appointments on a purely professional basis. Even before his inauguration, President Kennedy acted to meet this issue head-on through seeking an understanding with Chairman John Rooney of the House Appropriations Subcommittee that Congress endeavor to provide more adequate representation allowances. Further, the Kennedy administration issued a directive in April 1961 restricting the use of federal funds for holiday celebrations at embassies.

The result of the restriction was sharply to reduce the scale of Fourth of July celebrations in 1961. In London, Ambassador David Bruce at his own expense entertained 350 guests at Winfield House, compared with the 3,000 feted in 1960 by Ambassador John Hay Whitney at a cost of $16,400. In Paris, the reception did not take place, and in the afternoon Ambassador and Mrs. James Gavin flew to Lyons to join with citizens of the only French town that officially celebrates the American Independence Day. In Moscow, which was not affected by the State Department directive, Ambassador Llewellyn E. Thompson, Jr., gave a formal reception at Spasso House for 1,000 guests, including Premier Khrushchev and 200 top Soviet officials, financed through a special category of representation funds. In Rome the official reception was cancelled; in Tokyo an evening reception was limited to 1,200 Japanese guests and a dozen "representative" Americans; and in New Delhi the United States Embassy celebrated Independence Day with a "Dutch treat" party for Americans. While these acts of self-restraint, which Americans living abroad were encouraged to undertake, can hardly be said to have solved the problem, they are noteworthy for their broad application. The presence today of "professionals" without great personal fortunes as ambassadors in Moscow, New Delhi, Tokyo, Belgrade, Bonn, Rome, Paris, Vienna, Manila, Santiago, and Warsaw is a sign that the Kennedy administration is struggling to face up to the issues.

Protocol may also be linked with more appropriate American domestic responses to external challenges. Significantly, in a world of growing interdependence, the watchdog of international diplomatic procedures becomes the guardian of national democratic practice. The present chief of protocol, Angier Biddle Duke, has made it his business to investigate complaints from diplomats representing the new nations, to offer apologies when required, and, in his own words, "to see what could be done to make it unnecessary to make such apologies." In a nutshell, Mr. Duke has asked for more than empty apologies and, at least in certain areas, his diligence has borne fruit. When Ambassador Fitzjohn of Sierra Leone was turned away from a Hagerstown, Maryland, restaurant, the mayor following "consultation" took the initiative in inviting the ambassador back as an honored guest of the city, and the restaurant owner shortly thereafter desegregated his establishment. I am told that Mr. Duke's meetings with top real estate owners in Washington led to the opening of enough first-class apartment buildings to house most of the staff of the twenty-five new African states. There followed a meeting with state governors and state attorneys-general to seek improvement of public services in restaurants, motels, and gas stations along the so-called "Incident Highway" from New York to Washington, D.C. Taken together, these efforts reflect a serious endeavor to broaden the outreach of protocol to embrace some of our most vital internal and international problems—given new urgency by the "wind of change."

Then again at the pinnacle of government the problem of multiplying functions and responsibilities defies imagination. How is the secretary of state to coordinate the on-going work of approximately 100 American ambassadors, 200 consulates, of our representatives at the 394 international organizations of which the United States is a member, and keep abreast of a daily cable volume at least equal to the combined intake in Washington of the Associated Press and United Press? And what if he at the same time must fulfill social obligations and speak for the United States at a succession of foreign ministers' conferences in Asia, the Middle East, Europe, and Latin America? Is it any wonder that Secretary Rusk with other foreign ministers are seeking to curtail the symbolic and representative functions of their office. New and unprecedented problems require the secretary's attention, and only by modernizing the framework within which he works can he meet the challenge.

Many of the purely formal elements of protocol require a useless expenditure of time and energy and invite fairly drastic reforms.

The second Congress of Vienna necessarily focused attention on a limited sector of the formal aspects of protocol, especially diplomatic immunities and privileges. It dealt with the size, essential functions, and legitimate instruments of diplomatic missions. It put considerable stress on the authority of the receiving state to determine the maximum size of a mission and to control, through granting or withholding permission, the operation of radio transmitters and receivers. It reflected the fact that throughout the world, and particularly in the so-called underdeveloped areas, revolutionary programs cloaked in ideological trappings are organized to capture mass movements of nationalism and social progress. With this as a primary objective, an embassy becomes a base of operations or a control tower for carrying on and directing a combined missionary movement and espionage campaign.

Even for the free world, however, the objective of diplomacy has become more than the harmonizing of disputes; it entails the total involvement of the American or any other free people with peoples and governments abroad. Thus the American diplomatic community abroad includes military advisers, trade experts, cultural attachés, and agricultural specialists. Protocol must take account of the changing composition of representation abroad and the shifting patterns of foreign relations. An ambassador cannot regard his responsibilities as something left over after military assistance or foreign trade or cultural exchange or agricultural policy is extracted. The manifold threads of life and work abroad converge at the point of the ambassador's office. He must think, act, and report in the total context of a concrete foreign situation. In turn, his behavior must be ordered and controlled by a body of rules and procedures germane to his changing role, no longer the narrowly specialized one of representation, negotiation, and protection of property rights. A State Department publication,

The American Ambassador, explains: "Today, the American Ambassador is the administrator of a great complex of operations that this nation carries on abroad as part of our foreign policy."

Therefore, the concepts of diplomatic protocol must be broadened to allow reasonable definitions of the lawful means of reporting on developments within a state, of legitimate methods for promoting "friendly" economic, cultural, and scientific relations, of notification due ministries of foreign affairs of the arrival and departure of official members of missions, of restrictions upon the establishment of subsidiary missions outside national capitals, and of the right to inspect the personal baggage of a diplomatic agent if "there are very serious grounds for presuming that it contains articles" not for accepted use by the mission or for the personal use of the diplomat or members of his family. At the same time, it must be recognized that persons enjoying privileges and immunities must respect the laws and regulations of the receiving state and not interfere in the internal affairs of that state. Taken together, these reforms are a response to the new revolutionary era of total involvement in international politics requiring new rules and procedures.

If diplomatic protocol is to keep pace with events, however, it must also assist responsible officials to concentrate on their essential task without being continually diverted by secondary endeavors. Concretely, the foreign ministers of the world should continue to seek an understanding, or "gentleman's agreement," restricting their attendance at international conferences. The weight of international business and the task of coordinating the far-flung activities of foreign policy no longer permit a state the luxury of engaging its highest official in long and continued negotiation abroad. While John Foster Dulles earned the reputation of our most widely traveled secretary of state, his successor once removed, Dean Rusk, was obliged to attend four major conferences on the problems of Laos, NATO, SEATO, and CENTO during his first four months in office and has followed this with participation in the conference of foreign ministers in Punta del Este, Uruguay, calling for nearly two weeks of his precious time. However constructive and essential these missions are for highly placed officials, the secretary's absence from Washington gives rise to the question, "Who is left tending the shop?" Incidentally, Rusk's travel of 53,000 miles exceeded Dulles' 30,000 miles in their first six months of office.

The reluctance of serious observers to divert our highest officials from their most important constitutional tasks is based on solid considerations. In part, doubts arise because all agree that the secretary and *a fortiori* the President should be habitually at their posts. But also the setting in which high officials conduct negotiations makes for ineffectual diplomacy. They operate under serious time pressures, often with insufficient preparation, in a football stadium atmosphere where the contest for prestige is accentuated. They are often called away at the most crucial stage of the negotiations. Moreover, the process serves to downgrade still further the role of ambassadors who must continue the long and dreary task of accommodating conflicting interests when his chief departs, as he came, by jet plane. We do well to recall once again that the landmarks of diplomatic achievement of the postwar world, whether the Austrian Peace Treaty, the Berlin Blockade, or the settlement on Trieste, have been the product of long, tedious, and agonizing diplomatic preparation. Foreign ministers may ratify these accomplishments but they are unlikely to bring them about. Fortunately, the present secretary is profoundly aware of the problem and, through diplomatic correspondence, roving ambassadors and the wider use of first-class envoys like Ambassador Llewellyn Thompson in Moscow, is moving to provide an answer. We may hope that the proposal for the new office of Secretary for Foreign Affairs is still on the minds of our leaders.

Below the level of secretary of state, the social and symbolic functions of subordinate officials crowd out the time to think, to plan, or to innovate. The pressure of successive diplomatic functions prompts the question: Would it be possible to combine on a regional basis some of the more than one hundred receptions commemorating national days into, for example, a single Latin American reception or North African one, while giving due recognition to the attainments and public relations of separate nation-states? Could a more rational plan be devised for diplomatic entertainment at the United Nations which would be less onerous for delegates whose working agendas already tax strength to the limit? It is true that a diplomat can no more neglect his social duties than relax his political vigilance, but that a reasonable balance must be maintained. A nagging doubt persists that this balance has been upset by perpetuating and expanding social forms that have outlived their usefulness. Top United Nations officials are attending a decreasing fraction of the receptions, if this is any index of their diplomatic value.

The adjustment of diplomatic practice to a changing world can, of course, be measured in a more general way by the evolving techniques of the United Nations. I would recall again that the late Secretary-General wrote: "Within the framework of the Charter there are many possibilities . . . for variation of practices. . . . It is my hope that solid progress can be made in the coming years in developing new forms of contact, new methods of deliberation and new techniques of reconciliation." Although Mr. Hammarskjold spoke of possibilities "largely unexplored," variation in practice has already involved collective action for peace in Korea, off-the-record talks in United Nations cloakrooms, use of intermediaries, commissions of inquiry, peace observation teams, a United Nations "presence" and emergency force, and negotiations on regional problems pursued with reference to the universal framework. The rules of the game adjust to new problems and institutions. The United Nations intervenes in the domestic affairs of states on the theory of mutual involvement. It couples "trying on issues for size" in parliamentary debates with behind-the-scenes bargaining and give and take. Since no more than 20 percent of votes reflects action by instructed delegates, opportunities open up for a new form of diplomatic responsibility susceptible to influence from the outside. A novel system of internal protocol and practice has developed and those who master it show signs of multiplying their influence and effectiveness within and outside the United Nations. The secretary-general has functioned with advisory committees on Suez, Lebanon, and the Congo to implement United Nations resolutions. Parliamentary diplomacy as a blending of the old and new practices of states illustrates graphically both the necessity and limitations of modernizing the rules of diplomacy.

In summary, the second Congress of Vienna has put forward important but rather specialized reforms in diplomatic practice. At more informal levels, such as in the processes of new international institutions, other changes are being evolved. This pattern of change will continue and constructive reforms should be suggested and undertaken. Yet in certain rather fundamental ways, the underlying purposes of diplomacy being broadly constant, we can expect continuity as well as change.

3. The Test of Diplomacy in a Changing World

IF diplomatic practice is measured against present necessities and demands, the adequacy of any emergent pattern inevitably comes under question. For contemporary diplomacy is asked to bridge the seemingly unbridgeable chasm that separates East and West and frequently divides North and South, to support the foundations of an international order within which peoples remain free to opt for a government by consent, to proceed upon the fragmentary facts upon which diplomats must act in closed and sometimes in open societies, and to marshal support for unpopular undertakings across a broadly representative domestic and international front. To heighten the challenge, all this must be accomplished in an atmosphere of crisis in which the rate of challenge and response exceeds any known to man. Under the most favorable of circumstances, and given the happiest merger of practices and techniques, present-day diplomacy is destined to fall short of the mark. Its successes, however fleeting, must of necessity go unheralded, and this at a moment when the public clamors for results. Its methods must often seem at odds with the goals it seeks. And while other great nations have attuned their diplomatic instruments to public understanding over several centuries, American diplomacy must adjust within a decade or two.

Yet the course of events within and beyond the reach of contemporary diplomacy offers grounds for hope, however formidable and imposing the task. In Europe, a postwar generation of young and thoughtful leaders less dominated than their parents by gusts of ideological passion have hammered out new forms of collaboration. Change is the order of the day in Europe as in Africa and Asia; the new generation is more pragmatic, less anti-American, and more optimistic about the future, provided Europe can meet the challenge of democratic revolution and social change at home and abroad. In Jean Monnet's words: "The Soviet Union is changing, America is changing and Western Europe is beginning to change. A détente has no significance unless it represents facts. This process of change will go on until it produces new unity and strength in the West—then and only then will it be possible to negotiate an accommodation with Moscow." [13] Those who feel the pulse of change in Europe urge that the West, in the spirit of the Marshall Plan, concentrate on achieving new unity and strength through fashioning worldwide policies projected by the new European institutions. They assert that diplomacy should concentrate on things it can hope to change within the Western world instead of things it cannot hope to change in Russia.

Similarly, our friends in Latin America remind us that they, as our closest neighbors, stand on the threshold of the most far-reaching change. Leaders like Lleras Camargo of Colombia are with their peoples struggling to construct economically viable and politically representative societies. Opposing them are deep-rooted hierarchical structures of wealthy landowners, military power, and the ancient unities of church and state. Those who hope for the gradual achievement of social change and reform of the existing order should not fail to note that within these same hierarchies of blood and grace formidable new independent forces are emerging to join in the common historic task. The great enterprise for both the "haves" and "have-nots," defined in simplest terms, is to impose democracy on underlying feudal institutions, now moribund, in an era of rising social and political expectations. With all the profound divisions fed by memories of misunderstanding and abuse separating North and South, the central fact that transcends all others is the partnership willingly being forged by Latin American leaders and their friends in the United

[13] Quoted in James Reston, "The New Pragmatism in Europe," *The New York Times*, May 27, 1960.

States. The Alliance for Progress has given new dimension and concreteness to inter-American relations; it bids fair, despite all past errors, to render Castro impotent in the Southern Hemisphere much as the Marshall Plan turned back the tide of communism in Western Europe.

In Africa and Asia, the tides of history surge and flow past limits that were expected to stand for decades. Insistent demands for freedom from contempt, mutual respect, more and better education, and economic development resound through the halls of national and international assemblies. They are the felt needs of today's world community. Western intellectuals must do more than point up the difficulties and handicaps of the West in cooperating within primitive tribal cultures to bring about workable and free national societies. For if it is true that Marxism has latent appeal in cultures most nearly resembling those European societies emerging from feudalism to which Marx's original diagnosis was addressed, it is also a fact that the democratic revolution embodies values and achievements that are the product not of forty-five years of limited and inconclusive experimentation but of two thousand years of free discussion, trial and error, and stirring success. Americans ought never to allow moods of self-criticism, healthful in themselves, to obscure this essential truth. We need less discussion of the factors that divide men North and South of what by now is a totally imaginary line, and more of courage and unity in facing specific, identifiable common problems.

I see fear and uncertainty at the root of much of our present hesitation, both North and South, to unite in the latest, most noble adventure of contemporary civilization— fear that is spawned in the North by an exaggeration of differences, by obsession over balancing ledgers of profit and loss, by stubborn racial prejudice that always lies hidden just below the surface and is fed by counterclaims of racial superiority thrown off by roughriding nationalist movements, by doubts that technical assistance is worth the candle, particularly when it yields ingratitude and criticism, by worries over national bankruptcy and a balanced budget, and by the curious misreading of history that counsels leaving natives as we find them in their imagined bliss, harmony, and happiness—as if we and our ancestors in northern Europe a few centuries ago would have accepted this injunction. And with all respect, I must point the finger as well at fear in the South that clings to the comforting illusion that all the manifold frustrations, disappointments, and failures of developing societies are someone else's doing; that freedom from colonialism is an end in itself; and that leaders who seek power must speak more of racial differences and less of national sacrifices, more of economic exploitation and less of capital formation, more of equality with the rest of the world and less of inequality of caste or tribe within the new states that prevents true self-fulfillment, and more of driving expatriates from national soil and less of uniting men of all colors and faiths in the war against poverty and disease.

Courage is fear that has said its prayers. If those who accept the fateful burdens of responsibility North and South should gain the courage and strength to hold in check the passions that play on mass emotions, we could face the future together with courage and hope. When all is said and done, the forces that unite men are more lasting and enduring than those that divide them. In Paul Tillich's cogent statement, man through religion in its deepest spiritual sense is reunited with mankind and God. The hope of religion is that the union may be restored. To drive out this hope of reunion, as communism does, is to destroy the prospects of mankind. Lest he be misunderstood by those who confess other faiths, Tillich reminds us that the great mass of mankind may "serve God without ever knowing his name." Admittedly, the political and social order at best is a proximate order mediating justice through interest and power. Yet by any measure of justice that transcends class and nation, Western civilization hand in hand with Asian and African cultures must not shirk a common responsibility to broaden educational opportunities, to multiply the chances for man's fulfillment not in mere labor but in work, to increase the numbers who may enjoy a tolerably good life, and to enable men to do their best in the light of that divine spark which neither bondage nor pain, self-seeking nor pride ever quite snuffs out.

It is conceivable that worldwide goals of freedom and justice may be realized within a series of regional confederations linked through Article 51 of the United Nations. Winston S. Churchill's design in 1943 for the world community envisaged a network of regional organizations with a United Nations Organization at the summit, reserving to itself those problems and disputes not resolved at a regional level. History may have outstripped this grand design, since the nations of Asia, Africa, and Latin America have acquired a vital stake in the United Nations. Thus, while holding open the possible relevance of the federal idea, notably in western Europe, wise statesmen must continue to build on the limited but tangible unity already visible in the United Nations. In the Belgian Congo, the Gaza Strip, and at locations as yet undetermined around the world, the United Nations may fill existing political vacuums more effectively than rival factions within the region or the great powers or some concert of powers made suspect by a former colonial status. Indeed, for the foreseeable future —a future that even so great a statesman as Mr. Churchill could not have foreseen—any union of free nations within or outside a world region may be obliged to work through the instrumentalities of the United Nations.

Finally, the most severe and fateful test of diplomacy in a changing world arises from the life and death confrontation of East and West. Months and years of dreary and fruitless negotiations on disarmament suggest the prospects of agreement are not bright. If the world of change stops at Russian boundaries, the grounds for hope are fragile indeed. And if progress is impossible for two relatively secure and efficient empire-states, what are the prospects of agreement with the spread of nuclear weapons to the reckless and un-restrained revolutionary regimes on the march in Asia and Africa? Informed observers question whether we are likely in any foreseeable future to witness for a multipower world a repetition of the present threefold common interest of the Soviet Union and the United States: a common interest in restricting the spread of nuclear weapons, in halting the pressures of an uncontrolled arms race devouring most of their annual budgets, and in holding in check the expansionist war lords of Communist China at the risk of a general war. If these limited and tangible interests do not lead to an under-standing now, what of the future?

If I follow the discussion of responsible officials, they rest their hopes on three additional factors: the total destruc-tiveness of thermonuclear war, the possible influence of the wind of change within the Soviet empire, and the chance that new and more fruitful diplomatic approaches may be found. Only the latter falls strictly within the province of my sub-ject, but the others are inseparable from success at the con-ference table. Respecting the first, who is there among us who believes that nuclear warfare is a rational instrument of policy? And who would question Winston S. Churchill's bleak prediction on conflict on Central Europe, "that there is no chance of the world being spared the use of nuclear weapons if war came." [14] The specter of a devastating thermonuclear war may be driving the nations to accept the stalemate inherent in the balance of terror—a stalemate in which warfare has lost its function as a practical step to achieve on the battlefield the victory denied at the conference table. Talks may be broken off and contacts interrupted, but if hard-boiled realists prevail, the direct and deliberate involvement in war seems unlikely so long as both sides stand firm and remain strong.

Secondly, if we look within Russia our best experts seem agreed that since 1953, with Stalin's death, change has become

[14] *The New York Times,* April 21, 1959, p. 6.

the law of Soviet society. Some maintain that the Soviet state is transforming itself from a Byzantine despotism to a Western state in the earliest stages of its development. If indeed change is being effected, Communist doctrines must be supplanted by other less rigid and absolute principles drawn from contending philosophies. Stated in its most emphatic form, this trend of thought assumes that:

The Soviet economy and the Soviet society are becoming highly complex, much too complex to be run successfully by a centralized dictatorship. The same practical circumstances which brought the West its liberty—centuries after the ideas of liberty had been defined and propounded—are present in the Soviet Union. A complex society cannot be made to work without a large measure of personal liberty and personal incentive and popular consent.[15]

Correspondents like Harrison E. Salisbury point to growing pockets of liberalism within an essentially totalitarian state holding fast to the maintenance of the Soviet regime but believing "in a rule of law, of justice as it is known in the West, in freedom of the individual within socially recognized bounds, in freedom for the creative arts and in close and meaningful state and personal relations between the Soviet Union and the West." [16] These observers, despite the grave tensions of the last half year, see a second and more profound post-Stalinist thaw gaining momentum from day to day. Some of the most eminent figures in Soviet science—physicists, astronomers, and mathematicians—are turning not to formal religion but to a spiritual conception of the universe. Mr. Salisbury caps his analysis by asserting that: "Most leading Western diplomats in Moscow believe that Premier Khrushchev, despite all his threats and bluster, has made preservation of peace with the West the keystone of Soviet foreign policy. . . . A succession of unequivocal Soviet declarations that there no longer exists in

[15] Walter Lippmann, "Today and Tomorrow: Soviet-American Relations Today," *New York Herald Tribune*, February 13, 1962, p. 22.

[16] Harrison E. Salisbury, "Soviet Liberals Fighting Neo-Stalinists for Power," *The New York Times*, February 6, 1962, p. 1.

the world any sane alternative to peace has strongly bolstered the Western diplomats' conclusion." [17]

Alongside these more hopeful signs are the irrefutable and deeply troubling facts that Soviet negotiators persist in their attitude that "what's mine is mine, what's yours is negotiable"; that irrespective of peaceful sentiments, events may take command; that Khrushchev indiscriminately mixes talk of peace with threats of war, hostages, and destruction of the West; that American officials not noted for reckless language say we were closer to the brink of catastrophe last August and September over Berlin than at any time in history; that the prestige of both sides is irretrievably engaged throughout the world; that the Soviet-Chinese conflict is exerting a powerful centrifugal force that may draw the whole Communist world with it; that since the Geneva Conference in 1955 no tangible progress has been registered on a single outstanding problem; that the discrepancy between Chinese peasants living on 15 cents a day and Khrushchev's claim of equaling the American standard of living in twenty years breeds instability; that the rift has caused unsettling divisions within every national Communist movement; that if peace forces exist within communism, they have been weakened by six years of talk of peaceful coexistence bringing them no closer to a détente with the West; and that the failures of communism anywhere to resolve the problem of food production may lead to further crisis, conflict, and expansionism.

Thus diplomats, who must measure these competing estimates of trends in the Soviet Union, return to the center of the stage endlessly in search of peace with justice, moving through the drama from one unhappy act to the next, suspect among those whose claims and vital interests they protect, feared by an adversary whose intentions they test and probe, and despised by a world community neither strong nor effective enough in itself to end the cold war. How ironic that America—with its

[17] Harrison E. Salisbury, "A Return to the Soviet: Emphasis Is Put on Peace," *The New York Times*, February 5, 1962, p. 1.

preference for straightforward commercial relations, its love of free and open debate, and its heartfelt assurance that a chosen nation was rid of the toils and ambiguities of international diplomacy—should be guided along the knife-edge of peace by the diplomats it had once rejected. Might not the public grow more compassionate and understanding of diplomacy if it remembered the words of Justice Oliver Wendell Holmes in another connection: "Every year, if not every day, we have to wager our salvation upon some prophecy based on imperfect knowledge."

You will not be surprised that I perceive few novel and dramatic approaches through diplomacy to the cherished goal of peace. Nor will you expect me at the eleventh hour to urge that our government throw caution to the wind and meet at the summit where eighteen heads of state are expected in a few hours to achieve a program of disarmament that has escaped us for more than forty years. At the United Nations, or in a much publicized Geneva disarmament conference, it remains true that public debate of sensitive issues is a serious matter and drastic medicine to be used when less dangerous therapy has failed. In most circumstances, less dangerous therapy is possible through normal diplomatic channels with all their "privacy and gravity." Debate and personal diplomacy to an audience made up of scores of reporters, hundreds of bystanders, and millions of newspaper readers continues to be a substitute for more violent means, not a substitute for less dangerous techniques. Below the level of summit conferences or full-dress international conferences, these less dangerous techniques are many and varied. Sometimes great powers, whose national prestige is at stake and whose area of maneuver is hopelessly restricted, can put their claims in cold storage while working diplomats gnaw at the edges of a dispute—as with Laos—and, again, they can place them on deposit temporarily with the United Nations, as in the Berlin blockade. Occasionally they can talk an issue into suspense or delay in the hope that the fever will subside. Sometimes they can wait for other factors to operate—the force of world opinion, shifts in national attitudes, or the self-interest of an adversary. Above all, through channels that ought not long remain closed, they can seek answers to all-important questions that speculation engenders: Is there a change among responsible Soviet leaders? Does this or that announcement portend a shift in tactics? Are there reasons to believe a "no" may become "yes"? Assuming that "interests never lie," what is the Soviet interest in Laos or nuclear testing or Berlin?

Finally, what are the prospects of negotiating realistically and without appeasement on the issues underlying the perpetuation of great weapons systems which from either side of the Iron Curtain evoke terror and fear? Are there reasonable measures for ending the arms race? Could new approaches yield success? If we reflect on the problem, it is striking how many of the tensions that undergird the arms race involve third parties or states which find themselves caught between East and West. Not bilateral relations between the great powers but their associations with "in-between" states carry the seeds of conflict. We fear less what the Soviet Union may do to us and more what it might do to Berlin, the Belgian Congo, or Cuba, and they return the compliment with respect to Hungary, Poland, or East Germany. Is it reasonable to ask whether one or more of these points of conflict might be drawn out of the context of the cold war? Could the direct involvement of East and West be reduced in one or more of these areas? Are there regional approaches that might help to draw the two great powers from the center of a conflict? Is it conceivable, for example, that western Europe might eventually be strengthened and prepared to undertake its own defense against eastern Europe, with the forces directed from Moscow and Washington pulled back from the front line to a position of strategic reserve? Is it likely that in other world regions local countries might group themselves around the concept of a regional Monroe Doctrine committed to support their frontiers rather than depending upon the United States? Should they not be encouraged gradually and self-consciously to think more responsibly about their own security, calling on the United States for help, not expecting us to mobilize their forces for defense? Is the unanimous declaration of the nations of Latin America that communism is incompatible with the Organization of American States a first important step in this direction? Has the role of the United Nations in the Belgian Congo, while not eliminating the cold war, set it in a wider, more hopeful context? I acknowledge the immense difficulty of altering present patterns of international politics, but progress here can provide the preconditions for armaments control.

And if this approach has any merit, are there more hopeful ways of packaging the many disagreeable elements that make up a diplomatic understanding? From the Jay Treaty to comparatively recent times, arrangements with other states that have endured have been founded on give and take: we have given a little on one issue not central to our vital interests to gain something in return. There are risks in isolating each separate issue, dealing with it when one or both parties have nothing to offer in return. The United Nations, with its more than one hundred members, accentuates the existing practice of facing every issue in isolation from every other, although on membership issues, seats on the Security Council and disarmament, progress has nevertheless been made. Someone must give this the thoughtful attention it deserves if we are to move ahead toward disarmament.

Thus I end as I began. Diplomacy is the practice of ways and means. Those who ask of it grand designs or the transformation of society must forever be disappointed. The more profound changes take place outside the conference room. Yet the institutions of contemporary diplomacy are sufficient to the day if the diplomat uses them wisely and well. This is the one justification I know for turning the spotlight on the emergent patterns and changing practices of American diplomacy.

INDEX